Silent Rights

THE NINTH AMENDMENT

AND THE CONSTITUTION'S

UNENUMERATED

RIGHTS

Calvin R. Massey

D0141480

Temple University Press

PHILADELPHIA

Temple University Press, Philadelphia 19122
Copyright © 1995 by Temple University
All rights reserved
Published 1995
Printed in the United States of America

⊗ The paper used in this book meets the
requirements of the American National Standard for
Information Sciences — Permanence of Paper
for Printed Library Materials,
ANSI Z39.48-1984

Text design by Betty Palmer McDaniel

Library of Congress Cataloging-in-Publication Data
Massey, Calvin R.
Silent rights : the ninth amendment and the
constitution's unenumerated rights / Calvin R. Massey.
■   p.   cm.
Includes bibliographical references and index.
ISBN 1-56639-311-6 (cl: alk. paper). — ISBN 1-56639-312-4 (pb: alk. paper)
1. United States — Constitutional law — Amendments — 9th. 2. Civil rights —
United States.   I. Title.
KF4558 9th.M37   1995
342.73'085 — dc20
[347.30285]   94-36231

Portions of, and ideas from, the following articles appear in this book:

Calvin R. Massey, "Anti-Federalism and the Ninth Amendment," 64 *Chi.-Kent L. Rev.* 987 (1988). Copyright by the *Chicago-Kent Law Review*. Reprinted by permission.

Calvin R. Massey, "The Anti-Federalist Ninth Amendment and Its Implications for State Constitutional Law," *Wis. L. Rev.* 1229 (1990). Copyright by the *Wisconsin Law Review*. Reprinted by permission.

Calvin R. Massey, "Federalism and Fundamental Rights: The Ninth Amendment," 38 *Hastings L. J.* 305 (1987). Copyright by the *Hastings Law Journal* and Calvin R. Massey. Reprinted by permission.

Calvin R. Massey, "The Natural Law Component of the Ninth Amendment," 61 *U. Cin. L. Rev.* 49 (1992). Copyright by the *University of Cincinnati Law Review*. Reprinted by permission.

To Martha and Ellen

AMENDMENT IX

The enumeration in the Constitution,
of certain rights, shall not be construed
to deny or disparage others retained by the people

CONTENTS

PREFACE

Twenty-plus years ago, when I was a law student studying constitutional law, I was unable to make sense of the Ninth Amendment.
It seemed to be an important statement, both a recognition of the
existence of unspecified rights "retained by the people" and a directive that the Constitution's listing of protected rights should
not "be construed to deny or disparage" those unspecified retained
rights. I quickly learned, however, that inquiries about the substance of the Ninth Amendment were apt to be brushed aside as
inconsequential. The Ninth Amendment did not mean anything,
despite hints to the contrary dropped by a few scholars and judges.
My insistence that it must mean *something* merely elicited mild
exasperation, as if I were a bit of a constitutional crank, or perhaps
only a dull student who was unable to grasp the concept that parts
of the Constitution wilt and drop off like autumn foliage. Still, to
mix metaphors, the Ninth Amendment remained there, grinning
as enigmatically as the Cheshire cat, long after its substance had
apparently departed.

Since that time a great many scholars have begun to react as I did
when I first confronted the Ninth Amendment. Discussion of its
origins, its intended meaning and function, and its possible role in
contemporary constitutional adjudication has burgeoned in the
community of legal academics. The Ninth Amendment became a
focal point of the remarkable hearings regarding President Ronald
Reagan's nomination of Robert Bork as a justice of the Supreme
Court. But the discussion has engendered little, if any, judicial
acceptance of the Ninth Amendment as a meaningful aspect of

constitutional law. This is probably due, in part, to the fear that attempting to uncover the substantive unspecified rights protected by the Ninth Amendment would be like embarking on a voyage without charts, compass, or sextant. In short, the concern is that if the judiciary were to start taking the Ninth Amendment seriously, judges' political leanings would displace the collective political preferences of legislative assemblies.

The usual assumption is that the result would be so appallingly antidemocratic that it would be both constitutionally unprincipled and politically unpalatable. It does not have to be so. The Ninth Amendment can be taken seriously without threatening our treatment of legislative judgments as presumptively valid and our use of the courts to rein in legislatures and executives only when they transgress boundaries clearly understood to be rooted in our constitutional covenant. This book is an attempt to present a comprehensive explanation of a possible contemporary meaning of and function for the Ninth Amendment. I have tried to pay respectful attention to the historical debate surrounding the Ninth Amendment's originally intended meaning and function as I describe how the Ninth Amendment might better serve to explain some of our current conundrums of constitutional law. My intent is not so much to promote my perspective of the Ninth Amendment (though I like doing that too) as it is to stimulate real and serious discussion about the place of unenumerated rights in what Justice Robert Jackson termed our "constitutional constellation."

I am grateful to the many people who have sparked my thinking about the Ninth Amendment and its role in protecting the unenumerated rights of the Constitution. A partial list includes Randy Barnett, David Mayer, Bernard Siegen, William Wang, Philip Hamburger, Steven Heyman, James Bond, Thomas McAffee, and Hans Linde. I am indebted to the following people and institutions for giving me the opportunity to present some of these ideas for discussion at intellectual workshops, lectures, and other public places: the Liberty Fund and David Lips, former Dean James Bond and the Seattle University Law School, Doug Ross and the National Association of Attorneys General, and Dean Mary Kay Kane and my colleagues at the University of California's Hastings College of the Law.

The ideas presented here have been developing for some time, and this book is, in part, a refinement of thoughts that I have expressed earlier in more tentative form. I am grateful to the following journals for permission to use portions of my earlier articles: *University of Cincinnati Law Review, Wisconsin Law Review, Hastings Law Journal,* and *Chicago-Kent Law Review.*

I am also grateful to my father, Field William Massey, an intelligent man largely educated in the "School of Hard Knocks" (as he would have put it), who preached to me the gospel of diffusing the authority of governments in order to preserve the liberties of the people. My mature interest in the Ninth Amendment and the importance of preserving unenumerated rights undoubtedly developed from this early baptism in the faith of the people's residual rights and corresponding confinement of governmental prerogatives.

Part I

THE CONTEMPORARY PROBLEM

ONE

The Symbolic Constitution

When Americans experience governmental injustice personally, they are apt to declare, "That's against the Constitution!" Many of these claims would, of course, be swiftly punctured by a constitutional lawyer, but the fact that there is an American propensity to equate the Constitution with governmental justice suggests that there is a deep feeling in the U.S. political psyche that the Constitution protects individual rights that are otherwise not explicitly stated in the text of the Constitution.

It is not an attitude peculiar to those unschooled in the arcana of law. Thomas Jefferson declared for all rebellious Americans that among the "self-evident" truths was the proposition that all persons "are endowed by their Creator with certain inalienable rights." Nearly two centuries later, Justice William O. Douglas opined that "in our scheme of things, the rights of men are un-alienable. They come from the Creator, not from a president, a legislator, or a court."[1] Indeed, many of the rights that Americans take for granted as central parts of their constitutional inheritance are nowhere to be found in the text of the Constitution. Instead, they have been created by the Supreme Court as unenumerated rights implicitly part of the Constitution. Into this category fall such fundamental rights as the right to associate with others, the right to vote, the right to be accorded equal protection of the laws by the federal government, the right to be presumed innocent and to have that presumption overcome only by proof beyond a reasonable doubt, the right to travel, the right to marry or not, the right to have children or not, and the right to enjoy a zone of personal privacy or autonomy into which government may not intrude.[2]

The usual constitutional vehicle by which unenumerated rights have been brought into the constitutional family are the two due process clauses. The Fifth Amendment prohibits the federal government from depriving any person "of life, liberty, or property, without due process of law," and the Fourteenth Amendment imposes the same limitation upon the state governments. The due process clauses have always been regarded by U.S. courts as derived from the provision of Magna Carta that protected free men from governmental actions except "by the law of the land."[3] The meaning of the phrase "law of the land" in Magna Carta might be thought to convey the idea that the role of courts was simply to ascertain whether any given statute was enacted with the requisite procedural regularity. If so, it was the duly enacted "law of the land"; if not, the statute had no claim to status as enforceable law. But this "was not the view which American courts took of due process of law. [Rather] . . . most American courts agreed that the principle of law of the land, or due process of law, was one of the standards against which legislation could be measured and, if found wanting, declared void."[4]

These standards were never completely procedural, although courts often acknowledged the procedural dimension by noting that the phrase protected "the ancient established law and course of legal proceedings, by an adherence to which our ancestors in England, before the settlement of this country, and the emigrants themselves and their descendants, had found safety for their personal rights."[5] Rather, from early moments in our constitutional history U.S. lawyers and judges have perceived in "due process of law" a limitation upon all manner of governmental actions, whether taken by the legislature or the executive, that interfere with unwritten understandings of individual rights. As Daniel Webster argued in *Dartmouth College v. Woodward*,[6] "acts directly transferring one man's estate to another" could not possibly be said to be part of the "law of the land." In pressing the argument, Webster made no attempt to cite some more explicit textual limit on the legislative power; it seemed self-evident to Webster that such an act was illegitimate.

In more recent times, Supreme Court justices have hinged this judgment more squarely on the due process clauses, opining that they protect "not particular forms of procedure, but the very substance of individual rights to life, liberty, and property."[7] The refinement of this substantive dimension begins at a fairly high level of abstraction, and becomes ever more contentious as substantive due process is applied to specific claims. Few are likely to disagree with the sentiment voiced by the Court in *Twining v. New Jersey* that due process includes those "fundamental principle[s] of liberty and justice which inhere[ ] in the very idea of free government,"[8] or Justice Benjamin Cardozo's declaration that the concept of due process encompasses those rights that are "implicit in the concept of ordered liberty," such that "neither liberty nor justice would exist if they were sacrificed."[9] But violent disagreement has attended the Court's conclusion that the due process clauses protect the liberty of women to terminate an unwanted pregnancy. Whether on the general or specific levels, it has proven extraordinarily difficult to articulate why due process includes substantive "fundamental rights" otherwise unenumerated in the Constitution. Even harder is the task of determining in some principled way those specific fundamental rights that should be protected by due process. The difficulty of the effort has not prevented the inquiry, however, for there seems to be a deep need in the American character to preserve and protect some quantum of individual liberty not otherwise specifically accounted for in the charter of our liberties.

Webster had good authority for his *Dartmouth College* claim, for some Supreme Court justices had already declared that it was not necessary to rely on constitutional text as a device to secure the people's unenumerated rights. In 1798, two decades before Webster related his argument concerning legislative expropriations of property to Magna Carta's precursor to due process, Justice Samuel Chase opined that "a law which takes property from A, and gives it to B . . . is against all reason and justice" and, as such, was beyond the legitimate scope of legislative power. "There are," declared Chase, "certain vital principles in our free republican governments which will determine and overrule an apparent and flagrant abuse of legislative power."[10] Chase thought that these principles were implicit in the very idea of constitutional government and need not be recited in a written constitution as express limitations on government.

But Chase did not speak for everyone. His colleague, Justice James Iredell, eloquently expressed the contrary position.

> If . . . the legislature of the Union, or the legislature of any member of the Union, shall pass a law within the general scope of their constitutional power, the court cannot pronounce it to be void, merely because it is, in their judgment, contrary to the principles of natural justice. The ideas of natural justice are regulated by no fixed standard; the ablest and purest men have differed upon the subject; and all that the court could properly say . . . would be that the legislature (possessed of an equal right of opinion) had passed an act which, in the opinion of the judges, was inconsistent with the abstract principles of natural justice.[11]

Thus, to Iredell, the constitutional boundary upon legislation extended only so far as the text of the Constitution.

Daniel Webster would no doubt have agreed with Chase, and the modern progeny of Chase and Webster apparently include

Justices John Paul Stevens and William Brennan. Stevens has proclaimed "it self-evident that all men were endowed by their Creator with liberty as one of the cardinal unalienable rights. It is that basic freedom which the Due Process Clause protects."[12] Brennan has opined that the familial right to privacy "has its source . . . in intrinsic human rights."[13] These conceptions of implicit limits on governmental authority or, put another way, individual rights not enumerated in the Constitution, necessarily assume that there is some source of constitutional principles extrinsic to the Constitution.

Just as Samuel Chase's views have found contemporary adherents, Iredell's arguments have been echoed by other textualists. Justice Hugo Black contended that the function of judges was to eschew prudential, political, and historical judgments in interpreting the Constitution; rather, judges ought simply to give effect to the contemporary sense of the text of the Constitution.[14] Judge Alex Kozinski of the U.S. Court of Appeals, a leading modern textualist, asserts that "the first principle [of constitutional interpretation] . . . is textual fidelity. . . . Constitutional adjudication must be grounded in the words . . . actually used in the Constitution, not in words or concepts that are not there." Judge Kozinski also identifies "completeness" as an equally compelling principle of textually faithful constitutional interpretation. "When something was put into the Constitution it was meant to have a purpose and ought not be ignored. Yet . . . there are a number of provisions in the Constitution that have been ignored or emasculated by judicial interpretation."[15] As an example of a constitutional provision that has been ignored, Judge Kozinski offers the Ninth Amendment, which states that "the enumeration in the Constitution, of certain rights, shall not be construed to deny or disparage others retained by the people."

How should a textualist approach the Ninth Amendment? According to Judge Kozinski's precepts, the principle of completeness commands textualists to divine the purpose of this text and apply it conscientiously. Kozinski's principle of textual fidelity demands that constitutional decisions be grounded in the words actually used by the Constitution, but these actual words seem to refer us to some set of retained rights that are wholly unspecified in constitutional text. The only thing clearly stated in this text is the mandate that interpreters of the Constitution may not use the fact of enumeration of certain rights as an excuse to ignore or debase unenumerated rights. There may be other reasons to ignore unenumerated rights, but the bare fact that they are not written into the Constitution is not a constitutionally sufficient reason. Textualism seems to require us to look outside of text for the content of these unenumerated rights, which we are required to treat with a dignity equal to the Constitution's enumerated rights.

But textualism is not as simple as it seems. Various literary theorists argue, with some merit, that a text may have a distinct meaning to its author and a very different meaning to its reader. To illustrate, imagine a confined and unique Canadian island community with the postal code K0Z 1R0. A summer resident from the United States, driving around in an auto bearing U.S. license plates with the personalized message "K0Z 1R0" will be clearly understood *by that island audience* as expressing his bond with the community. But once the summer resident returns to the United States, the same message, "K0Z 1R0," is read entirely differently (What's a "koziro?" or "Hmm, the Motor Vehicles people have come up with a new alphanumeric sequence"), although the message continues to mean the same thing to its author. As with license plates, so with constitutions: The meaning of the Ninth Amendment to its authorial generation may have been entirely different from its meaning to our generation, to say nothing of those who will follow us. It may be that any serious textual theory of the Ninth Amendment will require a firm understanding of its past meaning (or meanings) as well as its current meaning (or possible meanings).

The problem of finding meaning in a constitution is compounded because textualism is not the only plausible mode of constitutional interpretation. Professor Philip Bobbitt has identified six modes of argument about the proper meaning of the Constitution: historical, textual, doctrinal, prudential, structural, and ethical. Historical argument, sometimes termed originalism, "marshals the intent of the draftsmen of the Constitution and the people who adopted" it. Textual argument is "drawn from a consideration of the present sense of the words of the provision." Doctrinal argument is the common law method applied to constitutional law, "argument that asserts principles derived from precedent or from judicial or academic commentary upon precedent." Prudential argument claims validity for "particular doctrines according to the practical wisdom of using the courts [or interpreting the Constitution] in a particular way." Structural argument involves "claims that a particular principle or practical result is implicit in the structures of government and the relationships that are created by the Constitution among citizens and governments." Ethical arguments rely upon "the character, or *ethos*, of the American polity . . . as the source from which particular decisions derive." Constitutional argument frequently employs simultaneously several of these modes. It is also a common practice for constitutional advocates to select the modes most congenial to the result they desire.[16]

Argument about the Ninth Amendment has not been immune from these practices. Much effort has been expended upon identifying the "correct" historical meaning of the amendment; lesser quantums of effort have been directed to textual, structural, ethical, and prudential arguments. Very little effort has been devoted to doctrinal argument for the simple reason that a majority of the

Supreme Court has never relied upon the Ninth Amendment as the basis for any decision.[17] Nevertheless, it is difficult to escape the force of Justice Arthur Goldberg's observation that "in interpreting the Constitution, real effect should be given to all the words it uses. . . . The Ninth Amendment . . . may be regarded by some as a recent discovery . . . but since 1791 it has been a basic part of the Constitution which we are sworn to uphold."[18]

What, then, does the Ninth Amendment mean? As might be supposed, there are many plausible answers. Some, like former Judge Robert Bork, contend that the amendment has no discernible meaning whatever. Others, including former Justice Stanley Reed, suggest that the amendment is merely hortatory and duplicative of the axiomatic reminder in the Tenth Amendment that the states retain all powers not surrendered under the Constitution. Still others, such as legal historian Raoul Berger, contend that the amendment prohibits the federal government from exercising any power with respect to the "rights retained by the people." To Berger, however, the very powerlessness that deters governments from invading the domain of retained rights also prevents governments from doing anything to enforce this prohibition upon governments. Thus, in Berger's view the Ninth Amendment becomes a guarantee that is entrusted exclusively to its potential violators.

Yet another view is one often claimed to be the true original understanding of the Ninth Amendment. Articulated best by Professor Thomas McAffee, this view asserts that the Ninth Amendment was merely a cautionary device to check unwarranted extension of the powers of the federal government. Some constitutional experts, like Professor Laurence Tribe, suggest that the amendment is best regarded as a constitutional rule of construction — a constitutionally mandated instruction to later generations regarding the proper way to interpret the Constitution. In Tribe's view, the Ninth Amendment is not a source of rights but, rather, a rule of interpretation. This rule invalidates argument that any given right (such as the right to use contraceptives) is not to be included within some enumerated right of the Constitution (such as due process) simply because the right to use contraceptives is not expressly enumerated in the Constitution. There may be other grounds for concluding that due process does not include the right to use contraceptives, says Tribe, but reaching that conclusion simply because the Constitution is silent about contraceptives is an avenue of reasoning expressly barred by the Ninth Amendment.[19] Finally, there are those, such as Professor Randy Barnett, who contend that the amendment ought to be treated as an independent source of substantive and judicially enforceable individual rights, determined without reference to any of the enumerated rights.

Every one of these views is laden with problems. Some of the problems are analytical, some are historical, some are political. Judge Bork regards the amendment as analogous to "an amendment that says 'Congress shall make no' and then there is an ink blot and you cannot read the rest of it."[20] But there is no ink blot obscuring the text of the Ninth Amendment. Justice Reed's conflation of the Ninth and Tenth amendments into a single axiom is historically incomplete and a poor reading of text, because the Ninth Amendment is pretty clearly concerned with "*rights* retained by the *people*" while the Tenth is equally explicit that its focus is upon governmental "*powers* . . . reserved to the States respectively, or to the people." To be fair, Justice Reed's conflation does bear some resemblance to the traditional account of the "original understanding" of the Ninth Amendment but Justice Reed and the "original understanding" suffer from a failure to account for an enormous amount of ambient constitutional change (such as the 1937 revolution that began the current process of centralized government), which has rendered obsolete the "original understanding." The originalists' contention that the Ninth Amendment was merely a device intended to prevent bloat of the powers of the federal government has adequate historical support, but, given the evident failure of the amendment's original purpose, this account is incomplete without provision of a plausible and viable contemporary purpose. Tribe's view is similarly incomplete. There is no reason to suppose that the amendment is *solely* a rule of interpretation. It may well make better historical and analytical sense to treat the amendment as both a rule of interpretation *and* an independent source of rights. Finally, Raoul Berger's view would transform a guarantee of rights into a hollow mockery of rights, rather like guaranteeing someone food but fulfilling the guarantee by displaying food within an inaccessible cage.

Yet, if the Ninth Amendment is treated as a source of individual rights effective against governments, a host of other problems emerge. What is the substance of these rights? How is that substance to be determined, given the Constitution's enigmatic and somewhat unhelpful reference to "rights retained by the people?" Whatever their substance, may these rights be enforced by the courts, Congress, the executive, or the states? If they may not be enforced by anyone, can it be said that these rights really exist, and, if that is the case, what are we to make of a Constitution that guarantees nonexistent rights?

Assume for the moment that we have overcome the considerable obstacles surrounding definition of the substance of Ninth Amendment rights. May these rights be enforced judicially? Some commentators take the position that the amendment merely declares an area in which governments have no power to act. According to Raoul Berger, governments may not act to invade unenumerated rights, but if they do so, the judiciary is powerless to intervene.[21] This is a curious conclusion, because it permits governments to do what they may not, and denies to the aggrieved citizen access to the most efficacious remedy for governmental impropriety. Berger reaches this conclusion because he perceives Ninth Amendment rights as arising outside of the Constitution and assigns to the framers an intent to vest the judiciary with power to enforce only those rights enumerated in the Constitution. Berger's view is considered in more detail later; for the moment note that his view wreaks havoc upon text.

The Ninth Amendment provides that enumeration of rights shall not "deny *or* disparage" the unenumerated rights. The very term "disparage" carries with it a strong implication that enumerated and unenumerated constitutional rights are to be accorded equal status. "Disparage" is derived from the Old French predecessor to *deparager*, meaning "to marry unequally." Its more modern meaning is given as "actions or words" that "depreciate, undervalue," or "degrade" that which is disparaged.[22] The common contemporary usage of "disparage" is to sum up in a single word a process of erosion of another's value. "Joe Bob disparaged Mary Lou" conveys a fairly nasty scene: a diminution of another's worth, a besmirchment of character or status. "The car salesman disparaged Hondas" is less emotionally laden but no less charged with the idea of undercutting the utility, attractiveness, or value of Honda autos. Whether by reference to its etymological roots or its contemporary meaning, the concept of disparagement has at its heart the denial of equal treatment, or parity, between the items drawn into comparison. But disparagement is not denial; to deny an appeal is to end the matter, to deny (with power) is to terminate, not just to denigrate. There being a difference between the two terms "deny" and "disparage," the Ninth Amendment must be taken to mean that enumeration of rights cannot be used to terminate *nor to besmirch* unenumerated rights. How better to besmirch than to say, "[J]udicial review is reserved for enumerated rights only." Thus, although the Ninth Amendment plainly indicates that enumerated and unenumerated rights are entitled to some sort of parity, Berger's limitation of the judicial enforcement power to enumerated rights alone appears to mock the parity principle.

But even if we were to conclude that Ninth Amendment rights exist, although not judicially enforceable, we must still determine whether they may be enforced by anyone. Disabling the judiciary from enforcing Ninth Amendment rights does not eliminate the problem of defining the scope of these rights or even the problem of their enforcement. Judicially unenforceable constitutional rights are still binding on government and remain paramount to other, inferior, sources of law. Governmental actors, whether legislators or executives, are required to determine the scope of these rights and to act to preserve and obey them. The difficulties of definition and enforcement have not gone away, but have simply ambled over from the courthouse to the legislative chamber and the executive office.[23] It may be that unenumerated rights will wither and die in those quarters, and although that possibility cannot be assumed, neither should it be dismissed.

Given that Ninth Amendment rights are, by definition, not spelled out in the Constitution, how do we divine their substance? This may be the toughest issue of all, for it forces us to articulate and defend a principled methodology of constitutional interpretation. Though it is not beyond dispute, let us assume that Bobbitt's modes of constitutional argument capture most, if not all, of the relevant ways in which we seek to make sense of our Constitution. The limits of text are obvious and quickly exhausted. Text alone provides a basis for at least two plausible readings for our generation: a rule of construction, whether Tribe's rule of interpretation or some other version, and the thesis that there are rights unspecified in the Constitution that are entitled to equal treatment with the constitutionally specified rights, whether judicially enforceable or not.

But text also provides some support for the historically based arguments of one original understanding. Historical argument provides much rich ore; the problem is that the smelted product is base metal of minimal value. As is so often the case, the history of the adoption of the Ninth Amendment has been susceptible to a wide variety of conflicting interpretations. Even if we were to settle upon a single historical explanation of the originally intended function of the amendment, we would still have to provide a persuasive rationale for preferring that intended function to some different, contemporary function that is securely grounded in structural or prudential argument. There is an absence of doctrinal argument because there is no doctrine. We may debate the specific structural functions to be served by the amendment, but the combination of text and historical context of its creation suggests strongly that the amendment is an important, if neglected, component of the constitutional structure. Reasons of prudence may dictate that we neglect the amendment, but if those reasons are rooted in the difficulty of defining unenumerated rights, it makes little sense to avoid the Ninth Amendment while simultaneously forcing the due process clauses to perform the Ninth Amendment's job.

The Ninth Amendment may be a hard nut to crack.[24] Cracking the Ninth Amendment nut is important for several reasons. The pretense that it does not exist undermines the legitimacy of all constitutional interpretation because there is no self-evident principled explanation why we should observe the strictures of equal protection and ignore the ligatures of the Ninth Amendment.

Ignoring the Ninth Amendment problem does not make it go away. It simply travels to other parts of the Constitution, where it serves the perverse function of distorting doctrine in some other area. It is far more difficult to justify the *existence* of a substantive component of due process than it is to justify the existence of constitutional unenumerated rights protected by the Ninth Amendment. Justifying their placement in the due process clauses unnecessarily garbles our understanding of due process without doing much to advance our understanding of the substance of these elusive unenumerated rights. Indeed, once we uncouple unenumerated rights from the pretense that they must be a species of "liberty" protected by "due process of law," we face a larger task:

sorting out an immense pool of possible rights. The enormity of that task may counsel some prudence as to the manner by which we declare these rights to exist. But freedom is always scary and requires good sense to keep.

Finally, recognition of the Ninth Amendment as an independent source of individual rights responds to the apparent need of Americans to regard their Constitution as an embodiment of justice. It is, of course, asking far too much of the amendment to secure "justice" in all its many facets. It is likely true that Americans treat the Constitution as a symbol. It is a symbol not only of our tradition of democratic self-governance, but also of freedom, of fairness, of the integrity of the individual, and undoubtedly of a host of other values projected onto it by a believing populace. As Sanford Levinson has suggested, there is a constitutional faith and, perhaps like all faiths, it is a faith that knows no bounds.[25] This is not to suggest that the Ninth Amendment ought to be regarded as similarly limitless; it is to suggest instead that the principled use of the Ninth Amendment as a source of individual rights effective against governments is a tangible and meaningful way to respond to the faith of constitutional adherents. The Ninth Amendment ought to be the preferred vehicle for dialogue concerning the actual manifestation of the symbolic Constitution.

Given the open-endedness of the Ninth Amendment, there is great risk that any such dialogue will degenerate into verbal mush, a kind of constitutional stream-of-consciousness that may grace literature but has little value to the judge who must decide concrete cases and, in the deciding, frustrate the genuinely held contentions and aspirations of a losing litigant. For this dialogue to have any practical value it must assume the familiar outlines of legal doctrine. Doctrine cannot spring all at once, as out of the head of Zeus. It is the nature of our constitutional system, deeply tinctured by the common law method, that legal doctrine is produced by the accretion of cases. One obstacle to the development of Ninth Amendment doctrine is the fear that, once one has embarked upon the journey, the path will prove to be quicksand. Some assurance to the contrary can be provided by sketching out a coherent theory of the meaning of the Ninth Amendment, one that makes sense of its history, text, and structural role in the Constitution, and one that responds to the doctrinal necessities of a principled quest for constitutionally guaranteed unenumerated rights. All of this is, in a very real sense, theoretical because the courts show no immediate signs of jettisoning our two-century-old tradition of ignoring the amendment. At the same time, courts show little likelihood of rejecting our almost equally well-established tradition of assimilating unenumerated individual rights to other parts of the Constitution. It makes little sense to preserve both traditions. Sustained attempts to articulate a comprehensive and sensible account of how the Ninth Amendment could be used to secure and preserve unenumerated rights will eventually overcome the tradition of ignoring the Ninth Amendment and destroy the reflexive and wrongheaded notion that it is appropriate to continue to treat the Ninth Amendment as a constitutional nonentity.

Part II

THE ORIGINAL MEANING
OF THE NINTH
AMENDMENT

TWO

The Political Context
of the Founding Generation

Before beginning the debate about the originally intended meaning of the Ninth Amendment, it is wise to ask why we care to know the answer, assuming that there is an answer we can know. It is often contended that we should be bound by the original intent of the framers of the Constitution because this will provide a reference point independent of contemporary value preferences, thus providing some neutrality and stability in the development of the law of the Constitution. There are a host of objections that can be, and have been, raised in regard to this premise.

It is not certain whose intent counts. Is it the intent of the fifty-five men who convened in Philadelphia in the summer of 1787? Is it the intent of the smaller set of men who actually drafted the text, or those who participated most vigorously in the deliberations in Independence Hall? Is it the intent of the delegates to the various state ratification conventions? What are we to do with the intentions of those who opposed the Constitution or any given amendment? Are their intentions relevant, in a negative way, to describing the intentions underlying the constitutional text? What of the pamphleteers? Is the Federalist troika of Publius the only one to count, or may we include the anti-Federalist opposition? What about the intentions of those people utterly excluded then but included now? Are we free to ignore them on the grounds that their intentions were not manifested or, if we take them into account, are we required to discount the present utility of original intention as the constitutional lodestar?

Assuming we have identified those people whose intent matters, are we to refer to their subjective intentions or can we infer their intent from the objective indications of the text that they adopted? One familiar example is that the Congress that adopted the Fourteenth Amendment also tolerated or approved of racial segregation in the District of Columbia. When confronted with the question of whether official, government-mandated racial segregation violated the equal protection guarantee of the Fourteenth Amendment, should the constitutional interpreter have been bound by the apparent subjective intentions of the framers or by the objective principle of equality embodied in the text?

Even if those knotty problems are overcome, history does not necessarily answer our questions. The question of whether our constitutional interpretation ought to be driven exclusively by the intentions of the founding generation is an issue of contemporary political theory, not history.[1] Moreover, the Constitution we possess consists of a text, not just a set of historical intentions. The utility of inquiry into original intentions is to illuminate the text, to provide a richer context for its interpretation, not to supplant it with an alternative text consisting entirely of historiography. At best, historical inquiry provides answers to the specific problems of concern to past Americans, not necessarily to us. The application of the equal protection clause to governmental discrimination on the basis of sex was not a concern to the generation of 1868, but it is to ours. Resort to history will not provide answers we need.

History is uncertain at best. It yields a range of probabilities, a set of "most likely" outcomes. In this milieu, we can never feel comfortable that we have divined the one, pure, nugget of fact. Indeed, as Jefferson Powell has put it, history yields interpretations, not facts. Those interpretations, like the facts upon which

they are based, are often contradictory. There are plausible historical accounts that differ substantially from one another.

Finally, it is a mistake to think of history as a series of snapshots
frozen in time, faded sepia images from the national photo album.
History is a dynamic event, constantly moving and changing. To
focus on the static imagery of the past, however "accurate" the
view may be, is to forget that such imagery is constantly rede-
ployed in the manufacture of new forms, which in turn become the
raw material for tomorrow. For example, history reveals a certain
concept of equal protection, circa 1868, that was perversely employed to create newer ideas of equal protection in 1896, at the
time of *Plessy v. Ferguson*.[2] And newer, more refined, ever changing
images that are by no means static are being formed today that
bear little resemblance to the faded views of a century ago.

Objections to the quest for original meaning certainly undercut
the utility of that quest as a tool for sculpting contemporary constitutional understanding. They do not, however, provide adequate
reason to remove the tool from our constitutional tool kit. The
soundest interpretation is one that comports with, or at least
makes sense of, the original intent that we can know as well as our
subsequent history, and that simultaneously makes a satisfactory
peace with text, fits smoothly into the structural edifice of governmental relationships created by the Constitution, does no violence
to precedent, and poses no insurmountable problems of politics.

The objective in grappling with the original intent of the Ninth
Amendment is not to reveal the talisman that will solve all our
interpretational difficulties with the amendment; it is simply to
identify clearly the shape of and image upon one more piece of the
constitutional jigsaw puzzle of the Ninth Amendment. In parsing
the past, it is easy to forget why we are doing so. In quarreling
about the original meaning of the amendment, scholars have over-
looked the rest of the puzzle.

Some maintain that the original purpose of the Ninth Amendment was to secure against governmental usurpation a host of individual rights not specified anywhere in the Constitution, but residing in extrinsic sources. The most popular extrinsic source is natural law, the conception that there are inalienable rights inseparable from one's humanity, rights that have no source in governmental arrangements and rights that cannot legitimately be abrogated by governments. But there are other conceivable sources, not connected to natural law but rooted in the positive law of governments. The most likely such source is state laws and, in particular, state constitutions. Whatever the source of extrinsic rights, adherents to this view usually assert that extrinsic rights are as enforceable as any other constitutional right, and urge that the Ninth Amendment be used by litigants and courts as a means to protect a wide variety of individual choices against governmental invasion. This reading is one that treats the Ninth Amendment as an independent source of judicially enforceable rights, the substance of which must be found in sources extrinsic to the Constitution.

Other scholars contend that the original purpose of the amendment was simply to prevent the implication that, because certain rights were enumerated as beyond the federal government's power, the federal government must implicitly possess powers beyond those specified in the Constitution or it would not have been necessary to curb governmental power by enumerating rights. On this view, the amendment's function was merely to restrain constitutional interpreters from construing too broadly the powers delegated to the central government. By doing so, it had the secondary effect of preserving individual liberties, because the "residual rights" of the citizenry were protected by the sheer absence of governmental power to curtail them. Significantly, adherents to this view reject the idea that the Ninth Amendment is itself an independent source of human rights capable of judicial cognizance.

No sensible attribution to the framers of an intended purpose for the Ninth Amendment can be made without some understanding of the intellectual background upon which they acted. The framers were widely read, reflective, and thoughtful consumers of diverse and often incompatible views on matters of political, economic, and social theory.[3] When Americans of the late eighteenth century sought to synthesize "the several traditions [they] had inherited from Britain and Europe, [the resulting] body of literature by Americans about America lacked explicit philosophical coherence. Nevertheless, it reflected the profound sense of openness and broad socioeconomic opportunity, the ambivalence about authority and about traditional conceptions of the social order . . . that were perhaps the most important elements determining how Americans received and used the many elements of their rich . . . intellectual inheritance."[4] It is thus not surprising that historian Forrest McDonald concludes that "it is meaningless to say that the Framers intended this or intended that: their positions were diverse and, in many particulars, incompatible."[5]

This rather formidable caution ought to temper the zeal of those who seek to reduce constitutional law to a matter of ascertaining some supposed unitary original intention of the framers.[6] Even granting the insuperable difficulties of locating with any degree of usable certainty the intentions of the framers, perhaps we can discuss intelligently and derive some value from the nature of the richly spiced intellectual stew that fed the creation of our Constitution.

To do so, let us examine the political context in which the founding generation acted. It is foolhardy to assign a particular original intention to the Ninth Amendment or, for that matter, any other part of the Constitution, without first having some understanding of the general assumptions and experiences that were common to the founding generation, particularly those related to the problem of judicial review based on unwritten law. In Chapter

Three I examine in greater detail the historical evidence that bears specifically upon the intended purpose and meaning of the Ninth Amendment.

From a political standpoint, the framers were Englishmen. "From the beginning of English settlement in North America, colonists believed themselves the equals of native Englishmen and entitled to the 'rights of Englishmen.' "[7] It is not as important to know whether these rights were instantiated by statute, common law, customary tradition, or inalienable "natural" and fundamental principles as it is to understand the revolutionary generation's eclectic and rather muddied conception of the nature of the rights of Englishmen.

Colonial Americans would most likely have associated their inherited rights with the English tradition of constitutionalism. This tradition recognized the unwritten English constitution, which "consisted of a mixture of custom, natural law, religious law, enacted law, and reason," to be fundamental "higher law . . . [that] existed and operated to make void Acts of Parliament inconsistent with that fundamental law." The mechanism of invalidation was, however, more problematic. Suzanna Sherry contends that judges were thought to be entitled to "use that fundamental law to pronounce void inconsistent legislative or royal enactments."[8] Helen Michael argues that, although such a power of judicial review might be found in the theories of Edward Coke, Viscount Bolingbroke, and the "Country" opposition party of late seventeenth- and early eighteenth-century Britain, it was not widely assumed by Americans, who preferred instead to vindicate fundamental law in more populist fashion — through legislation and, if necessary, revolution.[9]

Philip Hamburger has argued that natural law "was not a residual source of constitutional rights but rather was the reasoning that implied the necessity of sacrificing natural liberty to government in a written constitution."[10] In Hamburger's view, early

Americans assigned to natural law an aspirational role. Civil (or positive) law ought to conform to natural law precepts but courts were incapable of invalidating laws that did not so conform. As with so much that pertains to our revolutionary past, all of these views possess a modicum of accuracy, a result that makes it virtually impossible to dictate results for today from the verdicts of history.

There can be no doubt that colonial Americans were heavily influenced by Sir Edward Coke and the associated theories of the English country-party opposition. As Edward Corwin has noted, Coke "was first on the ground" in the colonies, which resulted in a pervasive "presence of Coke's doctrines . . . during the latter two-thirds of the seventeenth century." Indeed, "the seventeenth century was Coke's" and although "the early half of the eighteenth century was Locke's,"[11] American "independence brought with it the triumph, at least temporarily, of the anti-capitalistic, 'country-party' ideology . . . of the English Opposition."[12]

An integral part of the Cokean ideology was the idea, set forth most explicitly in *Bonham's Case*,[13] that courts possessed the power to invalidate legislation offensive to constitutional fundamental law. Dr. Thomas Bonham practiced medicine without a certificate from the Royal College of Physicians, although he held a medical degree from Cambridge. The college censors first fined him five pounds, then imprisoned him when he continued to practice medicine. Bonham sued the college censors and president for false imprisonment. The college asserted in its defense its statute of incorporation, which authorized it to regulate all physicians and punish with fine and imprisonment practitioners not licensed by it. The statute also gave the college one half of all fines imposed by it.

In deciding against the college, Lord Coke was of the opinion that "the censors cannot be judges, ministers, and parties; judges to give sentence or judgment; ministers to make summons; and parties to have the moiety of the forfeiture, since no person may be a Judge in his own cause; . . . and one cannot be Judge and attorney for any of the parties." But the enabling statute plainly granted this power to the College. No matter, said Coke, for "it appears in our books, that in many cases, the common law will controul Acts of Parliament, and sometimes adjudge them to be utterly void: for when an Act of Parliament is against common right and reason, or repugnant, or impossible to be performed, the common law will controul it, and adjudge such Act to be void."[14]

Scholars have argued whether Coke's decision was rooted in a constitutional mandate, vesting courts with the power of judicial review of legislative acts, or merely one of strict statutory construction, rendering the quoted passage merely *obiter dictum*.[15] Regardless of the weight of the declaration, it seems unmistakable that when Coke invoked "common right and reason" he was referring to "something fundamental, something permanent . . . higher law . . . binding on Parliament and the ordinary courts alike."[16]

Whatever its merits, the academic debate came later. Colonial Americans could read Coke for themselves, and did. Coke was popular in no small part because of his role in defending the rights of parliament and the people against Stuart absolutism. His views were clearly set forth in his *Institutes*, particularly in the *Second Institute*, which restated the rights of Englishmen under Magna Carta and succeeding statutes. In the prologue to the *Second Institute*, Coke cited parliamentary enactments that invalidated any law or action contrary to Magna Carta. As Professor A. E. Dick Howard has observed, "Coke was speaking of statutes which had thus enshrined Magna Carta, but his commentaries helped lay the way for the view, subscribed to in the American colonies, of the Charter as a kind of superstatute, a constitution placing fundamental liberties beyond the reach of Parliament as well as the King and his ministers."[17]

But Americans did not understand Coke to confine judicial review to cases of parliamentary invasion of Magna Carta or other written declarations of the rights of Englishmen. Following the

Seven Years' War the London government determined that colonial Americans should pay for the cost of securing the tranquility of their frontier. To that end, it sought to suppress the flourishing trade in smuggled goods. In Boston, King George's agents sought and received general writs of assistance, search warrants that enabled the bearer to search anyone at any time for evidence of smuggling. As might be imagined, this practice was greeted with extreme hostility by the mercantile classes of Boston, who had grown affluent with profits augmented by tax evasion. The legality of these sweeping searches was soon challenged. In *Paxton's Case* (the *Writs of Assistance Case*) counsel for the crown defended generalized search warrants by pointing to specific statutory authorization for their issuance. But when James Otis, Jr., thundered against the validity of general writs of assistance, he had no doubt that *Bonham's Case* was good authority for the proposition that courts could invalidate legislation on the grounds that it offended "fundamental Principles of Law."[18] John Adams, who witnessed Otis's performance, later declared that "then and there the child independence was born,"[19] for the clear implication of Otis's assertion was that any colonial court possessed authority to invalidate the legislation of the imperial Parliament. To Professor Corwin, this principle was nothing short of the birth of a uniquely American constitutional law.[20]

It was not a principle that went unused in the turbulent final years of colonial existence. A Virginia court declared the Stamp Act to be unconstitutional[21] and arguments in Massachusetts against the Stamp Act were that "the Act . . . is against Magna Charta, and the natural Rights of Englishmen, and therefore, according to Lord Coke, null and void." Even loyalist judges in Massachusetts agreed that "an Act of Parliament against natural Equity is void."[22] Nor was this principle confined to imperial legislation. George Mason relied upon Coke to argue successfully to a Virginia court that a 1682 act of the Virginia Assembly should be declared void.[23] This is not to suggest that Otis's argument in the *Writs of Assistance Case* sparked an unbroken trend toward vigorous exercise of judicial review in the service of unwritten fundamental law; rather, it is only to claim that the Cokean legacy was a powerful and influential aspect of the intellectual heritage of the framers.

If Coke provided the jurisprudential foundation for American lawyers, John Locke and his fellow thinkers of the Continental Enlightenment supplied much of the political theory that actuated the revolutionary generation.[24] "The Patriots turned to Locke rather than to the other great natural-law theorists — Hugo Grotius, Samuel von Pufendorf, Thomas Rutherforth, J. J. Burlamaqui, Emerich Vattel — for the reason that none of the others was so well adapted to their purposes."[25] Only Locke provided a convincing rationale for independence by declaring that governments that "act contrary to their Trust . . . put themselves into a state of War with the People, who are thereupon absolved from any farther Obedience."[26]

More generally, Locke posited that the original position of humanity was a "state of nature" — a social existence without government — in which people possessed certain inalienable rights, but that out of "strong obligations of necessity, convenience and inclination," people constitute governments.[27] The social contract thus made involves the surrender of some individual rights in order to secure the remainder more effectively.[28] The gospel of the Lockean social contract — "natural rights and the social compact, government bounded by law and incapable of imparting legality to measures contrary to law, and the right of resistance to illegal measures" — was regularly preached by colonial, particularly New England, clergy, who used their pulpits as much for political as theological instruction.[29]

Locke contended that the legislature was the supreme and exclusive lawgiver of the political commonwealth,[30] a position that Helen Michael has taken to mean a complete repudiation of any constitutional judicial review, whether based on positive or natural constitutional law.[31] Although that may be the logical result of Locke's statements, Americans blithely took liberties with the Lockean canon. Locke's political theory was frequently fused with Coke's views on jurisprudence to produce a peculiarly American brand of constitutionalism. Edward Corwin contended that the Massachusetts Circular Letter of 1768 blends Coke and Locke by asserting that, although "Parliament is the supreme legislative power . . . [it] derives its power and authority from the constitution, . . . [which] ascertains and limits both sovereignty and allegiance." Significantly, the Massachusetts colonists also contended that "essential, unalterable right[s], in nature, [were] engrafted into the British constitution, as a fundamental law, and ever held sacred and irrevocable by the subjects within the realm."[32]

The Massachusetts Circular Letter was more than a mingling of Locke and Coke; it was also alloyed with Enlightenment thought. Vattel, for example, was quite explicit in his assertion that the legislative and executive authority of government is subordinate to "the fundamental laws of the state."[33] Pufendorf and Burlamaqui contended that the sovereign was bound by natural law and that, should the sovereign violate natural law, the people were entitled to revolt to enforce their natural rights.[34] Grotius was more equivocal, for he flirted with the oxymoronic idea that people could alienate their inalienable rights but simultaneously expressed the presumption that people could not part with the right to resist a sovereign's misconduct.[35]

The colonial alloy was peculiar to America. It fused Lockean and Continental notions of natural law as a limit upon sovereignty (albeit one not susceptible to judicial enforcement) with the Cokean notion that judicial review was an appropriate and legitimate mechanism by which to enforce these limiting principles of fundamental law. Although Lockean and Continental Enlightenment political theory *standing alone* might "undermine . . . [the view] that judicial review was a logical outgrowth of the diverse natural law tradition that the American colonists embraced,"[36] the importance of these theories is that they cannot be considered in isolation. Just as birds use wildly disparate elements to construct their nests, the colonists fashioned their applied political theory from similarly incongruous sources. Colonial lawyers transformed their sources, rather than being constrained by them. It is myopic to think that they hewed carefully to the logical limits of the theories they embraced. These were men on a mission who were impatient with the intellectual details that preoccupy the modern, detached observer.

Among the other influences upon colonial political thought were a number of disparate egalitarian thinkers: radical Whigs like John Trenchard and Thomas Gordon (the authors of *Cato's Letters*), the Protestant clergy of colonial America, the Scottish Enlightenment, and such American radicals as Thomas Paine. As with Locke and the Continental natural law scholars, Americans absorbed these influences and put them to their own purposes.[37]

Trenchard and Gordon were, in a sense, radical Lockeans. They contended that political society rested on a compact between the people and their governmental agents, relied on the legislative agents of the people to safeguard their liberties, but recognized that the legislature was subject to the limits of fundamental law. Like Pufendorf and Burlamaqui, Trenchard and Gordon believed that the remedy for legislative action infringing upon fundamental law was to hold frequent elections and, if necessary, revolution.[38]

The eighteenth-century Protestant clergy of colonial America "taught their flocks political theory . . . [and, a]fter the Bible, Locke was the principal authority relied on by the preachers." Although the colonial clergy consisted of New England Puritans, Southern Anglicans, and dissenters of all kinds, their message was the familiar one of "natural rights and social compact, government bounded by [fundamental] law, . . . and the right of resistance to illegal measures."[39] To be sure, there were disturbing notes of extreme egalitarianism sounded by George Whitefield, the preacher at the center of the "Great Awakening" of the mid-eighteenth century. More established clerics recoiled from Whitefield's challenge to authority, but his message resonated with the mass of colonial Americans and contributed to the doctrinal cacophony that makes it so difficult to assess some shared intention with respect to any given practice or principle.

The Scottish Enlightenment thinkers were, perhaps, the most radical of all. They argued that all people are endowed with equal capabilities for moral reasoning and, as a result, concluded that this inherent, natural moral equality dictated political equality.[40] This sentiment, echoed in the Declaration of Independence's assertion that "all men are created equal," was "but a short step to radical democracy,"[41] in which "the spirit of the law . . . [should] be considered . . . only on appeal to the representatives of the people."[42]

Radical egalitarianism was also much in evidence in Thomas Paine's *Common Sense.* Paine asserted that "the equal rights of nature" compelled the conclusion that government should be perfectly egalitarian. In short, Paine espoused an unvarnished majoritarianism, in which there would be "no distinctions" and thus "no superiority" among those composing the polity.[43]

In one important sense, all of these egalitarian components of colonial political theory were at odds with Cokean theories of jurisprudence. Although the egalitarians and Coke might agree that the "law of nature is part of the laws of England . . . [and] is that which God at the time of creation . . . infused into his heart,"[44] the egalitarians would be far less likely to concur with Coke that only those "schooled in the artificial reason and judgment of the law" were entitled to decide when legislation contravened the fundamental law of nature.[45]

The revolutionary generation simultaneously employed two concepts of how fundamental natural law could be used to protect human liberty. The jurisprudential strain associated with Coke and his forebears relied upon judges to invoke natural law to check executive and legislative abuses. An admixture of the Continental natural law thinkers and various radical egalitarians counseled colonial Americans to rely instead upon majoritarian democracy to discern and apply the fundamental principles of natural law.

Neither of these visions can be said to have wholly captured the Revolutionary imagination. As Forrest McDonald has observed, independence produced only the temporary triumph of the radical egalitarian approach.[46] The initial reaction to independence was enthusiastic embrace of a radical vision of majoritarian democracy, but within a short time this vision began to be supplanted or augmented by the Cokean jurisprudential notions of political arrangement. An examination of some representative samples of the salient political events from revolutionary America provides some telling and paradigmatic examples of the evanescence of radical egalitarianism and is a useful background upon which to understand the specific events surrounding the creation of the Ninth Amendment.

In 1776, Pennsylvania adopted a constitution that reflected the ideals of radical democracy.[47] It relied almost exclusively upon the legislature to conduct the popular will into governmental action. There was no governor; rather, executive functions were to be performed by a popularly elected committee. The legislature controlled the tenure of judges, who in any case could only serve for seven years.[48] "To make the legislature more responsive to its theoretical master, the people, Pennsylvania required annual elections of representatives, required representatives to subject their acts to the instructions of their constituents, and required the legislature to submit proposed legislation to popular review."[49] The political climate that produced Pennsylvania's 1776 constitution and others imbued with its revolutionary zeal was one in which "few Americans except lawyers trusted a truly independent judiciary" or, for that matter, a strong executive or even a legislature much distanced from the people. It is likely correct to observe of these manifestations of revolutionary political doctrine that "the notion that the judges should be so independent as to have power to . . . pass upon the constitutionality of laws enacted by the legislative bodies was alien to [the egalitarian strain] of American theory and practice."[50]

The practical result of its 1776 constitution was to make Pennsylvania "the most unstable state in the country, . . . a sort of . . . late twentieth-century California." Accordingly, "as a means of redressing this instability, Pennsylvania conservatives managed in 1790 to create a new state constitution modeled on that of the federal government . . . [and] reflect[ing] its framers' desire to lessen popular influence."[51] If Pennsylvania's 1776 constitution may be regarded as the prototypical revolutionary charter "establishing legislative supremacy," its 1790 constitution was characteristic of "the reaction to legislative supremacy . . . , [enabling] a new appreciation of the role of the judiciary in American politics." As Gordon Wood has noted, "by the 1780's the judiciary in several states . . . was gingerly and often ambiguously moving in isolated but important cases to impose restraints on what the legislatures were enacting as law."[52]

Just as Pennsylvania sought to temper its radical egalitarianism through constitutional change, the nature of judicial review in the 1780s reflected a similar assimilation of radical egalitarianism and Cokean theories of jurisprudence. Because American political theory was in flux during the decade it is not surprising that the handful of known instances in which state courts arguably asserted the power to invalidate legislation as contrary to unwritten fundamental law are susceptible to differing interpretations.[53] But the existence of these cases, in which the paramount nature of unwritten law was seriously asserted by courts, indicates that the political climate in the decade preceding consideration and adoption of the Ninth Amendment was one in which judicial enforcement of unwritten rights was an established, if controversial, phenomenon.

• *Josiah Philips's Case.* Josiah Philips was a notorious brigand during the Revolution. In May of 1778 the Virginia legislature passed a bill of attainder providing that, unless Philips surrendered himself prior to the end of June, he would be automatically "convicted and attainted of high treason" and subjected to "the pains of death." Philips was apprehended sometime in June, 1778, prior to the effective date of the attainder. Because he had not voluntarily surrendered himself, however, there must have been some uncertainty surrounding the applicability of the attainder. Philips was tried and convicted in accordance with ordinary common law procedures, rather than pursuant to the attaint.[54]

Two radically different explanations have been offered for the failure to rely upon the attainder. According to St. George Tucker, "an associate of some of [Philips's] . . . judges . . . [and who] was familiar with the circumstances of the case,"[55] Philips "was brought before the . . . court to receive sentence of execution pursuant to the [attainder] . . . [b]ut the court refused to pass the sentence and he was put upon trial according to the ordinary course of law." To Tucker, this was "decisive proof . . . of the independence of the judiciary."[56] Because the 1776 Virginia Constitution contained no explicit prohibitions of bills of attainder, though it did contain explicit guarantees pertaining to trial procedures, the judicial intervention described by Tucker might have been based, in part, on some unwritten conception of fundamental law that ranked on a par with the Virginia Constitution.[57] The contrary explanation is that, because the bill of attainder had not become effective, there was no reason to do anything other than apply common law. On this view, "the case had nothing whatever to do with judicial review."[58]

Whatever the actual explanation may have been for the failure to apply the legislative attainder to Philips, when it became a subject of debate in the Virginia ratification convention the delegates who spoke to the matter uniformly, and wrongly, assumed that Philips had, in fact, been condemned pursuant to the attaint.[59] To William Crosskey, this was "sufficient to show that, among Virginians, in 1788, the Philips case was, very clearly, *not* regarded as a great landmark of judicial review."[60] That may well be so, for it was St. George Tucker, writing in 1803, who understood *Philips's Case* to be an instance of judicial review. Nevertheless, the Virginians of 1788, convened to debate ratification of the Constitution, debated the validity of the attaint in terms of natural justice, which suggests that they did not regard their written constitution of 1776 to have supplanted unwritten fundamental law. Patrick Henry, Governor of Virginia at the time of *Philips's Case*, defended the supposed attaint as "justified by the laws of nature and nations." Benjamin Harrison, chairman of the very House of Delegates that enacted the attaint, labeled Edmund Randolph's charges of its unconstitutionality "very unjust . . . [because Philips] was a man who, by the laws of nations, was entitled to no privilege of trial." Even those hostile to the attaint attacked its validity in terms of natural law. Edmund Pendleton, for example, asserted that the attaint was "repugnant to the principles of justice[,] . . . contrary to the Constitution, and the spirit of the common law."[61]

The Virginians' misunderstanding of their own contemporary history might indicate that they did not regard the case as an instance of judicial review, but it certainly underscores their ready acceptance of natural law as coexisting with a written constitution. Tucker's gloss may well have caused a later generation to regard the case as an example of judicial review; perhaps Tucker simply recorded a common understanding that came later; or Tucker, one of the foremost legal commentators and scholars of late eighteenth- and early nineteenth-century Virginia, may have accurately described an early, *and advisory*, instance of judicial review. If the latter explanation is correct, perhaps the Virginians' treatment of *Philips's Case* in the ratification debates reflects the advisory nature of the judicial opinion. On this view, the Virginia courts simply advised counsel that prosecution under the attainder would violate fundamental law, whether rooted in the Virginia Constitution or in principles of natural justice. Even though counsel heeded that advice, the Virginia delegates found it politically expedient to debate the legitimacy of the legislative act that went unenforced.

Though clouded by misunderstanding in 1788, it is clear that by 1803, when the influential Tucker wrote, *Philips's Case* had begun to be understood as an early exemplar of judicial review.[62] That this may have been due to what Crosskey derisively described as the "oral tradition and the transient memories of judges and lawyers" does not diminish its effect.[63] Oral traditions and transient memories reflect the current importance of past events. The importance of *Philips's Case* lies not so much in what actually transpired as in what the immediately following generation thought happened. Whatever the "true" understanding, *Philips's Case* epitomizes the transformative nature of political thought in the 1780s, a time in which radical egalitarianism (which treated natural law as a principle capable of apprehension only by democratic legislatures) became intermingled with the Cokean theories of jurisprudence that regarded the judiciary as the guardian of individual rights (whether derived from written or unwritten fundamental law). It is no surprise that St. George Tucker should have been an agent of that transformation with respect to *Philips's Case*, because he regarded judicial review as indispensable for the preservation of human liberty.[64]

• *Holmes v. Walton.* In 1778, the New Jersey legislature enacted a statute designed to prevent trading with the enemy by providing for forfeiture of goods taken in such trade. The statute, as applied, provided for a six-man jury trial. Prior practice applicable to cases of the type at issue was to require a twelve-man jury, and the New Jersey Constitution expressly guaranteed the right to a jury trial, though of an unspecified size. The New Jersey Supreme Court reversed the conviction and remanded for a new trial. Crosskey contends that the court did so because it found the trial judge's interpretation of the statute to be in error but admits that his conclusion is only a weighing of probabilities.[65] We do know that the New Jersey Supreme Court reversed the conviction and that it was urged to do so on the grounds that trial by six-man jury was "contrary to law, . . . the constitution of New Jersey, . . . [and the] practices . . . of the land."[66] Fused together in this argument without attempt to distinguish between them were appeals to custom, reason, and written and unwritten fundamental law. As James Whitman has pointed out, this form of discourse — the intermingling of sources of fundamental law — was characteristic of the revolutionary generation.[67]

We also know that the New Jersey Supreme Court was understood by contemporary observers to have declared the act unconstitutional. Residents of Monmouth County, where the case arose and was tried, petitioned the New Jersey legislature to complain "that the justices of the Supreme Court have set aside some of the laws as unconstitutional."[68] In neighboring Pennsylvania, Gouverneur Morris argued to the legislature that it would be unconstitutional for it to abolish a bank charter, and invoked *Holmes v. Walton* for the proposition that Pennsylvania judges possessed the power to declare legislation unconstitutional.[69]

There can be little doubt that, during the 1780s, *Holmes v. Walton* "was commonly regarded as a precedent for judicial review." It is also likely true that "there was, at that time, hostility to the whole idea of judicial review."[70] The two positions provide further illustration of the turbulence of political thought in the 1780s. Radical egalitarianism, exemplified by legislative supremacy, was beginning to shatter into a more complicated mosaic including, among other things, Cokean theories of jurisprudence.

• *Commonwealth v. Caton.* The defendants in this 1782 case were convicted of treason under a 1776 Virginia statute that vested the pardon power in both houses of the Virginia legislature. The House of Delegates voted to grant a pardon but the Senate refused. The defendants appealed to the Virginia Supreme Court of

Appeals, contending that the statute was contrary to the Virginia Constitution. The court found the statute to be in accord with the constitution,[71] but, in dicta, seven of the eight judges "were of opinion, that the court had power to declare *any* resolution or act of the legislature . . . to be unconstitutional and void."[72]

Were the power of judicial review to have been exercised in *Caton* it would have been with reference to a written constitution, but certain of the rhetoric employed by George Wythe suggests that he, at least, might in the proper case have regarded himself as entitled to range well beyond the written Constitution to void legislative actions violative of unwritten fundamental law. Wythe invoked the Cokean proposition that it was the duty of the judge "to protect the rights of the subject against the encroachment of the Crown" in order to declare that it was "equally [his duty] to protect . . . the whole community against [legislative] usurpations."[73] When speaking in revolutionary America of the "encroachment[s] of the Crown" Wythe could not possibly be thought to mean abuses wrought personally by the king; rather, the thrust of revolutionary animus was directed toward the claimed invalidity of legislation of the imperial Parliament.[74] Thus, when he invoked the power of *English* judges "to protect a solitary individual against the rapacity of the sovereign" he called upon a power rooted, if anywhere, in English traditions of an unwritten constitution.

Commonwealth v. Caton reflects the embryonic and tentative character of judicial review in the transformative 1780s. Just as in *Philips's Case*, where judicial review is likely to have assumed a purely advisory and nonbinding character, *Caton* is another example of judges claiming the power of judicial review without actually attempting to enforce the claim. It is reasonable to expect judicial review in the 1780s to assume that shape as revolutionary America groped toward a political rapprochement between the revolutionary ideal of democratic legislative supremacy and the other revolutionary tradition of fundamental law, rooted in a mixture of sources, as a judicially enforceable check upon legislative abuse.

• *Rutgers v. Waddington.* Elizabeth Rutgers sued Joshua Waddington, a British subject, for trespass resulting from his possession of her malt house pursuant to an order of the British military authorities in occupied New York. Rutgers's claim was founded on a New York statute that barred the defense that the trespass was ordered by the military occupation authorities. This statute was arguably contrary to the law of nations, however, which recognized the right of captors to use captured real estate, the 1783 Peace Treaty between the United States and the United Kingdom, which contained mutual releases of claims such as Rutgers's, and the Articles of Confederation.[75]

The court employed an artful dodge that seems typical of the period. It repeated the obligatory pieties about legislative supremacy,[76] declared that it was merely interpreting the statute to avoid unintended conflict with the law of nations or the Peace Treaty, and proceeded to uphold the statute but to deny relief. In short, the court exercised a judicial power that "it specifically declared no court had power to [exercise]."[77] Moreover, the court identified the problem as the conflict between the statute and the law of nations, which it "equated . . . with the law of nature."[78] Thus, the court's de facto exercise of judicial review was founded on unwritten fundamental law.

Rutgers differs from the prior cases in that judicial review was not advisory or hortatory. The court actually exercised the power, though it clumsily sought to camouflage the fact, no doubt due to the charged political atmosphere resulting from the reappraisal of radical egalitarianism. Accordingly, it is not surprising that, like *Holmes v. Walton*, the decision spawned protests of the claimed usurpation of legislative power. Nor is it surprising that the case was widely reported at the time, for it was vividly emblematic of the movement toward greater judicial control of legislatures in the name of fundamental law.[79]

• *Trevett v. Weeden.* Rhode Island imposed a penalty on all persons who refused to accept paper money in discharge of their obligations, and permitted no jury trial for prosecutions seeking to enforce the penalty. John Weeden contended that the statute was void because the denial of the jury trial right was contrary to fundamental law.[80] Because Rhode Island had no written constitution, Weeden's claim was a pure appeal to the primacy of unwritten fundamental law. The court granted the appeal and dismissed the complaint, noting cryptically that the prosecution was not "cognizable" before it. Despite the enigmatic disclaimer, the people of Rhode Island regarded the court as having declared the act unconstitutional. The legislature thought so too, for it summoned the judges before it for an explanation that, once delivered, was "highly technical" and wildly improbable.[81] The judges explained that, although Weeden's plea had been that the statute was void due to its repugnance to unwritten fundamental law, they had merely decided that the prosecution was not judicially cognizable, without specifying the reasons for the defect.[82] The judges convinced nobody. The legislature refused to reappoint them, the case was widely reported at the time as an example of judicial review based on unwritten fundamental law, and even Professor Crosskey, a vehement critic of judicial review, has characterized the judges' explanation as "mask[ing] their actual action."[83] Once again, the case illustrates the Janus-like nature of judicial review in the 1780s. Radical egalitarians denounced the thought of judicial enforcement of fundamental law, whatever its source; judges sought to preserve judicial review by indirection and obfuscation; and the people understood both the fact of the phenomenon and its implications to human liberty and majoritarian rule.

• *Bayard v. Singleton.* During the Revolution, North Carolina, like many states, enacted legislation that authorized the seizure and sale of loyalists' property. A 1785 North Carolina statute required judges, acting without juries, to dismiss all actions seeking recovery of such seized property, regardless of the merits of the claim. Bayard brought suit in ejectment to recover certain confiscated property that North Carolina had sold to Singleton. Singleton asked for dismissal of the action, citing the 1785 statute. The court, "after pretty clearly intimating its belief that the act . . . was unconstitutional,"[84] delayed its "decision for about a year and attempted to secure a compromise that would avoid a conflict between the law and the constitution."[85] The court finally denied Singleton's motion to dismiss, noting that "no act [the legislature] could pass, could by any means repeal or alter the constitution," and submitted the case to a jury, which promptly found for Singleton.[86]

Bayard is clearly an instance of the exercise of judicial review, albeit based upon a written provision of the North Carolina Constitution guaranteeing jury trials. It is possible that the *Bayard* court might also have felt entitled, in the proper case, to invalidate legislation as contrary to unwritten fundamental law.[87] The North Carolina court was not called upon to do so, however, and thus confined itself to enforcing the paramountcy of the written constitution. Like the other instances of judicial review in the 1780s *Bayard* engendered substantial public opposition,[88] reflecting the unsettled climate of political thought and the transitional stage from radical legislative egalitarianism to judicial constraint of the legislature.

The state precedents from the 1780s establish that judicial review was employed haltingly, sparingly, and with knowledge that its use would inspire popular opposition from dedicated radical egalitarians. Sometimes, as in *Philips's Case* and *Commonwealth v. Caton*, judicial review was claimed rhetorically but enforcement was not sought. The remaining occasions discussed are all instances in which judicial review was actually asserted, although in *Rutgers v. Waddington* and *Trevett v. Weeden* the judges sought to deny or obscure their true object. When lawyers urged judges to void legislation as repugnant to fundamental law, they were not careful to distinguish between written and unwritten sources of fundamental law. Indeed, the actual instances of judicial review reflect the advocates' haphazardness on this point.[89] *Trevett v. Weeden* and *Rutgers v. Waddington* are examples of judicial review based on unwritten fundamental law; *Holmes v. Walton* is an uncertain precedent; and *Bayard v. Singleton* is rooted in the written constitution of North Carolina. All of the decisions produced popular discontent from the disciples of radical egalitarianism, yet the decisions have endured and were cited by neo-Cokeans as examples of the judiciary's role as defender of human liberty.

Although some commentators treat the popular opposition to these precedents as evidence that judicial review — whether grounded in written or unwritten fundamental law — was not accepted at the time of the constitutional bargain in 1787,[90] they overlook the basic fact that the 1780s were times of intense upheaval and transition. John Adams declared that "the child independence was born" by James Otis's invocation in 1760 of Coke and the power of judicial review.[91] The sustenance of the newborn was radical egalitarianism embodied by the supreme legislature. That experiment soured and the 1780s represent the groping of the young United States toward a political structure that sought to secure revolutionary ideals in a more mature, sophisticated, and multidimensional fashion. The transition that occurred in that decade was a blending of revolutionary themes. Amid the fading bloom of revolutionary radical egalitarianism it is not surprising to find judges exercising the power of judicial review obliquely and tentatively. Nor is it surprising that even such indirect attempts to curtail legislative abuse were often greeted with public anger and resentment. The outcome, which could be only dimly foreseen in the 1780s, was a fusion of radical egalitarianism with Cokean theories of jurisprudence. Thus it is vain to pretend that, by understanding the tumult of the 1780s, we can be certain that *any single aspect* of those transitional times was of such paramount importance that it ought to be the rule of decision for today.

If the period leading up the 1787 Convention and resultant federal Constitution, were times of tumultuous transition in political thought, the period after 1789 presents a clearer picture of acceptance of the idea of judicial review and its employment as a device to insure the paramountcy of written and unwritten fundamental law. A brief review of some salient state and federal precedents will capture the flavor of the period.

In *Ham v. M'Claws* proceedings were brought to forfeit slaves imported into South Carolina in violation of a South Carolina statute. The slaveowners conceded the statutory violation but contended that, because they were induced to settle in South Carolina in reliance upon then existing law, and could not possibly have known of the recent alteration of the law, the statute should be regarded as contrary to "the rules of common right and justice." Counsel argued quite specifically that "statutes made against natural equity are void." The court agreed, charging the jury that "it is clear, that statutes passed against the plain and obvious principles of common right and common reason, are absolutely void, as far as they are calculated to operate against those principles." The court's embrace of Cokean principles of natural law and reason as authority for invalidation of the statute could hardly have been warmer.[92]

In *Kamper v. Hawkins* the Virginia Supreme Court concluded that a Virginia act reorganizing judicial districts was void because it was contrary to the Virginia Constitution. In seriatim opinions, the court concluded that where legislation and the Constitution collided, it was the judicial duty "to decide that the act is void." Similarly, Spencer Roane "conclude[d] that the judiciary . . . ought to adjudge a law unconstitutional and void, if it be plainly repugnant to the letter of the Constitution, *or the fundamental principles thereof.*" Lest there be any doubt about the relationship between the written Constitution and the unwritten fundamental principles appurtenant to constitutional text, Roane explained that fundamental principles were "those great principles growing out of the Constitution . . . ; those land-marks, which it may be necessary to resort to, on account of the impossibility to foresee or provide for cases within the spirit but without the letter of the Constitution."[93]

In *Bowman v. Middleton* a South Carolina statute transferring title to real property from one party to another was invalidated because "it was against common right . . . to take away the freehold of one man and vest it in another." Therefore, "the act was . . . void; and . . . no length of time could give it validity, being originally founded on erroneous principles." Once again the power of constitutional judicial review was squarely related to the primacy of unwritten fundamental law.[94]

To similar effect is *Merrill v. Sherburne* in which a New Hampshire court struck down legislation that awarded a litigant a new trial. The court concluded that the statute offended the New Hampshire Constitution because it both usurped the judicial function and was retrospective in its effect, but the court was sufficiently unsure of the specific constitutional textual foundation for its conclusion that it felt compelled to rest the decision "upon general principles."[95]

These state precedents are but the tip of the iceberg. Charles Haines has collected another two dozen state precedents from the period in which state courts declared legislation to be void as contrary to written constitutions or "against the law of nature."[96] It is hardly surprising that Haines concluded:

By a gradual development the American doctrine of judicial review of legislation had emerged through colonial and state precedents and dicta of judges into a fairly well understood and accepted principle. Referring on some occasions to an overruling law of nature, on other occasions to the fundamental principles embodied in the great English charters of liberties, and, finally, to formally enacted written instruments, colonial and state courts steadily asserted and maintained the right to invalidate acts, and thus they promulgated for the United States and put into an effective form Coke's theory of the supremacy of the courts.[97]

The contemporaneous federal precedents paint a similar picture. Well before the power of judicial review was definitively claimed in *Marbury v. Madison*[98] the Supreme Court had indirectly asserted the power and some of the lower federal courts had explicitly ruled legislation invalid on constitutional grounds.

In *Hayburn's Case*[99] five of the six justices, in their capacities as circuit justices, "rendered a decision for the first time holding an Act of Congress to be in violation of the Constitution."[100] Congress had enacted legislation that authorized pensions for disabled war veterans.[101] The federal circuit courts were required to entertain applications and to certify to the Secretary of War those applicants found eligible. The secretary, however, was free to disregard the judicial finding of eligibility and substitute his own judgment of ineligibility. The justices informed President George Washington that it was impossible to entertain pension applications because (1) "the business directed by this act is not of a judicial nature . . . [and] the courts . . . must, consequently have proceeded without constitutional authority," and (2) the power of the Secretary of War to revise judicial findings was "radically inconsistent with the . . . important principle [of judicial independence] which is so strictly observed by the Constitution of the United States."[102]

After the Eleventh Amendment overruled *Chisholm v. Georgia*[103] by stripping the federal courts of jurisdiction over suits against states brought by citizens of another state or country, the Supreme Court, in *Hollingsworth v. Virginia*,[104] dismissed all pending suits by citizens of one state against another. Even though the Eleventh Amendment had been ratified, Section 13 of the 1789 Judiciary Act continued to authorize suits in federal court by citizens of one state against another.[105] The Court's dismissal order, unaccompanied by an opinion, effectively treated that portion of Section 13 as invalid law due to the supervening constitutional amendment. Accordingly, "*Hollingsworth* may put to flight the conventional wisdom that *Marbury v. Madison* was the first case in which the Supreme Court held an act of Congress unconstitutional."[106]

In *Hylton v. United States*[107] a federal tax on carriages was attacked as an unconstitutional, unapportioned direct tax. The Supreme Court unanimously upheld the validity of the tax by concluding that it was not a direct tax, but was silent on the "threshold question whether the Court had power to declare an act of Congress unconstitutional. . . . Thus the Court began to accustom the country to the fact of judicial review without proclaiming its power to exercise it."[108]

By the time John Marshall asserted the power in *Marbury v. Madison* its pedigree had already been well established. As Suzanna Sherry has pointed out,[109] Marshall's opinion in *Marbury* relied almost equally upon written and unwritten fundamental law to reach the conclusion that a portion of Section 13 of the 1789 Judiciary Act was repugnant to the Constitution. Having concluded that William Marbury was entitled to his commission as a justice of the peace, Marshall concluded that Marbury was also entitled to a remedy, not because one had been given him by statute or the Constitution, but because the provision of remedies for violations of rights was "the very essence of civil liberty . . . [and] [o]ne of the first duties of government."[110] Evidently, the lack of a positive law source of a remedy would have violated some fundamental legal norm not to be found in the Holy Writ of the Constitution. The specific constitutional defect of Section 13 — the legislative authorization for the Court to assume original jurisdiction of suits seeking mandamus "to any . . . persons holding [federal] office"[111] — was, however, a incongruity between the written Constitution and the congressional act.

John Marshall's acceptance of natural law as a component of constitutional adjudication may be seen even more clearly in *Fletcher v. Peck*.[112] The 1795 Georgia legislature was bribed to convey vast tracts of public land for less than two cents per acre.[113] The following year a more virtuous legislature enacted legislation to cancel these so-called "Yazoo land grants." Fletcher, a successor in interest to an original Yazoo grantee, sued Peck, the immediate grantor, for breach of the covenant of good title. Fletcher contended that, because the Yazoo grants had been lawfully rescinded, Peck was in breach of his deed covenant.

The Supreme Court concluded that the Georgia legislature lacked the constitutional power to rescind its conveyance. In an opinion that "bristles with references suggesting unwritten limitations derived from natural law,"[114] Marshall concluded that "Georgia was restrained, either by general principles which are common to our free institutions, or by the particular provisions of the constitution of the United States,"[115] from revoking the Yazoo grants. Justice William Johnson, concurring specially on this point, was even more blunt: "I do it, on a general principle, on the reason and nature of things: a principle which will impose laws even on the Deity."[116]

All of this was evocative of Justice Samuel Chase's celebrated endorsement, in *Calder v. Bull*, of natural law as a principle by which judges may void legislation: "There are certain vital principles in our free republican governments, which will determine and overrule an apparent and flagrant abuse of legislative power. . . . An act of the legislature (for I cannot call it a law), contrary to the great first principles of the social compact, cannot be considered a rightful exercise of legislative authority."[117]

The early federal period is thus replete with cases that document the steady trend toward rejection of revolutionary-era legislative supremacy and return to the earlier idea that Cokean ideas of jurisprudence were the preferred methods by which to assure the continuation of individual rights.[118] In the course of this development, the cases rely upon written and unwritten fundamental law as a basis upon which to void legislation. That fact is reflective of a continuation in the early federal period of the revolutionary discourse that mingled together custom and reason, written and unwritten law, as sources of fundamental law.

To be sure, reliance upon unwritten law was a source of some controversy, as symbolized by the famous debate between Samuel Chase and James Iredell over the proper role of natural law in constitutional adjudication. Justice Iredell contended that judges could not void legislation "merely because it is, in their judgment, contrary to the principles of natural justice." Iredell objected to natural law because "ideas of natural justice are regulated by no fixed standard."[119] Although that objection might also be leveled against the written Constitution, Iredell thought that the idea of judicially enforceable unwritten limits on legislation was fundamentally incompatible with the concept of a written constitution.

Members of the 1787 Convention did not draft a written constitution that simply restated the existing understanding of fundamental law. Rather, they deliberately set out to create a new statement of fundamental legal principles, with no pedigree in history or experience, the validity of which was entirely grounded in the fact that it was a charter adopted by the people through their representatives in the ratification conventions. Though Iredell did not explicitly say so, his view that a written constitution wholly displaces unwritten sources of fundamental law must have stemmed from a belief that the *only* form of fundamental law was that which was adopted by the people. If Iredell did entertain such a view of popular sovereignty, it was one that comported uneasily with the Lockean political theory that actuated much of revolutionary political thought.

Locke and Iredell would no doubt have agreed that "law becomes binding solely because of the people's consent."[120] A central aspect of Locke's vision was "that the sovereign merely succeeded to the private rights given up to it by the contracting individual members of society." By assuming, as Iredell did, that the written Constitution delivered to the sovereign the power to invade every aspect of human behavior except where written limits were specified, Iredell stood Lockean and constitutional theory on its head. Lockeans thought that "the state itself had no claim to new and independent rights as against the person under its control," but derived its powers from explicit cessions from the people.[121]

It is true that many Americans of Iredell's era professed adherence to the Lockean social contract and also regarded it as possible that persons could cede to governments the power to invade all rights except those specifically reserved. But this possibility was supposedly guarded against by the creation, via the Constitution, of a central government with only carefully limited, enumerated powers, leaving the mass of all other powers and rights with the people. In this sense, although the written constitution might be the definitive instrument for determining the limits of that cession, it could not be the final authority regarding the limits of the people's rights, for Lockean thought posited that "government powers are islands in a sea of individual rights, not the sea encompassing islands of enumerated liberties."[122] Iredell and modern commentators who deny utterly the existence of unenumerated rights fall into the error of supposing that, because the Constitution defines the extent of governmental power, it must also define the limits of retained individual liberties immune from the exercise of governmental power. The one does not follow from the other. The lively presence of natural law thought in constitutional adjudication during the post-revolutionary period is proof that Iredell's error was not uniformly shared. Of course, over time the blandishments of positivism have captured the legal imagination and natural law has had to live a fugitive existence. Nevertheless, the continued persistence of natural law thought in constitutional adjudication, under whatever guise, suggests that we implicitly realize some degree of error in Iredell's position.

THREE

Dual Paths to a Single End

The Ninth Amendment was created in a political context that increasingly recognized the authority of courts to invalidate legislation in order to preserve unwritten liberties but that by itself, is no reason to ascribe to the Ninth Amendment a judicially enforceable power to protect unwritten liberties. Parsing the specific intended purposes of the Ninth Amendment is far more complicated.

Even if the daunting epistemological obstacles associated with original intentions are overcome we are left with the uncomfortable problem of demonstrating that original intentions ought to be the authoritative voice in contemporary constitutional interpretation. A constitution is a continuous organic act of political faith. It is an image of what we collectively affirm to be our essential political understanding.[1] It is our contemporary act of deciding to what we will consent and to what we will not consent. Original intentions are the legitimate voice of constitutional authority only if we agree today that it is so.

Given the apparent lack of a priori authority to original intentions it is reasonable to wonder why it is necessary to scrutinize the originally intended meaning and function of the Ninth Amendment. There are at least two answers. First, to the extent that contemporary constitutional interpretation is consistent with original intentions, when known, the objections of those in the political community who contend that *only* original intentions matter will be defused. While constitutional law can never be an exercise in unanimity, its authoritativeness increases as ever larger portions of the polity subscribe to the predominant understanding of the Constitution. Grounding today's interpretations in past intentions improves the contemporary legitimacy of constitutional lawmaking. Second, by attempting to understand past authorial intentions we provide additional texture to the current process of deciding precisely what it is we wish to consent to in our time.

Understanding the authorial intention of text does not necessarily force us to accept that intention as controlling, but it does force us to adjust our reading of text to account for the authorial intention. If we *know* irrefragably that Samuel Clemens intended *Huckleberry Finn* as a satire upon the peculiar mores of the antebellum South we may (but are not necessarily required to) adjust our understanding of the meaning of that text. If we know that the license plate "K0Z 1R0" means to its author an expression of affinity to a foreign community it may still be an odd alphanumeric sequence to us, but its meaning is amplified by our knowledge of authorial intention. Contemporary notions of constitutional law are not rootless, unconnected in any way from past understandings. Far from it. Constitutional understandings in any given period derive a considerable portion of their meaning from past views, whether such views be rejected or accepted. Understanding past intentions will thus aid the formation of our present interpretations.

In debating the intentions of the framers and ratifiers of the Ninth Amendment most commentators assume that there was only one intended purpose for the amendment. The nature of the debate then becomes an exercise in invoking historical sources in an attempt to demonstrate that any given view of the amendment is the most plausible one to attribute to the framers. There are at least two fundamental errors in any "single-purpose" approach. First, it ignores the multifaceted and contradictory political theories that actuated the framers' efforts, and second, it provides a poorer account for the entire historical record than does an approach that assigns multiple objectives to the Ninth Amendment.

It is familiar history that the 1787 Constitutional Convention took place amid a crisis of confidence in the new nation.[2] Most, but by no means all, of the leaders of the time thought that the difficulties of trade, public debt, and funding of a national government for common purposes such as defense, demanded a significantly stronger central government.[3] Participants at the convention in Philadelphia were more commonly beset by fears of state encroachment upon national power than fears of federal displacement of state power. In part this was due to the Confederation experience, which was marked by state jealousies, rival tariffs, artificial barriers to trade, and lack of a national currency or credit.[4] In part, it was due to sheer intellectual fascination with James Madison's pathbreaking conception of the "extended republic" as a device to check the ever-present dangers of majoritarianism. Madison contended that a large, diverse nation was suited to controlling factionalism by bringing diverse factions under a common roof, making it harder for any particular group to dominate the majoritarian machinery.[5]

Of equal importance, however, was the preservation of the independent status of the states. Madison contended that an advantage of the new Constitution was that "the federal and state governments . . . [would possess] the disposition and the faculty . . . to resist and frustrate the measures or each other." This was thought necessary in order to curb "ambitious encroachments of the federal government[ ] on the authority of the State governments."[6] Moreover, the framers acknowledged that the federal government would depend upon the states for its very existence, through such devices as state control over the qualifications of voters, the election of senators by state legislatures, and the use of the electoral college or voting by state within the House of Representatives to elect the president. To facilitate the independence of the states, the framers vested the central government with a "few and defined" number of powers, reserving to the states "all the objects, which, in the ordinary course of affairs, concern the lives, liberties, and properties of the people."[7]

Thus, the expectation of the framers was "that the protection of citizen rights was a matter to be governed by state constitutional law." In other words, sovereignty rested ultimately with the people of each state, who were responsible for safeguarding their individual liberties by using their state constitutions to reserve individual rights from the zone of authority otherwise ceded to state governments. A "federal republic . . . of both national and state governments was possible because the people, as the sovereign body, were superior to each government and could determine the precise amount of power allocated to each."[8] Therefore Madison could confidently declare that the federal and state governments were "different agents and trustees of the people, instituted with different powers, and designated for different purposes."[9] To Madison and the Federalists there was no need for an enumerated bill of rights, because the sovereign people had made an explicit, and quite narrow, delegation of power to the central government in the new Constitution.

The Antifederalists, however, had good reason to think otherwise. At the Constitutional Convention, George Mason made the irrefutable observation that the supremacy clause would render all federal laws "paramount to State Bills of Rights."[10] Toward the end of the Convention several unsuccessful attempts were made by Charles Pinckney of South Carolina and Elbridge Gerry of Massachusetts to persuade the framers to attach a bill of rights to the proposed Constitution. Typical of the thinking that led to rejection of these proposals was that of Roger Sherman of Connecticut, who argued that a proposed guarantee of freedom of the press was "unnecessary" because "the power of Congress does not extend to the Press."[11] Although the Federalist position prevailed at the Convention, the lack of a bill of rights became "the chief rallying point for the opponents to the Constitution during the ratification debates."[12]

The Antifederalists' central objection to the new Constitution was that it "would create an oppressive national government and destroy the political authority of the states."[13] Evidence of this was found in the "consolidated" nature of the new central government, a government with sweeping legislative and judicial powers and the authority to make its legislation supreme — displacing in the process any contrary state statutory or constitutional law. Because the practical necessity of a stronger central government was apparent, the Antifederalist opposition shifted "to a reluctant acceptance of the instrument provided that appropriate constitutional restraints were placed upon the powers of the federal government."[14] To George Mason, appropriate restraints would be those that would "point out what powers were reserved to the state governments, and clearly discriminate between [such powers] and those which are given to the general government."[15] Accordingly, every one of the eight states whose ratification conventions proposed amendments to the Constitution included an amendment reserving to the states all unenumerated rights and powers.[16]

Another key element in the Antifederalist opposition to the Constitution was the fear that this newly created consolidated government could invade with impunity the rights of the citizenry. Because the new central government was given broad power to tax, spend, and regulate commerce, as well as exclusive power to wage war, Antifederalists feared that these powers would be used to intrude upon all manner of human activity hitherto within the province of state governments. Even more ominous was the supremacy clause, which plainly provided that federal legislation would trump state law, including the individual rights guaranteed by declaration or reservation in the various state constitutions.

Although the new central government might be a government of limited and enumerated powers, to Antifederalists the powers enumerated were sufficiently encompassing to swallow all the individual rights carefully preserved in state constitutions.

Nor was this all that the Antifederalists feared. Many Antifederalists assumed that any individual rights not expressly reserved were ceded to the government, fair game for obliteration as the new government exercised its delegated powers. In arguing the Antifederalist cause at the Virginia ratification convention, Patrick Henry contended "that all nations have adopted this construction — that all rights not expressly and unequivocally reserved to the people are impliedly and incidentally relinquished to rulers, as necessarily inseparable from the delegated powers."[17]

It would be a mistake to assume that, by conceding this vast implied power to government, Antifederalists were simply unvarnished positivists who did not recognize any principles of "inalienable" natural right. An anonymous Antifederalist opponent of the Constitution, writing under the nom de plume of the Impartial Examiner, argued in the fashion of John Locke that in instituting governments the people "ought to give up no greater share [of their natural rights] than what is understood to be absolutely necessary." Despite the soundness of this principle the Impartial Examiner contended that unless an express reservation of rights was made in the political contract individuals may be presumed to cede to governments the power to invade their natural rights. Because this possibility was so alarming, the Impartial Examiner asserted that it was necessary to have "an express stipulation for all such rights as are intended to be exempted from the civil authority." To the Impartial Examiner, the political contract of the Constitution was especially alarming because the combination of the Constitution's supremacy clause and the lack of a bill of rights meant that natural rights secured by state constitutions were no longer safe. An express stipulation of some sort — preferably in the form of a bill of rights — was needed to prevent the loss of individual natural rights.[18]

To similar effect are the observations and arguments contained in the *Letters from the Federal Farmer*. The *Federal Farmer*, once thought to be Richard Henry Lee of Virginia though doubt on this point now exists, was a careful and thoughtful expositor of natural law. Like other Antifederalists he embraced and valued natural rights, but was practical enough to realize that they could be lost by aggressive governmental encroachment unless specific steps were taken to entrench natural rights into the positive fundamental law of the new nation. Like the Federalists, though, the *Federal Farmer* recognized that entrenchment might be accomplished by a carefully circumscribed enumeration of the powers delegated to the federal government, and was as sensitive as any Federalist to the dangers posed by an enumeration of specific individual rights:

> When we particularly enumerate the powers given [the federal government], we ought carefully to enumerate the rights reserved [to the people], or be totally silent about them; we must either particularly enumerate both, or else suppose the particular enumeration of the powers given adequately draws the line between them and the rights reserved[. P]articularly to enumerate the former and not the latter, I think most advisable: however, as men appear generally to have their doubts about these silent reservations, we might advantageously enumerate the powers given, and then in general words, according to the mode adopted in the 2d art. of the [Articles of] confederation, declare all powers, rights and privileges, are reserved, which are not explicitly and expressly given up. . . . But admitting, on the general principle, that all rights are reserved of course, which are not expressly surrendered, the people could with sufficient certainty assert their rights on all occasions, and establish them with ease, still there are infinite

advantages in particularly enumerating many of the most essential rights reserved in all cases; and as to the less important ones, we may declare in general terms, that all not expressly surrendered are reserved.[19]

To the *Federal Farmer* the express reservation needed to safeguard rights was necessary for two separate but related reasons: (1) to blunt the suggestion that the central government possessed implicit powers that could be used to invade the domain of individual rights, and (2) to make sure that an enumeration of rights did not lead to the conclusion that the enumerated rights were the only rights in existence. The *Federal Farmer* evidently thought of unenumerated rights as those natural rights of humanity that were never ceded to government. The express reservation proposed by the *Federal Farmer* was designed to secure those rights through two independent avenues.

Federalists reacted to these demands by making two related arguments. As James Wilson asserted in his famous State House Yard speech, delivered in Philadelphia in October 1787, less than a month after the conclusion of the Convention, the proposed federal Constitution was quite unlike state constitutions. The accepted theory of state constitutions was, as the Antifederalists observed, that the governments thereby established received "every right and authority which [the people] did not in explicit terms reserve."[20] The same condition was true in England, where the Crown possessed power to extinguish all rights except those which were the "enumerated rights of the people."[21] But, argued Wilson, because the new central government was given only limited, specifically enumerated powers to accomplish national objects, "the reverse of the proposition prevails, and everything which is not given, is reserved."[22] Accordingly, it was "superfluous to specify that the people would continue to enjoy privileges of which they had not divested themselves."[23] Moreover, continued Wilson, there was a danger implicit in adding a bill of rights to the Constitution. The "very declaration" that any given right existed might be "construed to imply that some degree of power was given [to invade the specifically enumerated right], since we undertook to define its extent."[24]

But the danger was even larger than that. Amending the Constitution to create a bill of rights might raise the implication that the only rights possessed by the people were those enumerated. Any enumeration of rights would necessarily be imperfect and would create the inference that no rights existed except those itemized. As Wilson put it in the Pennsylvania ratification convention: "If we attempt an enumeration [of rights], everything that is not enumerated is presumed to be given. The consequence is, that an imperfect enumeration would throw all implied power into the scale of the government; and the rights of the people would be rendered incomplete." To Federalists like Wilson, it would have been vastly preferable to enumerate imperfectly the powers of the federal government with the implication that powers not enumerated were reserved to the people, than to attempt an imperfect enumeration of rights reserved to the people, with the implication that rights not so reserved were impliedly delegated to the federal government. Wilson's arguments were widely circulated, for he was a well-respected lawyer, judge, and law teacher who had been one of the most influential and important members of the federal convention.[25]

Some variant of Wilson's two arguments — that a bill of rights was unnecessary and that enumeration was dangerous to individual liberty — were repeated by many of the principal Federalist defenders of the Constitution. In the North Carolina ratification convention, future Supreme Court Justice James Iredell contended that

> it would be not only useless, but dangerous, to enumerate a
> number of rights that are not intended to be given up; because
> it would be implying, in the strongest manner, that every right

not included in the exception might be impaired by the government without usurpation; and it would be impossible to enumerate every one. Let any one make what collection or enumeration of rights he pleases, I will immediately mention twenty or thirty more rights not contained in it.[26]

Iredell's remark reveals the duality of the problem of danger. A bill of rights might create the implication that the central government possessed unenumerated powers, which could be used to invade the unenumerated rights of the citizenry, but it might also create the equally dangerous implication that the rights of the people were completely expressed by the enumeration of rights in the bill of rights. Both implications would be calamitous. Modern observers who champion the "residual rights" reading of the Ninth Amendment — the idea that the amendment serves merely to prevent a latitudinarian construction of the powers of the federal government — read into Iredell's statement concern only that there be no implication of heightened powers to the central government by the creation of a bill of rights. Other modern commentators who are enamored of the "independent source of rights" reading — the idea that the amendment requires constitutional interpreters to enforce rights the substance of which are found outside of the Constitution — read into Iredell's statement concern only with the possibility that the enumeration of specific rights might give rise to the implication that the list is an exclusive and exhaustive one. Both views are half right, and to the extent that each view claims an exclusivity of concern for Iredell, both are half wrong. Iredell's preoccupation was with preserving the large mass of human rights — some important, such as the presumption of innocence or the right to marry, and some trivial, such as the right to grow a mustache — that would lie outside the zone of enumerated rights. He evidently saw two ways to accomplish the task: prohibiting illegitimate claims of implied governmental power and recognizing explicitly that the enumerated rights were not an exhaustive listing of the rights of humanity.

Speaking at the Virginia ratification convention, James Madison also reiterated the Federalist understanding that "every thing not granted [to the federal government under the Constitution] is reserved" to the people as a preamble to his argument that "if an enumeration be made of our rights [it will be] implied that every thing omitted is given to the general government." Like Iredell, Madison also contended that "an enumeration which is not complete is not safe."[27] Even at this relatively early stage of the gestation of the Ninth Amendment Madison was echoing the same duality of concern that may be seen in Iredell's argument to the North Carolina ratification convention. Madison's concern with dual objectives for the Ninth Amendment will become even clearer as we progress further into the development of the amendment.

Finally, Alexander Hamilton, in *The Federalist, No. 84*, argued that an enumeration of individual rights was

> not only unnecessary . . . but would even be dangerous. They would contain various exceptions to powers that are not granted; and on this very account, would afford a colorable pretext to claim more than were granted. For why declare that things shall not be done that there is no power to do? Why for instance, should it be said, that the liberty of press shall not be restrained, when no power is given by which restrictions may be imposed? I will not contend that such a provision would confer a regulating power; but it is evident that it would furnish, to men disposed to usurp, a plausible pretence for claiming that power.[28]

Hamilton's argument provides some of the best material for the "residual rights" theorists. Unlike Iredell and Madison, Hamilton seems concerned exclusively about the possibility that an enumeration of rights could lead to claims of implied governmental power.

However influential Hamilton undoubtedly was, it must be remembered that he was but one of the cadre of Federalist actors defending the unamended Constitution and seeking its ratification. It may be that Hamilton was more concerned than Iredell and Madison about the possibility of "constructive powers" arising from enumerated rights, or it may be that Hamilton simply was doing his best to defend the original structure of the Constitution — a structure that sought to insure individual rights by a carefully limited enumeration of governmental powers.

A third, and minor key, Federalist argument was to insist that the Antifederalist desire for an express reservation of rights was already supplied by the Constitution issuing from Independence Hall, either in the form of the "necessary and proper" clause or by the limitations on federal legislative power contained in Article I of the proposed Constitution. The argument is exemplified by Archibald Maclaine, who in the North Carolina ratification convention answered Antifederalist objections to the Constitution by asserting that "there is an express clause [the necessary and proper clause of Article I] which . . . demonstrates that [the federal legislative power is] confined to those powers which are given." To similar effect is the statement of Charles Jarvis in the Massachusetts ratification convention that Article I of the Constitution "is an explicit reservation of every right and privilege which is nearest and most agreeable to the people."[29] Predictably, this argument had little impact upon Antifederalists, who regarded it as specious, because the "express" reservation cited by Jarvis and Maclaine was hardly express, but one that could be ascertained only by much implicit scrutiny and application of considerable political logic. Patrick Henry derided this train of thought by observing caustically that "if you had a thousand acres dependent on this, would you be satisfied with logical construction?"[30]

The Antifederalists' response to the major Federalist arguments was that the enumeration of federal government powers was unbounded. For support, they pointed to the existence of the "general welfare" and "necessary and proper" clauses in the Constitution. To Antifederalists these seemed to convey to the central government great expanses of power, notwithstanding the lame Federalist attempts to characterize the necessary and proper clause as an express reservation of rights.

Even more damaging to the Federalist cause was the fact that the Federalist-dominated Convention in Philadelphia had already enumerated in the Constitution such rights as the right to jury trial in criminal cases, the right to habeas corpus, and the prohibition of bills of attainder and ex post facto laws.[31] Antifederalists pointed to these enumerated rights and demanded that their Federalist adversaries explain why these specific rights were enumerated if it was unnecessary and dangerous to enumerate rights. Does this mean, inquired Robert Whitehill, a Pennsylvania Antifederalist, "that every other right is abandoned?"[32] The Federalists had no answer to this charge; their neatly logical world was exposed as the hodgepodge that is the real world. As Leonard Levy has remarked, with quiet understatement, "[T]he argument that to include some rights would exclude all others boomeranged."[33] It is thus not surprising that, beginning with Massachusetts' ratification of the Constitution in early 1788, ratification in many of the remaining states came with a package of proposed amendments to the Constitution. As it became clearer that ratification was effectively conditioned upon amendment of the Constitution to include a bill of rights, Federalists and Antifederalists alike began to harbor ever greater reservations over whether an incomplete enumeration of rights could be overcome by a declaration that "all rights are reserved . . . which are not expressly surrendered."[34]

Early manifestations of this concern are apparent in many of the proposed amendments attached to state ratifications of the Constitution. Virginia and North Carolina proposed amendments that provided "[t]hat those clauses which declare that Congress shall not exercise certain powers, be not interpreted, in any manner whatsoever, to extend the powers of Congress; but that they be construed either as making exceptions to the specified powers where this shall be the case, or otherwise, as inserted merely for greater caution.[35] The evident concern of the Virginia and North Carolina draftsmen was the Federalist argument that it would be dangerous to enumerate rights, for fear that the enumeration would be read as an implication of federal power not otherwise existing. Missing from the resolutions is any apparent concern that an enumeration of rights might also lead to the conclusion that the enumeration was complete.

A similar preoccupation with the possibility of creating constructive governmental powers by adopting a bill of rights is also evident in New York's act of ratification, which provided

> that the powers of government may be reassumed by the people whensoever it shall become necessary to their happiness; that every power, jurisdiction, and right, which is not by the said Constitution clearly delegated to the Congress of the United States, or the departments of the government thereof, remains to the people of the several states, or to their respective state governments, to whom they may have granted the same; and that those clauses in the said Constitution, which declare that Congress shall not have or exercise certain powers, do not imply that Congress is entitled to any powers not given by the said Constitution; but such clauses are to be construed either as exceptions to certain specified powers, or as inserted merely for greater caution.[36]

New York's version provides a slightly more complete gloss. In addition to fear of creating implied federal governmental powers by enumerating rights, the New York proposal states unequivocally the principle of popular sovereignty, and underscores that point by its determination to hem in federal powers to those "clearly delegated," leaving the mass of all other powers that might be used to invade individual rights to the people themselves, for retention or disposal, at their discretion, to their agents of governments within the states. In effect, the New York proposal differs hardly at all from the Virginia proposal, but its greater emphasis on the sovereignty of the people and the limited grant of power conveyed by the people to government strongly suggests that although the New York draftsmen were aiming to secure individual rights by guarding against constructive powers, their overriding ambition was to secure every conceivable right from governmental encroachment.

In each case it is clear that the state ratification convention delegates conceived of individual rights as the complement of governmental powers. By carefully limiting governmental power they would secure individual rights, because rights could not lawfully be invaded by a government lacking power to do so. Today, we would be unlikely to converse in the same vernacular. We are likely to think of rights as trumping governmental powers. Thus, pursuant to the commerce clause Congress may have the *power* to enact a law forbidding the interstate shipment of Bibles, but its effective ability to do so is trumped by at least two First Amendment *rights* — freedom of speech and the right to free exercise of religion. It was, of course, equally possible for the founding generation to think of Congress as lacking the power to enact such a law, and to identify the lack of power with the same first amendment rights that operate as an exception to or reservation from the power Congress would otherwise possess.

Part of the modern disagreement over what the founders may have originally intended stems from this shift in perspective over the past two centuries concerning the nature of rights and powers. To many of the founding generation it seemed axiomatic that rights began where powers ended, and powers began where rights ended. Thus it might be entirely efficacious to secure rights solely by means of a narrow delegation of powers to the central government, but if an arguably unnecessary enumeration of rights was undertaken a further prohibition upon implied or constructive powers resulting from that rights enumeration ought surely to be enough to preserve individual rights. As we have seen, not every member of the founding generation was willing to rely entirely upon a limited enumeration of governmental powers, and once it began to be admitted that some enumeration of rights was inevitable nearly everyone agreed that any enumeration would be incomplete. To repeat James Iredell, an enumeration of rights "would be implying, in the strongest manner, that every right not included . . . might be impaired by the government . . . and it would be impossible to enumerate every one."[37] Thus, preoccupation with limiting governmental powers seemed incomplete even to many of the founding generation, which was accustomed to thinking of rights and powers as mutually exclusive. But to others of the same generation, careful limitations upon the accretion of powers to the central government were by themselves entirely adequate to the task of rights preservation. This duality of focus and emphasis reasserted itself as the Congress debated the creation of the rights that have become our Bill of Rights.

With ratification, events moved to the First Congress, where James Madison, formerly an opponent of a bill of rights on the standard Federalist grounds of inutility and danger but now a zealous advocate, began the task of shepherding a bill of enumerated rights through the First Congress. In language that responds to concern about the possibility that enumerated rights might be thought to be an exhaustive listing and to the concern that an enumeration of rights not give rise to implied governmental powers, Madison introduced his fourth resolution, which, after considerable revision, became the Ninth Amendment: "The exceptions here or elsewhere in the Constitution, made in favor of particular rights, shall not be so construed as to diminish the just importance of other rights retained by the people, or as to enlarge the powers delegated by the Constitution; but either as actual limitations of such powers, or as inserted merely for greater caution."[38]

In explaining this proposal on the floor of the House of Representatives, Madison declared:

> It has been objected also against a bill of rights that, [B]y enumerating particular exceptions to the grant of power, it would disparage those rights which were not placed in that enumeration; and it might follow by implication, that those rights which were not singled out, were intended to assigned into the hands of the General Government, and were consequently insecure. This is one of the most plausible arguments I have ever heard urged against admission of a bill of rights into this system; but, I conceive, that it may be guarded against. I have attempted it, as gentlemen may see by turning to the last clause of the fourth resolution.[39]

Modern observers disagree sharply over the import of the resolution and Madison's statement. One group regards Madison as treating the Ninth Amendment as a guarantee of unspecified individual rights that are as equally trumping of governmental powers as any enumerated right. The other observers regard Madison as simply reinforcing the conception of rights as inhering in the absence of governmental power. As is the case with disagreement over the nature of Iredell's arguments in the North Carolina ratification convention, each camp has depicted half the scene.

In the fourth resolution, Madison plainly expressed two independent purposes to be served by the resolution: as a prohibition upon using the enumeration of rights as reason to "diminish the just importance of other rights retained by the people" *or* "as [a device] to enlarge the powers delegated by the Constitution" to the central government. To be sure, the final clause of the resolution, which shifts from the prohibitory to the positive expression of the ends of the resolution, is more ambiguous. It inverts the prohibition upon use of an enumeration of rights to create constructive powers by a statement that rights enumeration is to be regarded "as actual limitations of [the enumerated governmental] powers." Of course, limitation might occur either by construing narrowly the grant of express powers or by affirmatively securing the unspecified rights retained by the people against otherwise lawful exercises of governmental power.[40]

As with the prior prohibitory clause, the positive expression proceeds with an alternative purpose of the resolution — "or as inserted merely for greater caution."[41] This latter phrase is susceptible to several constructions. It could mean that the "caution" is fear of constructive powers or fear that an enumeration of rights could be taken to be an exhaustive catalogue of rights. But in the immediately preceding phrase Madison had adequately addressed the fear of constructive powers arising from a bill of rights. Moreover, given the dual prohibitory objectives of the first part of the resolution it seems sensible to attribute a similar duality to the parallel, but positive, expression of the purposes of the resolution.

On the other hand, when speaking on the floor of the House, Madison referred to a *single* "plausible argument" against "admission of a bill of rights" but was maddeningly ambiguous in his characterization of the argument: "[B]y enumerating particular exceptions to the grant of power, it would disparage those rights that were not placed in that enumeration; and it might follow by implication, that those rights that were not singled out, were intended to assigned into the hands of the General Government, and were consequently insecure."[42] This could easily be taken to refer to either the fear of implied or constructive powers or the fear that enumerated rights would be the entirety of the universe of individual rights. The ambiguity is compounded by Madison's assurance that he had attempted to guard against this fear (but which one?) by the last clause of the fourth resolution, a clause that is itself ambiguous but likely addressed to *both* arguments, not one. Given the founding generation's strong propensity to conceive of rights as inhering in the absence of governmental powers it is possible that Madison simply collapsed the two fears into a single argument dealing with the fear of constructive powers. But it is also possible that Madison conflated the two fears into a single argument dealing with the fear that the enumerated rights would be construed to be a complete listing of rights. Because the fourth resolution undoubtedly owes something to the state proposals, particularly Virginia's and New York's, and those proposals focus relatively more on the constructive powers argument, it is tempting to conclude that Madison was shrewdly playing to the House in his speech. If the constructive powers argument was what it took to secure passage, so be it. Madison may have been a brilliant statesmen, but he was also a pretty successful politician.

This less-than-noble reading of Madison's House speech derives support from a source not open to inspection by Madison's political contemporaries: Madison's own notes prepared in connection with delivery of the speech. In his notes, Madison made the following cryptic observations: "disparage other rights — or constructively enlarge — [t]he first goes vs. St. Bills — both guarded vs. by amendts."[43] It seems fairly clear that Madison apprehended the fear that an enumeration of specific rights would lead to disparagement of unenumerated rights and the fear that rights enumeration might operate to enlarge governmental powers. Moreover, because Madison obviously thought that the fear of disparagement of unenumerated rights applied with equal force to state constitutions, which included their own declarations of enumerated rights, it is a fairly safe inference that Madison understood disparagement of unenumerated rights to mean the possibility that any enumeration of rights could endanger the security of unarticulated rights. Unlike the federal Constitution, which presumed in its structure that all rights were retained except those surrendered, the principle applicable to state constitutions was that all was given except that which was expressly retained. Thus, the risk that an enumeration of rights would be treated as a complete itemization was even greater with respect to state constitutions than with respect to the federal Constitution. Though Madison understood this, and the fourth resolution addressed the point, he failed to speak to the issue on the floor of the House. The package cannot be tied up neatly; the best that we can do today is admit that Madison understood both fears and both objectives that underlay the Ninth Amendment. To insist, as some modern commentators do, that Madison was single-mindedly in pursuit of one or the other objectives is like trying to force Cinderella's glass slipper onto her stepsister's foot.

Madison's fourth resolution is, of course, not the Ninth Amendment. The House created a select committee to which it referred all of Madison's proposals. The select committee altered the fourth resolution by proposing that it be adopted in the following form: "The enumeration in this Constitution of certain rights, shall not be construed to deny or disparage others retained by the people."[44] The entire House accepted this proposal with the addition of a comma and the change of "this Constitution" to "the Constitution."

The select committee's altered text might be taken to mean one or more of several possibilities. One possibility is that the select committee was concerned only about the fear that an enumeration of rights would be considered an exhaustive listing of rights, because the committee's language omits Madison's explicit prohibition upon using rights enumeration as a device to claim enlarged and implicit governmental powers. If so, this is mildly curious, because it is evident that Madison's fourth resolution owed much to the prior Virginia and New York resolutions and, as we have seen, those resolutions were focused almost entirely on the fear that seems unaddressed by the select committee's work—that rights enumeration would provide an argument for constructive powers.

Another possibility is that the changes might suggest that the select committee considered its text to be simply a more linguistically economical way of stating that the federal government was a government of limited, specifically enumerated powers and that, because the people retained all other rights (rights being thought of as the absence of governmental powers), an enumeration of rights was not to call into question the central fact that the U.S. government possessed only its explicitly delegated powers. But this reading is even less plausible than the first, for the work that is asked of the Ninth Amendment under this reading is almost precisely that assigned to the Tenth Amendment. Moreover, construing the select committee's work in this fashion necessarily implies that the committee ignored completely the parallel fear that rights enumeration would freeze the river of rights in place.

A third reading, which suffers from the inherent defects of compromise, is to assume that the select committee thought its version neatly encapsulated and addressed both of these fears. The problem with this reading is that, at least to us, it is certainly not self-evident that it does.

Fortunately, we are not confined to speculation. The House floor debate concerning the work of the select committee with respect to the entire proposed Bill of Rights adds texture to the changes made in Madison's fourth resolution. Massachusetts Representative Theodore Sedgwick charged that inclusion of a right of assembly in the Bill of Rights was unnecessary because "it is a self-evident, unalienable right which the people possess; it is certainly a thing that never could be called into question; it is derogatory to the dignity of the House to descend to such minutiae." In defense of the select committee, New York's Representative Egbert Benson replied, "The committee who framed this report proceeded on the principle that these rights belonged to the people; they conceived them to be inherent; and all that they meant to provide against was their being infringed by the Government." Sedgwick retorted that "if the committee were governed by that general principle, they might have gone into a very lengthy enumeration of rights; they might have declared that a man should have a right to wear his hat if he pleased; that he might get up when he pleased, and to go to bed when he thought proper."[45]

This floor colloquy between representatives Sedgwick and Benson helps but does not dispose of the uncertainty concerning the intentions of the select committee. Sedgwick asserted a standard Federalist argument — that inclusion of an assembly right was unnecessary — but not for the usual Federalist reason. Federalists argued generally that enumerated rights were not necessary because the new central government lacked delegated power to invade the rights of the people. Sedgwick, however, contended that an assembly right was not necessary because it was "a self-evident, unalienable right," and augmented that view by his declaration that such rights were simply too vast to enumerate. At this point, Sedgwick seemed to be voicing the concern that any enumeration of rights would not be extensive enough to describe the rights of the people and that such an imperfect enumeration might result in an exclusion of other rights. But in the same floor comment, Sedgwick also declared that inclusion of an assembly right was unnecessary because it would never be questioned and was not "intended to be infringed."[46] Sedgwick may have intended by these comments only to express the view that it would be politically unthinkable that any Congress would ever act to infringe upon such a basic "self-evident, unalienable right." But it is possible that, by these comments, Sedgwick shifted to the other argument and its related fear — that rights enumeration was unnecessary because the central government possessed only limited powers and to enumerate rights might suggest that the government also possessed implicit unspecified powers. Once again it is impossible to declare that only one of these fears was at work, but it is certainly safe to declare that the most prominent concern to Sedgwick was the fear that an enumeration of rights would be regarded as exclusive.

Further assistance may be gleaned from the fact that the House Select Committee used Madison's fourth resolution, in part, as the raw material for the Tenth Amendment as well as the Ninth. The Tenth Amendment provides that "[t]he powers not delegated to the United States by the Constitution, nor prohibited by it to the States, are reserved to the States respectively, or to the people." Madison's fourth resolution was designed to perform a dual function — prevention of the enlargement of governmental powers by implication and prevention of the implication that only the enumerated rights existed. Comparison of Madison's fourth resolution with the Ninth and Tenth amendments reveals that, at least linguistically, the Ninth Amendment deals with *rights* and the Tenth Amendment addresses the concern about enlarged *powers*. It is thus tempting to conclude that the House Select Committee intended the Ninth Amendment to perform solely the function of guarding against the possibility of the enumerated rights being regarded as a complete universe of rights, while the Tenth Amendment was intended to prevent against latitudinarian constructions of federal power. Although some additional support for this view may be garnered from an interesting exchange of correspondence among Hardin Burnley, Madison, and President Washington during the Virginia debates on ratification of the Bill of Rights, it is an imperfect explanation of the originally intended meaning of the Ninth Amendment.

In the fall of 1789, during the course of the Virginia legislative debate concerning ratification of the Bill of Rights, Hardin Burnley, "an intelligent member" of the House of Delegates according to James Madison,[47] corresponded with Madison about objections to the Ninth Amendment that had been raised by Edmund Randolph.

His [Randolph's] principal objection was pointed against the word retained . . . , and his argument . . . was applied in this manner, that as the rights declared in the . . . proposed amendments were not all that a free people would require the exercise of; and that as there was no criterion by which it could be determined whither any particular right was retained or not, it would be more safe, & more consistent with the spirit of the 1st. & 17th. amendments proposed by Virginia, that this reservation against constructive power, should operate rather as a provision against extending the powers of Congress by their own authority, than as a protection to rights reducable to no definitive certainty. But others among whom I am one see not the force of the distinction, for by preventing an extension of power in that body from which danger is apprehended safety will be insured if its powers are not too extensive already, & so by protecting the rights of the people & of the States, an improper extension of power will be prevented & safety made equally certain.[48]

Several salient points may be made by examining Randolph's argument and Burnley's reaction to it. First, it is clear that, as a staunch Federalist, Randolph continued to voice the fear that an enumeration of rights could lead to unwarranted inferences of constructive powers, and that it was better to guard against that possibility by addressing the constructive powers issue directly, as had the proposed Virginia amendment, than by the circumlocution of "rights retained by the people." Second, Randolph was equally clear that he understood that an enumeration of rights would necessarily be incomplete. Randolph's strategy for securing the unenumerated rights was, however, one-dimensional. Because Randolph evidently regarded rights as inhering in the absence of governmental power he was utterly content with protecting unenumerated rights by an explicit prohibition against constructive powers arising as a corollary to rights enumeration. The third relevant point is that Burnley (and "others") had a different understanding of Randolph's single-faceted strategy. To Burnley, it was "equally certain" that the "safety" of the people's unenumerated rights would be assured by "preventing an extension of power" or by explicitly "protecting the [unenumerated] rights of the people." Like Randolph, Burnley shared the supposition that rights began where powers ended but, unlike Randolph, Burnley saw that either tack — explicitly prohibiting constructive powers or preserving unenumerated rights — was equally efficacious to the goal of preserving the people's liberties. Both would have the effect of confining federal power and thus preserving liberty. Thus, it is no surprise that Burnley believed that "the supporters of the bill of Rights in the Virginia legislature deemed *both* the ninth *and* tenth amendments to be essential in order to assure the efficacy of the previous amendments."[49]

In writing to President Washington, Madison repeated Burnley's characterization of Randolph's argument and continued by observing that Randolph's distinction appeared to be "altogether fanciful. If a line can be drawn between the powers granted and the rights retained, it would seem to be the same thing, whether the latter be secured, ["whether" stricken out] by declaring that they shall ["be not be abridged violated" stricken out], or that the former shall not be extended. If no line can be drawn, a declaration in either form would amount to nothing."[50]

Like Burnley, Madison conceived of rights and powers as mutually exclusive spheres and regarded the two strategies — explicit preservation of unenumerated rights and prohibition of constructive powers — as equally efficacious. Madison's comments also reveal that he recognized that, for either tack to be effective, both must have real teeth. By noting that "if no line can be drawn [between granted powers and retained rights], a declaration in either form would amount to nothing," Madison evidently meant that in order for individual rights to be secure from governmental invasion it would be necessary for both amendments to constrain the powers of the newly established central government.[51] The Ninth would do so by guarding against either the inference of nonexistent unenumerated rights or the inference of constructive powers. The Tenth would do so by an explicit statement that the central government possessed only its specified powers. The Tenth Amendment may be seen as performing the principal function of rebutting the Antifederalist concern that the new government might be presumed to possess all powers not specifically retained, while the Ninth Amendment may be seen as primarily addressing the Federalist concern that any enumeration of rights might be viewed as recognition of the existence of implied governmental powers. But both amendments are more complex. The Ninth Amendment also addresses, in part, the fear that rights enumeration would eliminate other rights, and the Tenth also preserves to the people their discretionary authority to allocate (or not) powers to their state governmental agents. The complex and dual nature of the two amendments is deeply rooted in the founding generation's perceptions of the inextricable relationship between rights and powers. Thus, the lack of either amendment would be inimical to the preservation of a zone of individual autonomy where governments could not intrude.

Further historical evidence of this parallel intent is found in the congressional modification of the Tenth Amendment by which the phrase "or to the people" was added.[52] This phrase provides an important linguistic parallel to Ninth Amendment rights for Tenth Amendment powers. Without the change, the Ninth Amendment would have operated to secure the unenumerated rights "retained by the *people*," while the Tenth Amendment would have simply preserved the residual powers to the states alone. By adding the phrase "or to the people" the Tenth Amendment makes plain that the people, as ultimate sovereigns, retain both unenumerated individual rights and the residual powers of government, which may or may not be vested by them in their state governmental agents. Moreover, early constitutional commentators as diverse in political outlook as Joseph Story and John C. Calhoun interpreted the phrase "or to the people" to mean that "what is not conferred [to the national government], is withheld, and belongs to the state authorities, *if invested by their constitutions of government respectively in them*; and if not so invested, it is retained by the people, as a part of their residuary sovereignty."[53] In sum, both amendments were conceived as devices by which the sovereign people manifested their residual sovereignty. By the Ninth Amendment, they retained unenumerated rights; by the Tenth Amendment, they retained the nondelegated and unprohibited powers.[54]

Madison apparently did not regard selection of a particular strategy to preserve liberty and the people's sovereignty as a matter of great significance, for he observed to Washington that, even if Randolph's distinction was accurate "it does not seem to be of sufficient importance to justify the risk of losing the amendts of furnishing a handle to the disaffected."[55] Today, we appreciate Randolph's distinction more easily than did Burnley or Madison, for we perceive rights as uncoupled from governmental powers. Limiting governmental powers may indeed preserve liberty obliquely, but creating enforceable rights is a far more direct way of preventing governmental abuse of individual liberty, given our modern conception that rights "trump" powers. Because the actors of the founding generation did not see rights and powers in the way we do, they were more comfortable in treating the distinction between rights and powers as of no consequence and, thus, tolerated what we tend to regard as sloppy thinking about the methodology of protecting human liberty. Whatever degree of indifference there may have been in the founders' minds to the distinction between rights and powers, it is evident that many of the generation appreciated the fact that there were twin strategies that could be employed for the task of liberty preservation, for these dual approaches permeate the Ninth and Tenth amendments.

Although the Tenth Amendment appears reasonably well designed to confine the enlargement of governmental powers it fails that general objective in one respect and also fails to address the particular fear of "constructive powers" held by Federalists who opposed any enumeration of rights. Because the Tenth Amendment failed to limit federal powers to those "expressly" delegated, it has borne out Edmund Randolph's prediction that it would "not appear . . . to have any real effect."[56] But this problem could not be so surely known at the time. More problematic to the interpretation of the Tenth Amendment as the primary agent for preventing constructive powers is the fact that many Federalists were particularly concerned about the possibility that the enumeration of specific rights might trigger the inference that the federal government possessed unspecified powers to invade those rights. The Tenth Amendment addresses this fear obliquely; Madison's fourth resolution did so much more directly, a fact that has been used by some commentators to bolster their claim that the Ninth Amendment's sole function was to prevent constructive powers. But when it is recognized that the Ninth and Tenth amendments each employ aspects of the dual strategy of liberty preservation the force of the objection dissipates. Neither amendment was intended to perform a sole function; to insist to the contrary ignores the broader intellectual and political context within which the founders operated and the specific evolution of the amendments.

Yet it is true that the Ninth Amendment has never been widely regarded as a judicially enforceable guarantee of unspecified rights. There are likely many reasons for this state of affairs, but the principal one must be the prevailing conception of rights in the antebellum United States. In a world in which individual rights were thought to consist of the absence of governmental powers and in which one of the foremost political issues was the extent of the delegated powers of the federal government, it was easier for Americans to focus on the limits of expressed governmental powers rather than the substance of unspecified rights as the device for insuring the perpetuation of liberty. This tendency was reinforced by the fact that antebellum Americans generally regarded their state constitutions as their principal bulwark of liberty. Typical of the thinking is Oliver Ellsworth's declaration that he reposed his trust "for the preservation of his rights to the State Govts."[57] In a world in which state governments were the principal political actors upon the individual, state bills of rights were the more important. With respect to the new federal government the critical issue was the extent of the powers ceded to that government. In the antebellum United States individual and states' rights were thought of as the absence of powers in the federal government, although individual rights could be impaired by state governments in the absence of state declarations of individual rights. The natural focus was upon the scope of the powers of the federal government.

An early example of this focus is James Madison's argument in the House of Representatives that Congress lacked any power, implied from its enumerated powers, to charter a national bank. Madison contended that "[t]he latitude of interpretation required by the [bank] bill is condemned by the rule furnished by the Constitution itself[, instantiated in the Ninth Amendment] . . . as guarding against a latitude of interpretation [of the enumerated powers of Congress]."[58] This might be seized upon as proof that Madison understood clearly that the function of the Ninth Amendment was solely to prevent implied powers, but the way in which Madison employed the Ninth Amendment in his argument suggests that Madison also understood that an additional function of constraining governmental powers was to preserve unenumerated rights. Specifically, Madison argued that creation of a national bank was too remotely connected to any power delegated to Congress under the Constitution to be an aspect of the congressional power to "make all laws necessary and proper for carrying into execution" the delegated powers. Madison traced for his congressional colleagues the train of reasoning that was offered by bank proponents to link together the delegated power to borrow money with the establishment of a bank monopoly as a means to that end, and concluded that "if implications, thus remote . . . can be linked together, a chain may be formed that will reach every object of legislation."[59] Such a state of affairs was clearly regarded by Madison as an intolerable invasion of the rights of the citizenry, because it was almost axiomatic to view extensions of power as correlative invasions of rights. In our times we would regard Madison's concern as limited to the scope of governmental power, and treat invasions of rights as an analytically separate matter. The antebellum predisposition not to do so served to conflate the separate rights-protective dimensions of the Ninth Amendment into a single emphasis on its role as a device to curb implied powers.

Thus it should come as no surprise that a Federalist constitutional commentator like Joseph Story would, in his highly influential *Commentaries on the Constitution of the United States*, invoke the Hamiltonian Federalist account of the Ninth Amendment as intended merely to combat the possibility that federal power might be enlarged by implication from the act of enumerating rights.[60] The overpowering influence of Story's work is probably the reason that this narrow Federalist account has become the received wisdom. But other nineteenth-century constitutional commentators were not as dogmatic.

Thomas Cooley, who dominated the constitutional commentary of the latter portion of the century, wrote that "[t]he occasion for [the Ninth Amendment] is *supposed* to have been found in the apology of the Federalist for the absence of a bill of rights in the Constitution as first adopted, where the writer suggested that such a bill might be dangerous, since it would contain various exceptions to powers not granted, and on this very account would afford a tolerable pretext to claim more than were granted." At this point, Cooley was merely repeating the standard Federalist account, including the obligatory footnote reference to Hamilton's argument in Federalist No. 84. But Cooley continued with his own account: "There could be no harm in affirming by this amendment the principle that constitutions are not made to create rights in the people, but in recognition of, and in order to preserve them, and that if any are specifically enumerated and specially guarded, it is only because they are peculiarly important or peculiarly exposed to invasion."[61] By this explanation Cooley accounted also for the other fear—that the specified rights might be treated as the final and complete itemization of rights—and denied that the enumerated rights were complete. What is left unclear in Cooley's treatment is whether the unspecified rights are, as the text of the Ninth Amendment seems to require, entitled to the same degree of protection as the specified rights, or whether the unspecified rights occupy some nether world in the constitutional universe.

Many of Story's contemporaries treated the Ninth and Tenth amendments as analytically indistinct. Writing in 1834, Peter Du Ponceau quoted the text of the Ninth and Tenth amendments as a single article of amendment, noting that "this article differs from a similar one in the confederation in . . . that the word *expressly* is here left out, which leaves room for implied powers."[62] If the Ninth Amendment was universally understood to prevent implied powers, it is curious that Du Ponceau would have failed to mention such an obvious rebuttal to his statement that the unified Ninth and Tenth amendments permitted such implied powers.

One of the leading agrarian Virginians, Abel Upshur, espoused the theory of the union as a compact among sovereign entities and railed against the scope of implied federal power that was already evident by 1840. At the time Upshur wrote his *Brief Enquiry into the True Nature and Character of Our Federal Government,* he never mentioned the Ninth Amendment in the entirety of his argument. Although Upshur flatly claimed that "the Constitution allows no *implication* [of powers] in favor of the federal government, in any case whatever,"[63] his conclusion was based entirely upon consideration of the Tenth Amendment and the scheme of expressly enumerated powers of the federal government. Again, had there existed a universal understanding that the function of the Ninth Amendment was simply to prevent the development of implied federal powers, it is inexplicable that such a vehement critic of implied powers as Upshur would have let slip such a brilliant opportunity to skewer the advocates of an expansive reading of implied federal powers.

The question of whether the federal government possessed implied powers was, of course, a central focus of *McCulloch v. Maryland,*, where John Marshall relied upon the "necessary and proper" clause as the device to conclude that Congress possessed all manner of implied powers incidental to its enumerated powers. Marshall discussed and dismissed the Tenth Amendment as an obstacle to this result but never even mentioned the Ninth Amendment. Indeed, he declared that "there is no phrase in the [Constitution] which, like the articles of confederation, excludes incidental or implied powers."[64] If the Ninth Amendment had been understood as the residual rights theorists maintain it was, it is inexplicable that Marshall would overlook such an obvious rebuttal to his claim. Marshall's silence in *McCulloch* with respect to the applicability of the Ninth Amendment suggests that neither he nor any other member of that Court thought the Ninth Amendment had any relevance to the question of whether the federal government possessed implied powers.

Some enthusiastic proponents of the argument that the Ninth Amendment was intended solely to protect residual rights by guarding against implied powers, such as Professor Thomas McAffee, respond to these facts by making the much narrower claim that the Ninth Amendment "says nothing about how to construe the powers of Congress or how broadly to read the doctrine of implied powers; it indicates only that no inference about those powers should be drawn from the mere fact that rights are enumerated in the Bill of Rights." In this view, "the Ninth Amendment serves the unique function of safeguarding the system of enumerated powers against a *particular* threat arguably presented by the enumeration of limitations on national power. . . . If the government contended in a particular case that it held a general power to regulate the press as an appropriate inference from the first amendment restriction on that power . . . the Ninth Amendment would provide a direct refutation. That such arguments have never been made is a testimony perhaps to the efficacy of the Ninth Amendment, or perhaps to the speciousness of the original concern."[65]

But such arguments *have* been made. In the *Legal Tender Cases*, Justice William Strong, writing for the Court, argued that adoption of the Bill of Rights "tend[s] plainly to show that, in the judgment of those who adopted the Constitution, there were powers created by it, neither expressly specified nor deducible from any one specified power, or ancillary to it alone, but which grew out of the aggregate of powers conferred upon the government, or out of the sovereignty instituted." At that point in his argument Justice Strong was simply making the general argument for implied powers that the Hamiltonian Federalists insisted the Ninth Amendment was supposed to prevent, but Justice Strong went further and illustrated the general principle by making the very argument that McAffee contends has never been made and which the Ninth Amendment, in his view, was intended to prohibit. Strong noted that "[t]he power to suspend . . . [habeas corpus] is not expressly given, nor can it be deduced from any of the particularized grants of power. Yet it is provided that . . . [habeas corpus] shall not be suspended except in certain defined contingencies. This is no express grant of power. It is a restriction. But it shows irresistibly that somewhere in the Constitution power to suspend . . . [habeas corpus] was granted."[66] If McAffee is correct that the Ninth Amendment has only the narrow application he attributes to it, this is the very instance in which it applies, yet neither Justice Strong nor any of his cohorts even alludes to the Ninth Amendment.

Moreover, the Fifth Amendment's takings clause — "nor shall private property be taken for public use, without just compensation" — does not grant the power in question, but operates as "a tacit recognition of a pre-existing power."[67] But this "pre-existing power" is not enumerated anywhere else in the Constitution, save as part of the catch-all ancillary powers comprehended under the notion of powers "necessary and proper" to the execution of enumerated powers. If the Ninth Amendment operates simply as Professor McAffee contends, this is an instance in which the Ninth Amendment ought to prohibit governmental takings, or at least limit them to those takings necessarily adjunct to specifically enumerated powers. Of course, no one makes this argument. Indeed the practice of eminent domain is deeply imbedded in our pre-constitutional history and has continued unabated after adoption of the Ninth Amendment.[68] One might expect a challenge to the validity of governmental takings if the Ninth Amendment had been intended simply to prohibit the inference of specific implied powers (here, the power of eminent domain) from the enumeration of specific limitations upon governmental powers (here, the limitations upon eminent domain of public use and just compensation). The total absence of such challenges cast doubt upon the credibility of this claim of purported original intention.

Finally, when in the nineteenth century newly admitted states crafted their own constitutions, they typically added a Ninth Amendment of their own to their constitutions.[69] It is hard to understand why any group of state constitution makers would have done so if they had thought the Ninth Amendment was simply a device to confine federal legislative power. The clear inference is that, despite the nineteenth-century preoccupation with rights as the absence of powers, the understanding of the Ninth Amendment in 1819, for example, when Maine and Alabama adopted constitutions, was that it preserved individual rights as well as preventing unwarranted accretion to federal legislative power. This understanding was made explicit by five states that recognized that the Ninth Amendment preserved the dual role of cabining powers and preserving individual rights, for they expressly stated separately the two principles in their constitutions.[70] It is possible that the remaining nineteenth-century state constitution makers were simply attempting to confine the scope of the powers of state governments, but this seems an awkward conclusion in the face of the fact that state governments have universally been regarded as possessing all powers except those explicitly denied them in their constitutive documents. At least in the federal system a plausible claim may be made that the Ninth Amendment was a device to reinforce the limited grant of governmental powers, but in a scheme where the grant is presumptively unlimited a "Ninth Amendment" that operates to limit implied state powers is either futile, oxymoronic, or a poorly expressed intent to reverse the usual presumption that state governments possess all powers except those explicitly denied to them. The presence of Ninth Amendment analogues in state constitutions is reason to conclude that nineteenth-century legal actors continued to regard the federal Ninth Amendment as instantiating dual paths to a single end of preserving human liberty.

Nevertheless, the prevailing assumption that rights exist only in the absence of powers led nineteenth-century legal actors to focus on the powers of the federal government, but in doing so the Ninth Amendment was rarely, if ever, at the forefront of their concerns. Rather, the battle over governmental powers was largely fought over the extent to which the expressly delegated powers could be exercised, and that battle revolved not only over inter-pretation of the terms of the powers granted the federal govern-ment (as, for example, the scope of the power to regulate interstate commerce) but also over the degree to which the central govern-ment could employ means "necessary and proper" to the accom-plishment of the specified powers. The answer to these questions necessarily defined the frontier between federal and state powers proclaimed in the Tenth Amendment. The classic exposition in defense of implied federal powers, *McCulloch v. Maryland*,[71] em-bedded this approach by overlooking the Ninth Amendment en-tirely. If the Ninth Amendment was meant to contain implied federal powers, John Marshall's opinion in *McCulloch* effectively destroyed that purpose.

Although there is ample evidence that many nineteenth-century political actors regarded the Ninth Amendment as preserving un-written liberties, and despite its mixed parentage — sired of a desire to prevent the development of implied powers but born of a con-current desire to preserve other, unenumerated rights — the Ninth Amendment came to be regarded by judges as primarily a power limitation device. That conclusion was perhaps natural enough when rights were regarded as the void left outside the circle of powers, but as our conception of the nature of rights has changed the conclusion becomes ever more arid and unrelated either to our present circumstances or to the original multiple intentions sur-rounding the Ninth Amendment. Even though the Ninth Amend-ment has never been squarely relied upon by the Supreme Court as the constitutional root of an unenumerated right, a brief survey of the Court's changing treatment of the Ninth Amendment reveals this shift in the conception of the nature of individual rights and governmental powers.

In 1857, Justice John Campbell, concurring in the *Dred Scott* de-cision that Congress lacked the power to prohibit the introduction of slavery into federal territories, argued that because Congress possessed no enumerated power to prohibit slavery in the territories, and because "the ninth and tenth amendments . . . were designed to include the reserved rights of the States, and the people, within [the Constitution] . . . , and to bind the authorities . . . to their recognition and observance" it was improper to enlarge the enumerated powers of the federal government by implication or construction.[72] Campbell's argument is a straightforward nineteenth-century treatment of the Ninth Amendment as linked with the Tenth as dual barriers to the unwarranted extension of federal powers. No doubt Justice Campbell, an Alabaman who resigned his seat on the Court when secession came four years later, also regarded the ability to take one's slave (as a slave) into the territories as a valuable unenumerated right, but he did not so argue. Instead, intellectually bound by the prevailing conception of rights as bounded powers he argued entirely from the position that the Ninth Amendment's function, like that of the Tenth, was simply to constrict powers.

The view that the Ninth Amendment performs only the function of bounding federal powers received its clearest judicial endorsement almost a century later, in *United Public Workers v. Mitchell*.[73] In a decision by Justice Stanley Reed the Court upheld the validity of the Hatch Act's prohibition upon political involvement by federal civil servants. The Court conceded that the case involved "the nature of political rights reserved to the people by the Ninth and Tenth Amendments" but concluded that there was no incursion upon those rights.[74]

> The powers granted by the Constitution to the Federal Government are subtracted from the totality of sovereignty originally in the states and the people. Therefore, when objection is made that the exercise of a federal power infringes upon the rights reserved by the Ninth and Tenth Amendments, the inquiry must be directed toward the granted power under

which the action of the Union was taken. If granted power is found, necessarily the objection of invasion of those rights, reserved by the Ninth and Tenth Amendments, must fail.[75]

Like Justice Campbell, Justice Reed treated the Ninth and Tenth amendments as united in the performance of the single function of defining the boundary of federal powers. But by 1947 the Court, in common with other legal actors, no longer held to the conception that individual rights began where powers ended. Rather, individual rights were increasingly recognized as trump cards that invalidated exercises of power that might otherwise be unexceptionable. Given this change in the understanding of rights and powers, Justice Reed's Court simply conflated the power-limitations purpose of the Tenth Amendment (reserving a zone of legislative authority to the states) with the power-limitations purpose of the Ninth Amendment (preventing the growth of implied federal powers in order to preserve unspecified individual rights). Moreover, Justice Reed's conception of the Ninth Amendment simply ignored the dimension of the Ninth Amendment as a device to insure that the enumerated rights were not treated as a complete listing of human rights inviolate from governmental invasion.

Justice Reed's construction of the Ninth Amendment suffers from a variety of flaws. First, it renders the Ninth Amendment superfluous, a redundant appendix of the Tenth Amendment.[76] Second, and even more important, it creates several logical anomalies. If rights begin where powers end and, as Reed's opinion suggests, the Ninth Amendment is irrelevant to the question of the extent of granted powers, one might think that other *enumerated* rights are similarly irrelevant to the question of the scope of governmental powers. After all, the question is the extent of the powers of government, not the restrictions placed upon the exercise of those powers. Thus, if Congress has the raw power to ban the interstate shipment of Bibles, the First Amendment's guarantees of speech, press, and free exercise of religion should be as equally irrelevant as the Ninth Amendment. But that, of course, is not how we view the First Amendment nor is it how Justice Reed would have viewed the First Amendment.[77] Moreover, to treat rights secured by the First Amendment differently from those secured by the Ninth Amendment is to violate the Ninth Amendment's principle that unenumerated rights are not to be disparaged simply by virtue of their unenumerated status. Justice Reed's construction of the Ninth Amendment as a mere declaration of a constitutional truism, devoid of any independent content, effectively rendered its substance nugatory and assigned to its framers an historically untenable intention to engage in a purely moot exercise.[78]

The reconception of individual rights as analytically separated from and paramount to governmental powers has no doubt contributed to the recent interest in the Ninth Amendment as a source of substantive, judicially enforceable individual rights. Thus, when the Supreme Court recognized the existence of an unenumerated constitutional right of "privacy" in *Griswold v. Connecticut* it is hardly surprising that Justice Arthur Goldberg, joined by Chief Justice Earl Warren and Justice William Brennan, would concur in that judgment by reliance in part on the Ninth Amendment as an independent source for recognition of unenumerated constitutional rights.[79] If the old conception of rights and powers had dominated judicial thinking, one would have expected that claims of the Ninth Amendment as a source of an individual right for married persons to use contraceptives would have received as cold a reception as the Court, in *United Public Workers v. Mitchell*,[80] gave to the claim that the Ninth Amendment protected the political rights of civil servants.

Similarly, in *Richmond Newspapers, Inc. v. Virginia*[81] the Supreme Court recognized the existence of an unenumerated constitutional right of the public to attend criminal trials. In reaching the general conclusion that "important but unarticulated rights . . . share constitutional protection in common with explicit guarantees," Chief Justice Warren Burger relied upon the fact that James Madison had feared that any enumeration of rights would be incomplete and noted that "Madison's efforts, culminating in the Ninth Amendment, served to allay the fears of those who were concerned that expressing certain guarantees could be read as excluding others." The Court did not ground the public right to attend criminal trials in the Ninth Amendment, but rather chose to treat this unenumerated right as a right implicit in the First Amendment guarantees of freedom of speech and of the press. More generally, the Court declared that although "[t]he concerns expressed by Madison and others have thus been resolved; fundamental rights, even though not expressly guaranteed, have been recognized by the Court as indispensable to the enjoyment of rights explicitly defined." *Richmond Newspapers* thus represents a way station on the road toward recognition of the Ninth Amendment as the constitutional vehicle by which unarticulated individual rights are preserved. The Court could not bring itself to recognize that unenumerated rights are independently valid, rather than being applicable only just when appended to some explicitly recognized right.[82]

Most recently, in *Planned Parenthood v. Casey*[83] the Court upheld the "essential holding" of *Roe v. Wade*,[84] which itself held that the unenumerated right of a woman to terminate her pregnancy was an aspect of the liberty protected by the due process clause. In doing so, the Court in *Casey* cited the Ninth Amendment as support for the proposition that "neither the Bill of Rights nor the specific practices of States at the time of the adoption of the Fourteenth Amendment marks the outer limits of the substantive sphere of liberty which the Fourteenth Amendment protects."[85] Although the Court's reference to the Ninth Amendment was cryptic, the conclusion seems plain enough. Unenumerated rights derive their legitimacy, in part, from the fact that the Ninth Amendment explicitly recognizes their existence. *Casey* thus recognizes the dimension of the Ninth Amendment as a textual reminder that the stock of individual rights is not exhausted by reference to the enumerated rights.

We can draw several conclusions from this lengthy excursion into the history of the formation of the Ninth Amendment and its subsequent interpretation by courts and commentators. There does not seem to have been any single intention underlying the amendment. It may be that the dominant motivation for its adoption was the desire to prevent the argument that enumeration of certain rights carried with it the implication that the federal government must, therefore, possess unenumerated powers to invade rights (else the enumeration would be unnecessary). It is evident that the foregoing argument is not inconsistent with the argument that any enumeration of rights was dangerous because it would necessarily be an imperfect and incomplete enumeration of all the rights individuals might possess. The arguments differ in that the first is directed entirely toward the objective of cabining implied governmental powers, the object of the second is to recognize the existence of and to secure the enjoyment of a host of unspecified rights and liberties. But in an intellectual milieu in which rights were thought of as the absence of governmental powers the difference between the two arguments was blurry at best. Thus, it was natural that later observers of the events that produced the Ninth Amendment would ascribe to it merely the first objective. As time went on, that objective seemed to be ever more synonymous with the quite different purposes served by the Tenth Amendment — to preserve a separate sphere of state powers. It is in this error that the received account of the Ninth Amendment reached its full blossom. If the Ninth Amendment was simply designed to curb the extension of federal power, that function was also served by the Tenth Amendment, and it was appropriate to treat the amendments as a pair of constitutional Siamese twins, as did Justice Reed and his cohorts. But this treatment was wholly oblivious to the

Ninth Amendment's concurrent objective of insuring that the cat-
alog of constitutional rights did not stop with the enumerated
rights. As rights no longer were thought of as the absence of governmental powers, but rather as independent restraints upon governmental powers, it was inevitable that the lost function of the
Ninth Amendment would again be perceived.

Of course, simply perceiving that the Ninth Amendment could
be a proper constitutional basis for unenumerated rights does
nothing to solve the enormous problem of selecting *which* unenumerated rights deserve designation as constitutionally protected. There are a seemingly infinite set of possibilities, and recognition of the textual legitimacy of unenumerated rights carries
with it the responsibility of articulating some principled methodology by which such rights can be located. Sheer preference will
not do, for if unenumerated rights are merely a matter of judicial
preference there is no good reason why the preferences of a coterie
of judicial life tenants should be privileged over the preferences of
the people, as manifested through the aggregation of preferences
implicit in the legislation crafted by their elected representatives.
Whether the search for these rights is done under the rubric of the
Ninth Amendment, under the due process clauses, or as part of the
quest for fundamental rights entitled to heightened judicial protection under the equal protection clause, the problem is essentially the same. It may be, however, that employing the Ninth
Amendment as the constitutional foundation for unenumerated
rights would provide a different, and preferable focal framework
for that search.

Part III

PRINCIPLED PREFERENCES: DETERMINING NINTH AMENDMENT RIGHTS

FOUR

Constitutional Cy Pres

Even if we were to grant the validity of the argument that the Ninth Amendment was originally intended to perform *only* the role of preventing the establishment of implied federal legislative powers, and even if we were to concede the still more debatable point that in the course of contemporary constitutional interpretation we are obligated to effectuate the framers' intent, it by no means follows that we are compelled to regard the Ninth Amendment as simply a judicially unenforceable, hortatory restatement of the structural limits upon congressional power created by Article I of the Constitution. After two centuries of constitutional development, we no longer make any serious attempt to control the extent of the implied powers of Congress. If the Ninth Amendment's original intent was only to provide a rule of construction by which claims of implied congressional power would be rejected, that function has been irretrievably eclipsed by the awesome breadth of contemporary federal power.

In order to preserve the supposed original function of preventing implied federal powers, it is necessary to apply to the Ninth Amendment a sort of constitutional cy pres doctrine. When faced with the problem of an expressed testamentary intent that is impossible to achieve, courts seek to effectuate as nearly as possible (cy pres) the testator's intent. If the Ninth Amendment's intended purpose was simply to confine the extent of congressional power by preventing a latitudinarian interpretation of the scope of that power, it is evident that, apart from a radical reconstruction of existing doctrine, that intent can no longer be accomplished. To effectuate the original intent as nearly as possible it is necessary to constrain governmental power by reading the Ninth Amendment as a source of judicially enforceable individual rights that operate to limit the exercise of governmental power.

Reconceiving the Ninth Amendment in this fashion is also consistent with the shift in perception of the nature of rights and their relationship to governmental powers that has occurred from the time of the adoption of the Ninth Amendment. When the founding generation contemplated rights they regarded them as inhering in the absence of governmental power. Thus, the prevention of implied federal powers was simply a strategy to preserve individual rights. To some extent the founders' conception of rights was passive. Rights were residual; they were the air that surrounded the tangible organism of governmental power. The founders were not oblivious to the fact that governmental powers were capable of growth. Indeed, they feared the possibility that the organism of governmental power might grow at such a prodigious rate that it would consume a very large portion of the residual rights existing just outside the ever-growing grasp of the governmental monster. Hence, at least in part, the Ninth Amendment. But we no longer view rights in this fashion. Rather than seeing rights passively, as residual crumbs left after the governmental power creature has gorged at the table, we regard rights as fences that corral powers, as swords that chop off the greedy reach of powers into domains that have been marked as beyond the legitimate range of the exercise of powers. This active notion of rights, as power-restraining, to borrow Randy Barnett's phrase, is inextricably linked to the cy pres conception of the Ninth Amendment. If the original intention of the amendment was to confine governmental power, the reason for doing so was entirely to preserve rights. We have failed to confine those powers, partly because we now regard the affirmative assertion of rights as the vehicle for controlling the unwarranted assertion of governmental power. Thus, the only way the Ninth Amendment can be applied in our times to accomplish its original purpose is to regard the amendment as an independent source of individual rights.

The notion of "constitutional cy pres" is not without precedent. By prohibiting states from making or enforcing "any law which shall abridge the privileges and immunities of citizens of the United States," the creators of the Fourteenth Amendment intended "to embrace [the rights] . . . guaranteed by the first eight amendments and other basic liberties."[1] Of course, those intentions were promptly throttled by the *Slaughter-House Cases*,[2] in which the Supreme Court assigned to the privileges and immunities clause the role of protecting only the rights of national citizenship, and then proceeded to treat all the important and fundamental rights of citizenship as aspects of state citizenship, ultimately "left to the unfettered discretion of the local governments."[3] Given the lack of will to overturn directly the *Slaughter-House* decision, the original purposes of the privileges and immunities clause have proven impossible to implement. In a de facto application of constitutional cy pres, the Court has given an expansive reading to the due process and equal protection clauses of the Fourteenth Amendment in order to accomplish the intended purposes of the privileges and immunities clause.

Application of the Bill of Rights to the states has been largely accomplished by the selective incorporation of various guarantees of the Bill of Rights into the Fourteenth Amendment's due process clause. The Court's response to the desire to protect against state invasion "fundamental right[s] which belong, of right, to the citizens of all free governments"[4] has been to read into the due process clause protection for certain implied fundamental rights, such as privacy, and to subject state infringements of fundamental rights, consisting of rights "explicitly or implicitly guaranteed by the Constitution,"[5] to the most stringent judicial scrutiny under the equal protection clause.

Another case of constitutional cy pres is that of the Eleventh Amendment, which provides that "the Judicial power of the United States shall not be construed to extend to any suit in law or equity, commenced or prosecuted against one of the United States by Citizens of another State, or by Citizens or Subjects of any Foreign State." The Eleventh Amendment was adopted in 1798 as a response to the Supreme Court's decision, in *Chisholm v. Georgia*,[6] that the jurisdiction of the federal courts extended to suits seeking damages from the states. Within days of the *Chisholm* decision resolutions were introduced in Congress proposing a constitutional amendment to overrule the Court's judgment. The first proposals would have clearly introduced a constitutional rule of state sovereign immunity from suit in the federal courts, but the pending amendment was modified to narrow its focus in order to exclude from the federal courts only those cases asserted against states by citizens of foreign countries or other states.[7] This modification reflected a specific intent behind the nascent Eleventh Amendment: to render the federal courts unavailable to pass judgment upon the many claims of British creditors against the state governments. In the absence of federal jurisdiction British creditors would be forced to pursue their claims in state courts, where they would be frustrated by state rules enacted to deny relief to British creditors.

The Eleventh Amendment was never given the opportunity to perform its intended function because Jay's Treaty of 1794,[8] which created an international commission to adjudicate the claims of British creditors, effectively diverted this litigation from the U.S. courts. After the Civil War, when the original purposes of the Eleventh Amendment were no longer germane, the Supreme Court invested the amendment with a new, and broader, meaning derived from the originally intended function of the amendment.

In doing so, it effectively applied the cy pres principle to the Eleventh Amendment.

In the wake of the Civil War many southern states repudiated their bond obligations. This blatant effrontery to the Constitution's contract clause was deadly serious and no empty threat, because in the wake of the Compromise of 1877, which restored white rule in the defeated states of the Confederacy,

> the federal government lacked both the will and the power to enforce judicial decisions seeking to enforce the states' bond obligations. Thus, the Court was faced with the unpalatable choice of abandoning accepted contract clause doctrine or watching helplessly as state governments refused to submit to the Court's decisions. The Court's solution to this dilemma was to read the eleventh amendment as establishing, as a constitutional principle, [all-encompassing] state sovereign immunity from suit in federal court.[9]

The tale culminated in *Hans v. Louisiana*,[10] in which the Court found that the Eleventh Amendment barred suit in federal court against Louisiana by one of its own citizens, despite the fact that the Eleventh Amendment is utterly silent with respect to such claims. To achieve this effect, Justice Joseph Bradley concluded that what the Eleventh Amendment had been intended to do was to grant to the states a blanket immunity from suit in the federal courts. In so reconceiving the original purposes of the Eleventh Amendment Justice Bradley "turn[ed] somersaults with history" but he did have a point of sorts, albeit one he never articulated.[11] If the purpose of the Eleventh Amendment had been to stave off federal court claims against the state treasuries by a disfavored class of (British) creditors, it is entirely understandable how Justice Bradley could have resuscitated this purpose and applied it to new, wholly unforeseen domestic circumstances that were effectively beyond the power of the Court to control. Louisiana and other southern states possessed immunity from suit in the federal courts because the federal judiciary was unable, and the president and Congress unwilling, to enforce decrees adverse to the financial interests of the states. Thus, Justice Bradley fastened upon a blanket state immunity from suit in federal court as a way of permitting southern states to repudiate their public debt while still leaving the general fabric of the contracts clause untouched. Bradley's interpretation may not have comported with the original purposes of the Eleventh Amendment, although Bradley claimed that to be the case, but it was a reasonable adaptation of the Eleventh Amendment's original purposes to the circumstances of the late nineteenth century.[12] In short, the Eleventh Amendment was originally rooted in specific political issues of insulating states from the claims of foreign creditors (while using a repeal of federal jurisdiction or the creation of a party-based barrier to jurisdiction as the device to do so), but when that device could no longer fulfill the original intent of blocking politically disfavored claims against state treasuries, the Court altered the amendment to state a general principle of state sovereign immunity.

Still another example of constitutional cy pres is presented by *Brown v. Board of Education*.[13] There is no plausible evidence that the originally intended function of the equal protection clause of the Fourteenth Amendment was to eliminate racial segregation in the public schools.[14] The Congress that proposed the Fourteenth Amendment permitted racially separate schools in the District of Columbia, mandated racial segregation in its visitors' galleries, and consistently evidenced "a pervasive assumption that segregation should remain."[15] But that was the precise issue that was presented to the Court in *Brown*, and the Court's conclusion that equal protection prohibited racial segregation in the public schools sparked scholars to ponder whether the decision, for all its moral grounding, was a principled decision of constitutional law.[16] If principle inheres entirely in adherence to original intentions,

Brown is presumptively unprincipled. Still, no one is about to declare *Brown* to be wrong; indeed, a virtual talisman of contemporary constitutional theory is to explain why *Brown* is right. Even so ardent an originalist as Robert Bork justifies the result in *Brown*. Bork begins by contending that, although the framers of the equal protection clause were not concerned with racial separation, they did intend to insure racial equality under law, a principle that the framers thought was consistent with racial separation. Although the framers perceived no inconsistency in their original intentions, we do, with the result that a conflict is posed between two differing intentions. *Brown*, according to Bork, resolves the conflict by choosing to observe the more general intention.[17]

Bork's explanation of *Brown* is a form of constitutional cy pres, but it is not the only cy pres explanation of *Brown*. As Mark Tushnet has noted:

> If we asked . . . the framers of the Fourteenth Amendment . . . whether the amendment outlawed segregation in public schools, they would answer, "No." [They] had in mind a relatively new and peripheral social institution. [In] contrast they thought that freedom of contract was extremely important because it was the foundation of individual achievement, and they certainly wanted to outlaw racial discrimination with respect to this freedom. . . . [In *Brown*] education as it exists today — a central institution for the achievement of individual goals — is in fact the functional equivalent not of public education in 1868, but of freedom of contract in 1868.[18]

If it is true that the original intent of the equal protection clause was to eliminate hardships imposed by the state uniquely upon newly freed African-Americans, particularly by assuring to blacks the "right to contract, sue, give evidence in court, and inherit, hold, and dispose of real and personal property," it is equally true both "that the proposed constitutional amendment was couched in more general terms" and that the modern vitality of the original intentions are unlikely to be achieved without recharacterization of the equal protection guarantee as a bar to racial line-drawing by governments.[19] Chief Justice Warren, writing for the Court in *Brown*, eschewed history as "inconclusive" but the Court need not have done so. In effect, if not declared fact, the entire enterprise of dismantling official race consciousness is an exercise in constitutional cy pres.

Constitutional cy pres should not be regarded as a concept of unlimited flexibility. As with the more traditional cy pres doctrine, the idea is to come as close as possible to the original intention, given changed circumstances that have rendered a literal application of original intent impossible. It is a way of adhering to original intention, so far as it can be known, not of avoiding it altogether. To return to *Brown* and equal protection, it is fairly clear that while the framers did not intend to bar official racial separation they did intend to provide a guarantee of a fair and race-blind governmental process. The framers' preoccupation with rights to contract and inherit, for example, is indicative of an intent to bar governments from erecting racial barriers to economic autonomy and security. Their concern with insuring that race could not be employed as a selection criteria for jury service, to say nothing of the Fifteenth Amendment's guarantee of race-blind access to the polls, suggests that the framers wished to guarantee to all Americans race-neutral access to and participation in the democratic polity. Those intentions are surely a conception of equal protection as a guarantee of a color-blind process. Of course, it seems preposterous to us that the framers could have simultaneously aspired to a race-blind process and tolerated official racial segregation. But they did; it took *Brown*'s unspoken use of constitutional cy pres to end that dichotomy.

Today's controversies over equal protection center on whether the clause assures a fair, color-blind process or requires equality of outcome. The latter proposition is asserted in two ways. First, it is well established that deliberately race-conscious remedies are permissible if narrowly drawn to rectify past constitutional violations. Thus, race-based pupil assignment plans or race-based affirmative action programs are permissible to redress specific prior instances of unlawful racial discrimination. Second, and more radical, is the vogue assertion that, regardless of past constitutional wrongdoing, equal protection requires, as a substantive matter, equality of outcome. If blacks compose 15 percent of the population but only 3 percent of the mathematics faculty at State University, equal protection is said to mandate an increase in the proportion of mathematics professors of African ancestry. Constitutional cy pres repudiates this argument, for if the intention of the framers was to guarantee a color-blind process rather than a set of specific outcomes, it is plainly beyond the scope of the original intentions to transform a process guarantee into an outcome guarantee. However much cy pres might modify intentions to suit contemporary circumstances, it must bear some correlation to original intention.

Skeptics will observe that the art of constitutional cy pres lies in the characterization of original intentions. Constitutional cy pres does require parsing of original intentions at a specific level and at progressively more general levels. It requires asking, first, what is known about the specific intentions of the framers with respect to any given constitutional provision. Assuming that we can settle upon a set of specific intentions, we must ask whether those intentions can be realized today. If they cannot, due to ambient constitutional change or altered social conditions, we must ask how it is possible to realize the original intentions through other, unintended, means that are more in harmony with contemporary constitutional law. To do so we may usefully inquire of more general original intentions and implement the more general intention if possible, and if not possible, search for alternate ways of instantiating the more general intent in today's Constitution. Similarly, if no specific intention can be located, or if a known specific intention collides with a more general original intention (as was the problem in *Brown*) we can usefully employ the general intention. Of course, at some point intentions can be so generalized that they evaporate. No doctrine can prevent the unprincipled use of airy speculation as a method of constitutional law-making. All one can do is acknowledge the limits of any theory of constitutional interpretation and recognize that no single interpretational method will suffice as the measuring rod of constitutionality.

Accepting for the moment the legitimacy of constitutional cy pres, there are three major ways in which constitutional cy pres can be applied to the Ninth Amendment. The amendment can be seen as securing against federal invasion individual rights having their origin in state constitutions.[20] The amendment can also be read as "a rule of interpretation . . . [that] acts as a presumption in favor of generalizing" about the scope of explicit constitutional terms in order to protect unenumerated "rights which are *consistent* with the enumerated rights."[21] Finally, the amendment can be treated as an admonition to locate and enforce rights having their origin in natural law.

In order plausibly to read the Ninth Amendment as protecting individual rights having their origin in state constitutions it is necessary to consider the symbiotic relationship between the Ninth and Tenth amendments. The Tenth Amendment, regarded today as a truism that the states retain those powers not delegated to the central government, was intended to complement the power limiting aspect of the Ninth Amendment. If the Ninth Amendment was intended in part to prevent the accretion of federal power implied by virtue of the existence of enumerated rights exempt from the reach of federal power, the Tenth Amendment was designed to prevent the accretion of federal power by implication from any other source in the Constitution. The Ninth Amendment may have been intended to preserve individual rights by cabining federal powers, but the Tenth Amendment was intended to preserve the people's right to assign, if they wished, the residual powers of government to their state agents of government.[22]

Thus, the Ninth and Tenth amendments were conceived as a tandem device by which the sovereign people manifested their residual sovereignty. By the Ninth Amendment, the people retained their unenumerated rights; by the Tenth Amendment, they retained all powers neither delegated to the central government, conferred by them upon their state governments, nor prohibited to the states by the Constitution. Both amendments were intended to preserve to the people of the states the sovereign's prerogative to confer powers upon their state governmental agents (recognized in the Tenth Amendment) and to maintain all manner of individual rights secure from governmental invasion (recognized in the Ninth Amendment). An intended medium for doing so, in both cases, was the state constitution. Because the Ninth Amendment recognizes that individual rights stemming from a source other than enumeration in the federal Constitution may, nevertheless, not be treated any differently from individual rights that are expressly enumerated in the federal Constitution, it follows that if the state constitutions are a source of Ninth Amendment individual rights, state polities possess the power to define rights that the federal government may not invade. Both enumerated and unenumerated rights are entitled to parity of treatment under the federal Constitution; Congress is effectively disabled from infringing either type. The Tenth Amendment "simply recognizes that the people of the states and their state governmental agents retain residual authority to act in the shade of federal powers. Thus, the Ninth Amendment creates federal rights, independent barriers to federal action, while the Tenth Amendment recognizes the existence of concurrent state powers beyond the frontier of federal power."[23] The implications of this view to state constitutional law and the powers of Congress are of considerable scope and require a reconsideration of some of the basic premises of federal constitutional law. That is the project attempted in Chapter Five.

Another device by which constitutional cy pres may be implemented with respect to the Ninth Amendment is to admit that the amendment secures against governmental invasion individual rights that have their source in none of the civil institutions of government but which, instead, are rooted in the ineffable, often gossamer, rubric of "natural law." When the intellectual background of the colonial, revolutionary, and post-revolutionary periods are recalled, it is difficult to dismiss the influence of natural law in influencing the creation of the Ninth Amendment. Indeed, Roger Sherman's draft of the Bill of Rights expressly declared that "the people have certain natural rights which are retained by them when they enter into Society."[24] Randy Barnett has accurately described this as "reflect[ing] the sentiment that came to be expressed in the ninth [amendment]."[25] Thus, even if we grant for the sake of argument that the sole function of the Ninth Amendment was to prevent bloat of the powers delegated to Congress, the framers' reason for selecting that purpose was because they regarded it as the most effective way of preserving the natural rights that they had never ceded to the government they created. Because, on this view, the framers labored under the misconception that rights were simply the absence of powers it is crucial, now that we perceive that rights can trump powers and that the Ninth Amendment has failed of its original purpose, to recreate the framers' vision by preserving directly the natural rights the framers sought to preserve indirectly.

It is not easy to do this in a world filled with skepticism about whether there is any such thing as natural law. One object of Chapter Six is to overcome that skepticism by describing briefly what natural law is and is not, and by providing an account of a principled method of locating natural rights that can be judicially enforceable through the Ninth Amendment.

Yet another device by which constitutional cy pres may be applied to the Ninth Amendment is to read the Ninth Amendment as instantiating a general "rule of interpretation" to be applied to the many open-ended enumerated rights, but not as a separate source of individual rights. This view, suggested by Professor Laurence Tribe, is based on the assumption that "the Ninth Amendment tells interpreters of the Constitution how *not* to 'construe' that document." Tribe takes the position that the Ninth Amendment was designed to prevent "the argument that [claimed] rights are not there just because they are not enumerated in the Bill of Rights." In a sense, this is an inversion of the residual rights argument that the Ninth Amendment was designed to prevent the argument that because enumerated rights are exempt from federal power the federal government must possess implied power to invade rights not enumerated. Tribe has quite sensibly shifted the focus from governmental powers to individual rights. He then argues "that to make sense of the Ninth Amendment's *proscriptive* role requires readers of the Constitution to assume that it also plays a *prescriptive* role." Because Tribe has already shifted the "proscriptive" role of the Ninth Amendment from one preventing arguments for implied powers to one preventing arguments against the existence of unenumerated rights it is not surprising that the "prescriptive" role he envisions for the amendment should also reflect this shift.[26]

To a residual rights enthusiast, the prescriptive role of the Ninth Amendment would simply be a general rule against reading the Constitution to legitimate implied federal powers. But, of course, *McCulloch v. Maryland* killed this role and, although resurrections may occur in theology, they rarely appear in constitutional law. The prescriptive role urged by Tribe is to justify a generous reading of the scope of the enumerated rights in the Constitution. Although this is a reasonable role for the Ninth Amendment to perform in its reincarnation through constitutional cy pres, it is one that need not be so limited. After all, the text of the Ninth Amendment demands that the enumerated and unenumerated rights be treated equally. If we reduce the Ninth Amendment to an aid to construing the enumerated rights we have poorly served the ideal of parity between the enumerated and unenumerated rights. Of course, by giving explicit rights a wide scope we would, in effect, be protecting implied or unenumerated rights. This is an approach that has much to be said for it, but it is by no means mutually exclusive from other remedial approaches and can be considered within the natural law function addressed in Chapter Six.

There are multiple ways by which the Ninth Amendment can be restored to constitutional vitality. Indeed, there is no readily apparent reason why any of these methods have any claim to exclusivity, nor is there any immediately compelling reason to create a hierarchy of preferred methodology. The problems and advantages of these approaches to finding substance in the Ninth Amendment will be considered in succeeding chapters. For the moment, the issue is whether or not to accept as valid the notion of constitutional cy pres as applied to the Ninth Amendment.

There are other bases, apart from the claim that the idea of constitutional cy pres has actually manifested itself with respect to the Fourteenth and Eleventh amendments, for advancing and defending an idea that initially seems alien to constitutional adjudication. If we are to have any faith at all in the power of constitutional text as an aid to interpretation, it is important to account for all of the text. Judge Alex Kozinski calls this the principle of completeness — the idea that every bit of constitutional text "was meant to have a purpose and ought not be ignored."[27] But we do ignore some text. The fugitive slave clause, or the three-fifths clause, for example, are still in the Constitution but are rendered obsolete by the Reconstruction amendments, mute and impotent reminders of a less-equitable constitutional covenant of another time. The principle of textual completeness surely does not require that we breathe contemporary life into these ghoulish relics.

What, then, is the difference between the lifelessness of constitutional text that commands the rendition of fugitive slaves and text that recognizes the existence of rights retained by the people? By virtue of an explicit alteration of our constitutional understanding the former case is no longer one of constitutional interpretation. Its interpretational status, at least as applied to the issue of fugitive slaves, has been settled forever by the Thirteenth Amendment. But that is not so with respect to the Ninth Amendment. The moribund constitutional status of unenumerated retained rights is a product entirely of an interpretative convention, rather than the explicit moral choice embodied by the constitutional termination of the institution of slavery. Interpretative conventions ought not command our allegiance in the same definitive way as do explicit alterations of the fundamental covenant. Thus, as an abstract proposition, there is room for the operation of constitutional cy pres on other hibernating bits of constitutional text as, for example, the Second or Third amendments. Indeed, in recent years there has emerged a small corpus of literature pondering the possible contemporary role of the Second Amendment.[28] Nothing similar has occurred with respect to the anachronistic Third Amendment, although it was conscripted into modern constitutional duty by Justice William O. Douglas, who invoked it in *Griswold v. Connecticut* to enlarge the penumbral shadow cast by the Bill of Rights. This is not to suggest that there is a constitutional imperative immediately to manufacture a contemporary purpose for the Second or Third amendments, or the guaranty clause, or any other sliver of text that has been paralyzed by interpretation. It is to argue that when there is a pressing reason to do so we ought not to avoid the responsibility of recasting moribund text into modern terms that approximate its original function and place in the constitutional scheme. With respect to unenumerated individual rights, it is quite apparent that a pressing reason is evident — we have burdened the due process clause with more of a logical load than it can reasonably be asked to bear. We risk utter and complete incoherence if we continue to pretend that it is due process that protects us against substantive deprivations of liberties that lack much textual connection to the Constitution.

If we continue to believe that the intentions of the framers have any relevance to contemporary constitutional law we ought to revive those intentions, where possible, in a form that strives to accomplish as closely as possible the original purposes of constitutional text in our vastly altered contemporary setting. This is not an endorsement of the bogus claims of fervid originalists that constitutional law can be manufactured entirely by reference to some chimerical original intention. Rather, my contention is much narrower. Although the epistemological problem of determining original intentions is so daunting as to be impossible in many cases, and the theoretical question of whether we are bound by those intentions, once authenticated, is equally problematic, those problems are reduced in size by adopting principles of constitutional cy pres. When acting in a cy pres mode, we are not making the strained claim that we *know* what the framers intended, nor are we making the contestable claim that we *must act now* in accordance with those eighteenth-century desires. Instead, we are stating only that we wish to keep faith with the historical covenant, as best we can understand it from our current removal in time and distance, and that we do so by adapting what we know of past intentions to our current needs in a way that does justice to both.

Moreover, when constitutional cy pres can operate to reinforce rather than undermine the structural relationships created by the Constitution it is a positive force in constitutional adjudication. Today, we pay relatively little attention to the structural relationships between governments and governmental actors, and focus our structural analytic energies upon the relationships between governments and individuals. In doing so we slight the founders' design that human liberty may be enhanced by preserving structural checks upon the powers of various units of government. We need not return to the founders' conception of federalism to employ constitutional cy pres but we may utilize the cy pres doctrine to create some contemporary checks upon the unconstrained powers of governments. That is the essential task of the aspect of constitutional cy pres applied to the Ninth Amendment that seeks to locate the amendment's substantive content in state constitutional law. The problems attendant to that endeavor are the subject of the following chapter. In applying constitutional cy pres in that fashion it is possible to respond to the founders' structural vision that individual autonomy and liberty is most efficaciously maintained by dividing governmental powers between the states and the central government and to the modern conception that individual autonomy is best preserved by constructing affirmative limitations on the powers of any government to invade identified individual liberties.

Constitutional cy pres is well-adapted to the need for some degree of prudential discretion in the manufacture of constitutional law. Constitutional law is inherently political. Lacking the powers of purse or sword, the Court must necessarily step deftly and carefully in the mad dance of politics. Cy pres is but an additional tool with which the Court can chart its course. The question of when to invoke constitutional cy pres is necessarily the stuff of prudential judgment. There is no warrant for using cy pres as a pretext for melting down the existing coinage of constitutional law in order to stamp out some entirely new product. The role of cy pres ought to be limited to those instances where the original function of constitutional text has effectively been rendered incapable of realization, there is some good prudential reason for resuscitating that original function in a new manner, and there exist no sound reasons of prudence to forebear from the use of cy pres.

These principles may be applied to the Ninth Amendment as follows. The Ninth Amendment had two original purposes; one was to prevent the implication of governmental power arising from enumeration of rights and the other was to prevent the implication that the enumerated rights were the only rights of the people capable of blocking governmental action. The first purpose is plainly impossible to realize because we have thoroughly embraced the principle of implied governmental powers. The second purpose is not literally impossible, for in fact we have recognized a host of unenumerated rights by attaching them as unspoken appendixes to one or more of the enumerated rights, but the legitimacy of the endeavor is badly eroded by our undue reliance upon an inappropriate and ill-suited vehicle — the due process clause — for the task of providing constitutional recognition to unenumerated rights. Straightforward recognition of the Ninth Amendment as the vehicle for this project would be consistent with the founding intentions as well as provide a more ready answer to those critics of unenumerated rights who loudly question the connection of those rights to constitutional text.

There are at least two good reasons to employ cy pres with respect to the Ninth Amendment. We are committed, whether we like it or not, to constitutional recognition of unwritten rights. We have almost lost sight of the possibilities for preservation of human liberty that inhere in a living federal system of dual sovereignties. The contemporary rebirth of state constitutional law is evidence of a partial reawakening of our legal imagination to these possibilities. That project can and should be developed further by using the Ninth Amendment to recapture for federal constitutional law the promise of state constitutional law. To do so would respond innovatively to the original design of the amendment and to the burgeoning interest in state law as a device to insure greater human freedom. The prudential costs of this innovation remain to be examined, but they are not so large as to dictate abandonment at the outset of the idea of cy pres applied to the Ninth Amendment.

Constitutional cy pres need not conflict with preexisting doctrine. The prudential quality of its invocation is one way to avoid conflict, in that the Court can and probably should refrain from application of cy pres whenever it appears that considerable doctrinal conflict, upheaval, or confusion will be the result. But when an old and dormant constitutional purpose can be put to use in modern garb without placing tremendous stress upon our existing understanding there is no reason to invoke fidelity to doctrine as an excuse for refraining to do so. As will be seen, there are no insuperable doctrinal conflicts presented by reconceptualizing the Ninth Amendment in the fashion I propose. Indeed, although application of constitutional cy pres to the Ninth Amendment would necessarily require the Court to fashion *new* doctrine it would not require it to uproot old doctrine. There is no principled reason grounded in doctrinal adherence to reject cy pres simply because it would demand that the Court think.

There is a sound argument for recognition of the very idea of constitutional cy pres. There is an equally strong case to be made for applying the cy pres principle to the Ninth Amendment. The task that remains is to describe that application. The description is necessarily of an imaginary body of law. To bring that description back to earth I have set out to confront the problems that would be encountered in creating this new doctrine and to suggest avenues of resolution. Some avenues may be preferable, and I have attempted some normative judgments where appropriate, but the focus of this exercise is to provide an account of where we could go, and to do so in a fashion that is persuasive of the possibility of its accomplishment and the desirability of embarking upon the venture.

FIVE

The Positive Law Component

It is common to observe that the overwhelmingly English colonists of America regarded themselves as endowed with all the rights of Englishmen. True, they were living in a remote, often primitive, outpost of North America under social, economic, and geographic circumstances quite different from those prevailing at the heart of the empire, but predominantly British they were, in political affiliation, ethnicity, temperament, and cultural inclination. Like all Englishmen of their time they cherished their inherited political rights, guarding them with what sometimes appears, from our perspective, to be an irrational passion. Thus, when in the wake of the Seven Years' War (or the French-and-Indian War, as the colonists styled the conflict) the imperial Parliament began to levy taxes upon the colonists for the purpose of defraying the considerable expenses of garrisoning the American frontier, to say nothing of recouping the treasure expended in divesting France of partial control of North America, Americans reacted with an assertion of the rights of Englishmen that seemed entirely inappropriate to Englishmen who had never left their native isle.

Taxes, said the colonists, were not a thing that could be levied without the consent of the taxpayer, for "taxation is no part of the governing or legislative power. . . . [T]axes are a voluntary gift and grant of the Commons alone."[1] With this position the English agreed, but argued that the colonists *were* represented in Parliament and thus the consent of Parliament to the tax measures re-

sented by American colonists was, legally speaking, the consent of
the American colonists themselves. This was a remarkable position, given the fact that colonists were not permitted to vote for
representatives in the imperial Parliament, but Thomas Whately, a
British Treasury official, justified it on the grounds that the colonists were "virtually" if not actually represented in Parliament.
Because Englishmen were Englishmen, wherever their immediate
residence, they composed a single political community, and the
member of Parliament from Leeds, for example, represented not
just the voting constituency of Leeds but every Englishman, no
matter what part of the vast, geographically scattered, British political community in which he resided.[2]

To the colonists, this position was pernicious nonsense. The
colonial attitude was that the only legitimate form of representa-
tion was one by which a representative was actually selected from
among the very people he claimed to represent. In theory, this
would permit the colonists to elect some of their own to journey to
London for service in Commons. In practice, the colonists rejected this idea because it was impracticable and, if actually implemented, would create the danger that a colonial representative in
London would lose his colonial character by virtue of residence in
the vastly different circumstances of London. Thus did the colonists assert, "without at first being aware of what they were doing,
that the American colonies were different national communities
from the one that was represented in Parliament."[3]

When the rupture was complete and Americans undertook the
task of creating the institutions of governance for their new national community it is not surprising that the rights enumerated in
various state constitutions were, by and large, the inherited "rights
of Englishmen" as adapted to colonial circumstances and previously secured by colonial charters and statutes.[4] It would thus
seem to be a safe point of departure to assume that the unenumerated rights contemplated by the Ninth Amendment were intended

to be the remaining such "rights of Englishmen." But, of course, with the success of revolt from British rule, Americans possessed only the rights of Americans. To be sure, the rights of Americans might have a source in the traditional fount of English common and constitutional law but, to the extent such rights were of statutory dimension, the relevant statutes became those enacted by the states. Indeed, the sentiment of many, if not most, of the framers was to look to the states not only as the source of, but as the vehicle for, protection of their cherished liberties.[5]

This body of rights had two segments. The framers understood and observed a distinction between "natural" rights and "civil" or "positive" rights. James Madison, for example, exemplified the framers' understanding when he articulated his perception of the distinction between natural rights, "those rights which are retained when particular powers are given up to be exercised by the Legislature," and positive (or civil) rights, those that "may seem to result from the nature of the compact." Madison illustrated the distinction by citing trial by jury as a right "which cannot be considered a natural right, but a right resulting from the social compact which regulates the action of the community"[6] Freedom of speech, by contrast, was regarded by Madison as a natural right.[7] But, despite the distinction drawn, Madison thought positive rights were "as essential to secure the liberty of the people as any one of the pre-existent rights of nature."[8] Consequently, the founding generation did not use the distinction between natural and positive rights as a basis for selection of the rights worthy of constitutional enumeration. The package of rights expressly enumerated in the Constitution contains natural and positive rights. It is a fair inference, then, that the unenumerated rights of the Ninth Amendment were thought to consist of both varieties. Positive rights had their source in state common, constitutional, and statutory law. Natural rights stemmed from Lockean notions concerning the inalienable rights of the people.

Nor were rights constitutionally enumerated simply for the purpose of insuring their judicial enforceability. As the prime mover
for adoption of the Bill of Rights, James Madison undoubtedly
thought enumeration would lead to judicial enforceability, because
he urged Congress to adopt a Bill of Rights on the grounds that if it
were "incorporated into the Constitution, independent tribunals
of justice [would] consider themselves in a peculiar manner the
guardians of those rights; they [would] be an impenetrable power
against every assumption of power in the legislative or executive;
they [would] be naturally led to resist every encroachment upon
rights expressly stipulated for in the constitution by the declaration of rights."[9] Yet, he also entertained larger hopes for the entire
Bill of Rights: "The political truths declared in that solemn manner acquire by degrees the character of fundamental maxims of
free Government, and as they become incorporated with the national sentiment, counteract the impulses of interest and passion."[10] As we have seen, one of the political truths that Madison
hoped would become a fundamental maxim was that the unenumerated rights retained by the people were of equal constitutional
dignity with the specified rights as a means of preserving human
liberty.

It is perhaps most telling that when Madison introduced the Bill
of Rights to Congress and made his comment concerning judicial
enforceability of the Bill of Rights, he drew no distinction between
the clause that ultimately became the Ninth Amendment and
other enumerated rights. Indeed, the future Ninth Amendment
was offered by Madison as just one more clause to be shoehorned
into Article I, section 9 of the Constitution, along with clauses that
later became the First, Second, Third, Fourth, Fifth, Sixth, and
Eighth amendments. So far as one can tell from the context created by Madison himself, the Ninth Amendment was as much an
enumerated right for purposes of judicial enforcement as any other
aspect of the Bill of Rights. It would thus be too hasty to assume

that the principle of judicial enforceability of constitutional rights, while clearly extending to the enumerated rights as we think of them today, was also intended to stop there.

Madison correctly observed, when introducing the Bill of Rights in Congress, that there had been much popular opposition to ratification of the Constitution "because it did not contain effectual provisions against encroachments on particular rights, and those safeguards that [the people] have been long accustomed to have interposed between them and the magistrate who exercises the sovereign power." This suggestion that the enumerated rights were a contemporary expression of the traditional rights of Englishmen is partly undermined by Madison's further assertion that it was necessary to enumerate rights because "some States have no bills of rights, there are others provided with very defective ones, and there are others whose bills of rights are not only defective, but absolutely improper; instead of securing some in the full extent which republican principles would require, they limit them too much to agree with the common ideas of liberty."[11]

It was not merely traditional understandings of rights that must be preserved. The enumerated rights must also be a proper expression of republican principles, conforming to "common ideas of liberty." In so formulating the criteria for rights enumeration Madison edged into political theory. The Revolution had created a republican government founded on the social contract of the consent of the governed. Any enumeration of the people's rights must be congruent with the foundational postulates of that social contract. Thus it is not surprising that Madison declared to the House that "the great object in view is to limit and qualify the powers of Government, by excepting out of the grant of power those cases in which the Government ought not to act, or to act only in a particular mode."[12] The key premise of the Lockean social contract — that governments possessed only those powers explicitly conveyed to them by the people — was also evident when Madison noted:

It has been said, by way of objection to a bill of rights . . . that they are unnecessary articles of a Republican Government, upon the presumption that the people have those rights in their own hands, and that is the proper place for them to rest. It would be a sufficient answer to say, that this objection lies against such provisions under the State Governments, as well as under the General Government; and there are, I believe, but few gentlemen who are so inclined to push their theory so far as to say that a declaration of rights in those cases is either ineffectual or improper.[13]

Although the logic of the social contract and the gospel of natural law might lead to the conclusion that it was unnecessary to state explicitly the people's rights because, being inalienable, they were beyond governmental invasion, Madison was plainly unwilling to rely on natural law as wholly preservative of the people's liberties. Madison acknowledged, of course, that the federal government was one of limited powers, "the great residuum being the rights of the people,"[14] but he also recognized that such grants of authority as the necessary and proper clause were potential vehicles for governmental abuse. Accordingly it was necessary to express limiting principles in order to fence in the wandering and often overreaching power of government.

Thus, although rights were enumerated in the federal Constitution to provide a clear barrier to federal action there were no illusions that the enumeration was complete. The specific guarantees selected for enumeration were derived from the English constitutional tradition, the perceived principles of republican government, and similar specific guarantees then in existence under state charters, constitutions, or declarations of rights, all of which, taken together, created a potpourri of "natural" and "positive" rights. The inclusion of the Ninth Amendment was, in part, an attempt to be certain that rights protected by state law were not supplanted by federal law simply because they were not enumerated.[15] But the Ninth Amendment was intended to do more than secure unenumerated state-sourced rights from federal invasion. It was also to serve as a barrier to encroachment upon natural rights retained by the people.[16]

It is thus reasonable to conclude that the Ninth Amendment protects two distinct categories of rights: positive or civil rights that originate in state law, and natural rights that are grounded in societal conceptions of the inalienable rights of humans. The difference compels differing analytical treatment of their content and enforceability. If the reserved positive rights of the Ninth Amendment may be determined by reference to state law, either existing in 1791 or later created, there is no genuine theoretical obstacle to their judicial enforcement. The idea of judicially enforceable unwritten natural rights leads ineluctably to the objection that the dimensions of these rights are so amorphous as to endanger the validity of the judicial process by legitimating license to import subjective personal values into constitutional adjudication. This objection is a serious and legitimate obstacle to judicial enforcement of reserved natural rights, and will be considered separately in Chapter Six. But this objection lacks force when brought to bear upon the positive dimension of Ninth Amendment rights. When courts look only to state law to provide the boundaries of reserved positive rights they are no more subjective, and probably less so, than when courts interpret the more conventional textual guarantees of the federal Constitution.

The Ninth Amendment contains an explicit command that unenumerated rights are not to be denied or disparaged by virtue of their lack of textual location in the federal Constitution. As earlier discussed, this prohibition upon disparagement of rights by reason of their nontextual status carries with it a strong implication that enumerated and unenumerated constitutional rights are to be accorded equal status. Given a strong constitutional directive to treat these unwritten rights equally with the more familiar written ones, our job is to locate them. Let us begin with positive rights.

Positive rights were thought by the founding generation to be those rights that came into being by reason of the social compact. By the time of the Constitution, pre-existing social compacts had established colonial polities, and those newly independent political communities were groping toward the creation of another, virtually unprecedented, political community: the federal, or national, community. The federal community was both a union of sovereigns and the creation of a new government that was ceded power directly from the ultimately sovereign people. That duality produced enormous political conflict and, with the additional volatile element of human slavery, the bloody expiation of civil war. But at the moment of constitutional founding, positive and natural rights could be seen in two separate dimensions. To the extent the federal government derived its powers directly from one common people, the rights retained by the people were both natural (e.g., free speech) and positive (e.g., the right to a jury trial). But to the extent the new federal government was a union of sovereign governments the pool of natural rights necessarily melted away, leaving only positive rights. Governments do not possess natural rights, people do. But people represented by state governments might usefully be thought to possess a positive right, created by the act of federal union, to continue to define their individual rights within their respective state polities. To do so, they would necessarily employ the media of their state constitutions, judicial decisions, and statutory laws. Although that media might represent, with respect to each state, a variety of natural and positive rights, from the perspective of the newly formed federal community the entire package of state-law based rights might be thought to represent a positive retained right of the people of each state.

Thus, even originalist commentators such as Russell Caplan have concluded that the Ninth Amendment "simply provides that the individual rights contained in state law are to continue in force under the Constitution until modified or eliminated by state enactment, by federal preemption, or by a judicial determination of unconstitutionality."[17] And Judge Robert Bork, certainly no friend of unenumerated constitutional rights, opined at his confirmation hearings, "I think the Ninth Amendment says that . . . the enumeration of rights shall not be construed to deny or disparage rights retained by the people *in their State Constitutions*. That is the best I can do with it."[18] As Caplan indicates, positive rights defined entirely by state law are limited by the paramount nature of federal law, but the operation of the supremacy clause upon Ninth Amendment positive rights is less certain than in the usual case of state law in conflict with federal law. Ninth Amendment rights are, by definition, federal constitutional rights, whatever their ultimate source may be. Thus, a positive Ninth Amendment right is a federal constitutional right even though its substance may be partly or wholly controlled by state law. Moreover, if we are to adhere to the parity principle between enumerated and unenumerated rights we are forbidden to permit to Congress the power to preempt positive Ninth Amendment rights but to deny Congress the power to preempt First Amendment rights.

In short, if both enumerated and unenumerated rights are entitled to the full panoply of protections accorded individual liberties secured by the Constitution, and if the Ninth Amendment was intended to preserve individual liberties secured at least by state constitutions, the necessary conclusion is that individual liberties secured by state constitutions against governmental invasion are federalized by the Ninth Amendment. Just as the Fifth Amendment prevents Congress from using its delegated powers to compel a criminal defendant to testify against herself, the Ninth Amendment should prevent Congress from using its delegated powers to contravene an unenumerated federal right contained within a state constitution. Thus, citizens of the states ought to have the power, through their state constitutions, to preserve areas of individual life from invasion by the federal Congress in the exercise of its delegated powers.

This is radical stuff, for it seemingly amounts to a form of reverse preemption. The normal understanding is that Congress, through the supremacy clause, possesses the power to displace provisions of state law, whether embodied in statutes or the state constitution, whenever it acts within the scope of its delegated powers. The reconceived positive law component of the Ninth Amendment, however, is an additional brake upon the exercise of congressional power. Just as Congress may not use its legislative power to establish a state religion, it may not use its legislative power to trench upon Ninth Amendment rights. This conclusion is derived from three premises: first, that the Ninth Amendment's purposes can only be realized by reading it as a source of substantive rights; second, that one source of those substantive rights is state constitutions; and third, that in order to make sense of the Ninth Amendment's text and its structural role within the Constitution it is necessary to conclude that Ninth Amendment rights are to be treated on a par with the other enumerated rights.

As discussed in Chapter Four, the first, or constitutional cy pres, premise is grounded in the specific political history of the amendment's creation. This is especially so when it is considered in the broader context of the intellectual construct in which the founding generation existed and in the alterations over time to the allocations of power between state and federal governments. These alterations have been so substantial that the original framework exists today only in caricature.

The second and third premises rely upon several disparate elements. The founding generation regarded the states as their principal organ of government and, although they generally conceded that state governments possessed all powers not explicitly denied them, they simultaneously and inconsistently contended that many important liberties were not explicitly protected by the various state constitutional declarations of rights. In the heady initial years of republican self-governance the founders often placed what we would regard as undue faith in the good sense of their elected representatives to refrain from invading the unexpressed but vital rights of the people. The founding generation was far less willing to repose a similar trust in the federal government. Accordingly the new central government received only a few, albeit important, enumerated powers. It is thus reasonably clear that, at least with respect to the federal government, the founders manifested in the constitutional framework a deep belief that individuals composing a political society cede to government only a limited, enumerated portion of their freedoms; all other individual rights are inviolate. This proposition leads to the principle — plain in the text of the Ninth Amendment — that unenumerated constitutional rights are entitled to the same constitutional protection as enumerated rights. If only enumerated rights are susceptible to meaningful protection, unenumerated rights are thereby effectively denied or disparaged by the enumeration of other rights, precisely the condition forbidden by the Ninth Amendment.

This understanding, in turn, requires us to locate unenumerated rights outside the Constitution. Yet, because this principle rests on the bedrock notion that governments possess legitimate power to invade only those individual freedoms ceded by the act of political union, it carries a corollary belief that there is a domain of private choice with which government may not legitimately interfere. If this is so, it is a likely inference that the unenumerated rights intended as sacrosanct are of necessity "negative" ones: rights that inhere in individuals to negate the actions of government seeking to invade the individual, or private, sphere rather than "affirmative" rights of entitlement to receipt of benefits from government. Although it is fashionable nowadays to contend that the legal proclivity to separate life into public and private domains is analytically incoherent and falsely dichotomous, it is an undeniable aspect of human experience that we regard parts of our lives as private and other parts as public.

The public-private distinction results from an attempt to account for two opposing, but mutually dependent, attributes of human existence. We attempt simultaneously to recognize in our forms of social organization that people are autonomous and independent and that they are socially interconnected and dependent. The former point of view recognizes a realm of private choice, the latter presumes a public domain. We are committed to both principles, although they are inherently in tension. Individuality must be respected for freedom to flourish, but for that respect to be meaningful and the resulting freedom of any real value, it is vital that the communities in which people exist and of which they are a part be healthy and viable. But when community needs assume absolute priority there is the danger of suffocation of the individual spirit. When one pole or the other of this diad is accentuated excessively, democratic life falls out of balance. American democracy has, from its inception, attempted with varying degrees of success to mediate these competing, but mutually dependent, principles.[19] Justice Oliver Wendell Holmes's famous and pithy observation that "the life of the law has not been logic: it has been experience,"[20] is an epigrammatic confirmation of the pragmatic mediation between public and private realms that is and always has been at the heart of democratic community. It is thus unnecessary to enter the unrewarding debate concerning the continued vitality of the public-private distinction.

In any case, while in late eighteenth-century America no single theory of political union was universally accepted,[21] Americans were virtually united in their desire to free individuals from what they regarded as oppressive state control. The Hobbesian ideal of an omnipotent state was decisively rejected. If Americans were not orthodox Lockeans, they were at least, in today's parlance, highly libertarian. Those eighteenth-century views were simply one aspect of the continual mediation between public and private spheres. Although the Ninth Amendment is one fruit of that attitude, we are required today to place the Ninth Amendment into our contemporary balance of private and public spheres. Its primary role is likely to continue to be as a bulwark against the state, preserving the domain of private choice, but it is possible that in a world in which private choice may be ever more dependent on public choices the Ninth Amendment might require governments to exercise public choices in a way that accommodates or strengthens the ability of individuals to make private choices or in a fashion that maintains healthy and viable communities.

The Ninth Amendment is also part of the founding generation's concern with the preservation of the states as autonomous units of government and as structural bulwarks of human liberty. The amendment, like the rest of the Bill of Rights, in essence was a device to insure that the national government would be disabled from intruding upon the fundamental rights of its citizenry. It accomplished this by endeavoring to preserve natural rights (those transcendent of political union) and positive rights secured or maintained by state law (created or preserved by the people in the act of state political union). Given the accepted belief with respect to state governments that states possess all conceivable power except that which has been expressly denied them by the constitution creating them, the only source of state law for these positive rights is a state's constitution.

The idea that the Ninth Amendment contains within it judicially enforceable rights that are substantively rooted in the state constitutions and that such rights act as a barrier to congressional action is, at first, almost jarringly counterintuitive. Although there are a number of difficulties with that view none are indisputably insuperable.

The first question posed is whether the state-sourced positive "rights *retained* by the people" are a set of rights antecedent to the federal Constitution and, thus, effectively frozen in time and content, or whether such rights are a dynamic, evolving list that change as sentiment shifts within the states. There is much to be said for the proposition that Ninth Amendment rights are static. The word "retained" surely suggests that these rights existed prior to the Constitution. One must remember, however, that the Ninth Amendment was likely intended to be a source of both natural rights (which certainly predated any government) and positive rights (those created by, or incidental to, the act of political union).[22] Thus, it is plausible that the term "retained" was meant to apply only to those Ninth Amendment rights that were natural rights.[23] Yet, from the perspective of 1791 natural rights and all rights enumerated in state constitutions would have predated federal constitutional union. It is equally logical to suppose that both categories of rights would be "retained" by the people. Moreover, the rights specifically enumerated in the Constitution were not confined to either the category of natural or positive rights. It is thus unconvincing in method and result to contend that the word "retained" was originally meant to apply only to natural rights.[24]

Fortunately, there are other sources, more definitive than reliance upon supposition concerning original intent, that aid resolution of this issue. The addition over time of new states both complicates and simplifies matters. A frozen concept of Ninth Amendment rights would deny to the citizens of newly admitted states the most fundamental right apparently preserved by the Ninth Amendment: the right to decide the limits of governmental power to invade individual liberty and to make that decision effective against the people's federal agents. Moreover, denial of this right to newly admitted states while conferring it upon the original states through the device of a frozen concept of Ninth Amendment rights would violate the principle that each newly admitted state is admitted "on an equal footing with the original states in all respects whatsoever,"[25] a principle that has been uniformly followed from the beginning of the American union. This objection might be partially overcome by concluding that, while only the state constitutional rights in existence in 1791 became transmuted into federal Ninth Amendment rights, such rights are universally available to all citizens of the United States. Although this would make Ninth Amendment positive rights universally accessible to citizens of every state it would deny to the citizens of new states, while preserving to the founding citizens of the original states, the opportunity to specify in detail the precise nature of the rights retained by operation of the Ninth Amendment.

A static concept of Ninth Amendment rights is one that would undermine the principle that Ninth Amendment rights are to be treated on a par with the other rights enumerated in the Constitution. With the possible exception of the Seventh Amendment's civil jury trial right, no other enumerated constitutional right is treated as frozen in time. Even the Seventh Amendment right is one that necessarily bends with the times, given the necessity of fashioning analogues from 1791 practice to present-day causes of action unknown two centuries ago.

Finally, treating Ninth Amendment positive rights as only extending to those rights secured by state constitutions in 1791 undercuts the collateral intention of the founding generation that the Ninth Amendment would act as a device to prevent the possibility that the enumerated rights would be treated as an exhaustive listing of the people's fundamental rights. As Edmund Pendleton put it in a letter to Richard Henry Lee, "[M]ay we not in the progress of things, discover some great and Important [right], which we don't now think of?"[26] Pendleton's observation emphasizes the more general conclusion of such legal historians as Jefferson Powell that the founding generation intended that its intentions would not govern future generations.[27] According to Powell, the founding generation provided an open-ended constitutional text precisely because they anticipated that changing events would require re-interpretation of the specific meaning of such grand generalities as "due process," "cruel and unusual," and "retained rights." We need not take Professor Powell's word, however, because the Philadel-phia Convention's Committee on Detail and Style, charged with the responsibility of casting the Convention's decisions into a Con-stitution, left some quite pertinent evidence of its intentions. When Edmund Randolph penned the rough draft, with fellow committee members John Rutledge, James Wilson, Oliver Ells-worth, and Nathaniel Gorham hovering about him offering crit-icisms and suggestions, he expressed in marginal notes some of the principles that had guided the committee:

> In the draught of a fundamental constitution, two things de-serve attention:
>
> 1. To insert essential principles only, lest the operations of government should be clogged by rendering those provisions permanent and unalterable, which ought to be accommo-dated to times and events; and
>
> 2. To use simple and precise language, and general proposi-tions, according to the example of the several constitutions of the several states; for the construction of a constitution neces-sarily differs from that of law.[28]

Limiting the positive strand of "retained rights of the people" to those expressed in state constitutions in 1791 would undermine the general intentions of the framers with respect to constitutional guarantees and their specific intentions and aspirations with re-spect to the Ninth Amendment itself.

Thus, given the inherent shortcomings of the static view of rights, a dynamic concept holds more promise. The dynamic view, however, requires us to confront the issue of whether federal Ninth Amendment rights can ever be applied uniformly across the coun-try. Further, it raises the problem of whether such rights, once created by a state constitution and federalized by the Ninth Amendment, thereafter may be altered by unilateral action of the state polity. If a dynamic concept of Ninth Amendment positive rights is employed, uniformity of Ninth Amendment rights is problematic, for it presents the courts with the truly Herculean task of stitching together a common — and presumably consistent — fabric of rights from fifty different sources. What is the U.S. Supreme Court to do if California expressly preserves in its constitution a right of privacy and Alabama expressly repudiates such a right? Would the Court resolve this problem as it has done with recent death penalty cases — by simply calculating which scheme is the more prevalent?[29] A more likely problem is the possibility that any given right — privacy, for example — would be recognized in different state constitutions but given different substantive meanings by the supreme courts of the relevant states. At least in this case it would be plausible for the Court to assume the task of defining the substance of the right, without reference to differing state interpretations, inasmuch as the right involved would have become a federal Ninth Amendment right.

It is thus theoretically possible for the Court to use all fifty state constitutions as *potential* sources of the federal Ninth Amendment rights retained by the people, with the decision remaining with the Court as to *which* of these possible rights is to be recognized as a federal constitutional right. If, however, the Court were to attempt this task, it would be required to articulate some principled basis for preferring one state constitutional norm to any other. It is not impossible to do this. In the latter part of this chapter I suggest a tentative set of guidelines that might aid the performance of this task, but the job is one of considerable difficulty and uncertainty.

There are several advantages to leaving to the Court the responsibility of selecting which state constitutional guarantees are part of the set of positive rights preserved by the Ninth Amendment. First, positive Ninth Amendment rights would be uniformly applied across the entire nation, at least with respect to the federal government. Complete uniformity could only be accomplished by applying federally determined positive Ninth Amendment rights to the states as well, a complicated problem whose resolution I defer for the moment. Second, although these rights would owe their *origin* to their expression in one or more state constitutions, once recognized as part of the federal guarantee of "retained rights" they would be presumably be immune from elimination as a constitutional right at the hands of the state polity that sowed the seed of the federal right.

A disadvantage of this scheme, however, is that it would require the Court to confront the issue of whether the set of uniform positive Ninth Amendment rights is enforceable only against the federal government, or whether such rights are also enforceable against the state governments, presumably on the theory that Ninth Amendment rights are incorporated into the Fourteenth Amendment's due process clause, the constitutional vehicle by which most of the federal Bill of Rights are made applicable to the states as well as the federal government. There is a certain dissonance in making positive Ninth Amendment rights applicable to states that have never recognized the existence of the asserted right. Rooted as they are in state constitutions, the very existence of such rights is justified by the founding generation's desire to preserve states as autonomous governmental institutions.

On the other hand, failure to incorporate positive Ninth Amendment rights into the Fourteenth Amendment's due process clause would diminish the uniformity of Ninth Amendment rights. Although such rights would be uniformly applicable against the federal government they would have no applicability against the states. Under state law, however, the substantive Ninth Amendment right, or some close variant thereof, would be applicable to those states that had expressed the right in their constitutions. This is a condition virtually identical to the present, in which state constitutional rights vary considerably from state to state. Every American has the same federal constitutional rights, but by virtue of their state citizenship, Americans enjoy a greater or lesser degree of protection from state abuse. Discussion of this vexing question of whether positive Ninth Amendment rights might be incorporated into the Fourteenth Amendment's due process clause will follow. For the moment it is enough to note the existence of the problem.

A quite different approach to positive Ninth Amendment rights would be to acknowledge frankly that, because these rights have their origin in state constitutions, the substance of federal positive Ninth Amendment rights varies with the differing state constitutions. On this view, Ninth Amendment decisional law would develop a richly variegated pattern. A federal Ninth Amendment right of privacy would be recognized with respect to Californians and Alaskans, for example, because both states explicitly recognize such a right. In contrast, Missouri does not recognize that right. As a result, the citizens of each state would be uniquely and separately entitled to define the nature of their relationship with *all* of their governmental agents. They would be able to do this immediately (with the state via the state constitution) and, within the other constraining limits of the federal constitution, mediately (with the national government via the Ninth Amendment's incorporation of state constitutional guarantees).

The principal advantage of such a system is that it would respect the differing choices of separate state polities, insuring each that only their own choices of retained individual rights would be insulated against governmental invasion at either the state or federal level. To the extent that positive Ninth Amendment rights are historically grounded in a desire to retain for the states maximum flexibility in defining the content of retained rights, such a result is consistent with the concerns that animated the Ninth Amendment. This is part of the legacy of a system of dual sovereignty and may be a virtue.[30] The practical problems of judicial administration of such a scheme are not necessarily enormous. It has not proven burdensome for the federal courts to manage with fifty-one different legal regimes in diversity cases under the rule of *Erie Railroad Co. v. Tompkins*.[31] Thus, it is unlikely to be much more difficult for the courts to rely on state constitutional law to breathe life into this substantive dimension of the Ninth Amendment.

Skeptics will observe that the natural consequence of viewing Ninth Amendment rights as both dynamic and state-specific is that some Americans would enjoy more individual liberty than others. They would. But *all* Americans would enjoy the same package of federal constitutional rights that owe their substance to federal law. Only with respect to the positive dimension of the Ninth Amendment would federal constitutional rights vary with one's residence. Thus, for example, if Californians believe privacy to be constitutionally desirable and Missourians do not, Missourians can hardly complain if Congress invades their personal privacy in a fashion the Ninth Amendment would not permit with respect to Californians. To the extent the package of individual liberties provided by the federal Constitution and a state constitution is insufficient, state citizens can be expected to respond by altering their state constitutions or departing to other, more generous, jurisdictions. This objection is little different from the current situation where, for example, Alaskans possess the right to smoke marijuana in their homes while the citizens of every other state face fines or imprisonment for the same conduct.[32]

Acceptance of the dynamic and state-specific concept, however, poses another problem. Once a state polity has created a right under its own constitution, and thereby transmuted the right into a federal constitutional guarantee via the Ninth Amendment, may that same state polity rescind the *federal* Ninth Amendment right by rescinding the underlying state right? The answer is suggested by the nature of a state-specific view of the content of positive Ninth Amendment rights.

States, as a matter of independent state constitutional law, may alter their own constitutions. They may direct courts in their respective jurisdictions to interpret independent state guarantees of individual liberty more generously than their federal analogues but may not enforce interpretations of the state constitution that are more restrictive of human liberty than permitted by the federal Constitution.[33] Although positive and state-specific Ninth Amendment rights would be federal, their substance would be derived wholly from state constitutional law. Because one major concern of the Ninth Amendment's proponents was to reserve to the people their rights under local law, and to insulate those rights from federal invasion, it seems appropriate for a state polity to have within its own control the matter of the continued vitality of any given state constitutional right. Thus, states would control the continued existence and substance of positive Ninth Amendment rights which owe their initial viability to state constitutional action. Ninth Amendment rights originating in state constitutions would be dynamic organisms. Their dynamism would be rendered less destabilizing than it might otherwise be because such rights, although federal, would operate only as a barrier to federal and state governmental action with respect to the specific state of origin. They would thus be dynamic in substance but cramped in geographic application.

This scheme would be quite similar to established *Erie* practice. In diversity cases, federal courts are required to follow the rule of law announced by the highest court of the state whose law is applicable.[34] For this reason, and the fact that through the "adequate and independent" state grounds doctrine states are free to determine their own law,[35] the law applicable in federal diversity cases is of state origin. The law applicable in federal diversity cases changes as the state polity determines. It is not federalized by virtue of its application in federal court.

The same virtual result would be true in Ninth Amendment cases. The asserted right, though federal, would owe its entire substantive vitality to state constitutional action. Through the adequate and independent state grounds doctrine, the states remain free to establish and alter their constitutional law to the extent it does not violate federal constitutional law. That such alteration would have a collateral impact on a federal constitutional right would simply be a unique part of the design of the Ninth Amendment.[36] Because *state-specific* positive Ninth Amendment rights would only operate against the federal government within the jurisdictional authority of the specific state in question, the policies underlying the supremacy clause would not be applicable. The supremacy clause mandates the paramountcy of federal law in large part because it is a necessary mechanism for assuring uniformity of result within the sphere of federal jurisdiction. But if the sphere of federal jurisdiction with respect to positive Ninth Amendment rights is conceived as limited to enforcing against the federal government fifty different state constitutional choices, the premises behind the supremacy clause are simply not operative. Of course, those same premises may provide a more solid basis for arguing that the state-specific concept should be rejected in favor of a national, and uniform, concept of the content of positive Ninth Amendment rights.

The national concept of positive Ninth Amendment rights is attractive because it offers the promise of national uniformity to such rights and because it avoids the seemingly odd result of a *federal* constitutional right disappearing at the discretion of a state polity. Yet, the national concept necessarily raises questions of the applicability of positive Ninth Amendment rights to the states. Without such application uniformity would be incomplete, for positive Ninth Amendment rights would impinge only upon the federal government. In order for positive Ninth Amendment rights, nationally conceived, to apply to the actions of state governments it is necessary either to conclude that such rights ought to be incorporated into the Fourteenth Amendment's due process clause or that, independently of the due process guarantee, positive Ninth Amendment rights ought to bind state governments.

Most commentators agree that the Ninth Amendment operates, if at all, only against federal action.[37] It is, of course, quite clear that the Bill of Rights was intended to bind only the actions of the federal government.[38] Those intentions were supervened, however, by the incorporation doctrine, pursuant to which most of the guarantees of the Bill of Rights have been read into the Fourteenth Amendment's due process clause, thereby binding the states as well as the federal government. The Ninth Amendment has, of course, never been so incorporated because, at least at this point in our constitutional history, there is thought to be virtually nothing to incorporate.[39] Moreover, because positive Ninth Amendment rights would originate in and derive substance from state constitutional law they would also apply to the state of origin through the independent constitution of the state. Thus, in the case of state-specific positive Ninth Amendment rights there would be no need for the Ninth Amendment to act directly upon the states. Indeed, limiting the Ninth Amendment to bar only federal action would simplify matters.

Unfortunately, it is unrealistic to embrace without question the idea that positive Ninth Amendment rights should apply only against the federal government. First, it is not clear that the best concept of the substantive content of positive Ninth Amendment rights is state-specific. If the national concept of their content is preferred, doctrinal and political desire for uniformity of these rights would exert tremendous pressures to make them completely uniform, by rendering positive Ninth Amendment rights enforceable against state governments. Second, we should not lose sight of the fact that, as discussed in Chapter Six, the Ninth Amendment should also be regarded as encompassing a "natural law" dimension. The unenumerated rights that develop in that strain have no necessary foundation in state constitutions. Indeed, much of the logic of natural law is that natural rights are transcendent of political arrangements. It would be strange to recognize the existence of natural rights in the Ninth Amendment but permit state governments freely to invade them. Moreover, in order for natural Ninth Amendment rights to be treated on a par with enumerated rights (most of which have been incorporated into the Fourteenth Amendment's due process clause) it may well be necessary to enforce natural Ninth Amendment rights against the states. Of course, it is possible to enforce against the states only *natural* Ninth Amendment rights, leaving *positive* Ninth Amendment rights as barriers only to the exercise of federal power. Although it might be untidy to develop a Ninth Amendment doctrine that applies only selectively against the states — with respect to natural Ninth Amendment rights but not with respect to positive Ninth Amendment rights — that is a result that is no more illogical than the current state of the selective incorporation doctrine that has grown up around the Fourteenth Amendment's due process clause.

Superficially, it would appear that Russell Caplan is correct when he contends that it is not "logically possible to 'incorporate' the ninth amendment through the fourteenth to apply as a prohibition against the states, because the ninth amendment was designed not to circumscribe, but to protect the enactments of the states."[40] Caplan seeks to reinforce his point by observing that, in its modern dimension, the Fourteenth Amendment protects only unenumerated *federal* rights against state action. Thus, the right of privacy, grounded in the substantive due process clause, and the closest analogue to an enforceable Ninth Amendment right, owes its legal existence to a conclusion that it is a federal right, not one grounded in state law.[41]

There are several things wrong with this view. Although Caplan's observations have force when considered in the context of state-specific positive Ninth Amendment rights, they lack punch when transported into the realm of national positive Ninth Amendment rights. This is because national positive Ninth Amendment rights *are* federal rights; they owe their origin but not their entire substance to another source of law. Moreover, at least with respect to those states that in their own constitutional law recognize the existence of what would become a federal positive Ninth Amendment right, "the federal character of Ninth Amendment . . . rights derives from state action . . . [and] application of the Ninth Amendment to the states would merely amount to a federally enforced right to make the states abide by their own law."[42] Surely, a requirement that a government abide by its own law is the essence of due process.[43] Curiously enough, the U.S. Supreme Court has begun, perhaps unwittingly, to do something very similar under the equal protection clause of the Fourteenth Amendment.

In *Allegheny Pittsburgh Coal Co. v. County Comm'n of Webster County*[44] a West Virginia county tax assessor assessed property on the basis of its recent purchase price, but made only minor modifications to assessments of land not recently sold. As a result, the taxes imposed on similar property were wildly disparate. The Supreme Court held that this practice violated the equal protection clause of the Fourteenth Amendment because the West Virginia Constitution provided that "taxation shall be equal and uniform throughout the State, and all property, both real and personal, shall be taxed in proportion to its value."[45] While conceding that West Virginia was free to "divide different kinds of property into classes and assign to each class a different tax burden so long as those divisions and burdens are reasonable,"[46] the Court concluded that because the state's constitution had expressly directed otherwise, the tax assessor had violated Allegheny Pittsburgh's federal equal protection rights. This is nothing more than a conclusion that West Virginia must comply with its own law, and that a federal court may compel a state actor to do so. Although the Court used the rubric of federal equal protection law for this purpose, it could just as easily have relied on due process or, were it justiciable, the guarantee clause.[47]

Although the Court made no mention of it, the result in *Allegheny Pittsburgh* is seemingly at odds with *Pennhurst State School & Hospital v. Halderman*,[48] which held that the Eleventh Amendment prohibited a federal court from enjoining a state official from further violations of *state* law. The holding may be harmonized by observing that *Allegheny Pittsburgh* posed an issue of *federal* law, albeit one the substance of which was supplied by a state Constitution, while *Pennhurst* raised a claim of pure state law, with no claimed federal medium to transmute the asserted state right into a federal guarantee. *Allegheny Pittsburgh* thus suggests that the Court is prepared to accept state sources of law as the substantive core of federal guarantees. There is no theoretical or conceptual reason to suppose that this approach is one that must necessarily be confined to the equal protection clause.

The argument that the states may be required to observe federally defined positive Ninth Amendment rights because it amounts to making them obey their own law breaks down in two areas. First, the substance of the constitutional norm the states would be forced to obey would be fashioned by the federal courts, primarily the U.S. Supreme Court, and any resemblance to the specific state constitutional right from which it is extracted might become, over time, merely accidental. Second, national positive Ninth Amendment rights would inevitably consist of rights not recognized by every state constitution. With respect to any given national positive Ninth Amendment rights, some state constitutions would be silent on the subject and others might be explicitly adverse. It would be Orwellian to contend that these states were merely being asked to comply with their own law. Of course, states that have explicitly disavowed a national positive Ninth Amendment right might be treated as having, as a matter of Ninth Amendment entitlement, opted out of the coverage of the national positive Ninth Amendment right, but the creation of such a doctrine would undermine the justifications for having chosen to regard positive Ninth Amendment rights as national in the first place. There are costs to any choice, and this dilemma simply illustrates a disadvantage of the national positive Ninth Amendment rights concept, especially when coupled with the incorporation doctrine.

It could also be argued that because the founding generation was concerned with preservation of rights rooted in state law, positive Ninth Amendment rights, unlike the remainder of the Bill of Rights, were intended from the beginning to be applicable to the states. The problem with this argument is that it cannot serve as support for forcing states to abide by positive Ninth Amendment rights. This is because the substance of such rights are determined by federal judges and their content might be quite remote from the specific state guarantees that spawned their recognition. At best, this is an argument that supports applicability to the states of the state-specific concept of positive Ninth Amendment rights, and there is no consequence to that rule because it merely requires the states to do what, presumably, would be required of them independently under their own constitutional law.

The incorporation problem would be experienced most acutely if a national concept of positive Ninth Amendment rights were adopted. The state-specific concept of positive Ninth Amendment rights avoids these problems. In addition to the incorporation problem, there are other problems that are presented by the two different possible concepts of positive Ninth Amendment rights. To explore them, consider the following hypothetical case.

Mary is prosecuted in state court on the basis of evidence obtained by a warrantless police search of her household garbage deposited by her in a closed container at curbside for collection. The evidence is introduced despite Mary's contention that it was seized in violation of the state constitution's version of the search-and-seizure guarantee of the federal Constitution's Fourth Amendment. Mary and the state prosecutors agree that the federal Fourth Amendment poses no barrier to the admissibility of the evidence,[49] so the legal issue is one purely of state constitutional law. On appeal, the state supreme court concludes that the evidence was properly admissible under the state constitution. Mary, now imprisoned, files a habeas corpus petition in federal district court, alleging that her federal Ninth Amendment rights were violated by the introduction of the evidence. Does the federal district court have the opportunity to revisit the same legal issue and decide it differently from the state supreme court, on the ground that the issue is one of federal constitutional law? The answer to this hypothetical case ought to depend on whether the Ninth Amendment right is regarded as state-specific or national.

Although state-specific positive Ninth Amendment rights would be federal, their substance would be wholly derived from state constitutional law. Given that the federal right would not exist but for constitutional action of a state polity, and that it would extend only to the limits of the jurisdictional authority of the state from which the right originated, it seems consistent with this view of the positive dimension of the Ninth Amendment to defer to the states for final decision on the substantive meaning of a state-specific positive Ninth Amendment right. Just as in an *Erie* case, the federal courts would look to state law to supply the rule of decision. The difference here, of course, is that it is a state rule that drives the federal *constitutional* decision. Thus, in a state-specific regime the federal court in our hypothetical case would be required to deny Mary's habeas corpus petition, at least on Ninth Amendment grounds, because the state supreme court would have authoritatively defined the substance of the right adversely to Mary.

That result reinforces the earlier conclusion that because state polities retain the power to alter state constitutional rights they should also possess a corresponding power to alter the substance of state-specific, positive Ninth Amendment rights. If state-specific Ninth Amendment rights were of a "ratchet" type — once created by state constitutional action they could never be reclaimed from the federal Constitution — it would be necessary to concede to federal courts the power to review such rights *de novo*. Such rights would have acquired a peculiar federal status, wholly disembodied from their state origins. This would be at odds with the state-specific view of the nature of Ninth Amendment rights and would ultimately erode the state-specific view because, over time, the putatively state-specific right would acquire a federal substance bearing no necessary congruence with the state right from which it was born.

Finally, the principle of "comity" between the states and the federal government suggests, if not compels, deference to state authority. In *Garcia v. San Antonio Metropolitan Transit Authority* the U.S. Supreme Court appeared to abandon any meaningful judicial effort to define the point at which Congress was disabled from invading the realm of state authority by adopting the principle that, in general, "state sovereign interests . . . are . . . protected by procedural safeguards inherent in the structure of the federal system."[50] Those safeguards exist because Congress is made up of a congeries of legislators elected by the people of the various states. State interests are thereby protected because federal legislation is the product of state representatives. But, as *Garcia* noted, "any substantive restraint on the exercise of Commerce Clause powers . . . must be tailored to compensate for possible failings in the national political process."[51] The Court has begun to fashion several doctrines that define when Congress has acted in a fashion that evidences such failings. When a state is excluded from the deliberative legislative process, when it is singled out for special treatment, when a state's legislative process has been commandeered by Congress, or when Congress simply fails to make a plain statement of its otherwise legitimate exercise of power to regulate state functions, it has acted in a fashion that signals a sufficient failing of the political process to merit judicial intervention to protect the integrity of the states as autonomous sovereigns.[52]

Moreover, the Court continues, even after *Garcia*, to conduct a "judicial patrol of the frontier between federal and state sovereignty" with respect to the exercise of federal judicial power under Article III of the Constitution.[53] The principles employed by the Court to check federal judicial power — abstention, the adequate and independent state grounds doctrine,[54] the *Erie* doctrine, exhaustion of state administrative remedies, to name just a few — are better thought of as constitutional "guarantees, or . . . rooted in [constitutional] principles of residual sovereignty, rather than seemingly unconnected and disparate doctrines."[55] Thus, the Constitution's structural principle of state sovereignty, instantiated in the limits on federal authority sprinkled throughout the Constitution, and reinforced by the axiomatic declaration of the Tenth Amendment that the states retain all powers not surrendered, would receive further buttressing by the state-specific view of the nature of positive Ninth Amendment rights.

By contrast, a national concept of positive Ninth Amendment rights would lead to at least a different method for resolution of Mary's habeas corpus petition, if not a different result. Under the national view, the right claimed by Mary would be indisputably federal in content as well as nomenclature. There would be no necessary correlation between the substance of the federal right and any state analogue that may have spawned the federal right. Let us suppose that in Mary's case her specific contention is that, because the state constitutional law of a number of states other than her own is to the effect that a warrantless search of her garbage is impermissible,[56] courts should recognize a positive Ninth Amendment right to that effect, quite independently of the Fourth

Amendment's more lenient treatment of warrantless searches of garbage. Whatever the merits of this claim, a national view of positive Ninth Amendment rights would require the federal judge ruling on Mary's habeas petition to evaluate her claim independently of the state supreme court's determination of the issue.

One problematic aspect of the national approach to positive Ninth Amendment rights is that it would provide a second opportunity to relitigate issues of state constitutional law in a different forum and under a different substantive rubric and to relitigate issues of federal constitutional law under the Ninth Amendment. Thus, in Mary's case she would have the opportunity essentially to contest the continuing validity of settled federal Fourth Amendment law pertaining to warrantless searches of garbage as well as the opportunity to contest the determination of her state supreme court that the state constitutional protection against unreasonable searches and seizures was no more protective than the federal Fourth Amendment. This is a doctrine that carries enormous potential for chaotic and endless relitigation of seemingly settled issues. Of course, there are tempering devices to control the apparent mischief, such as the rule adopted in *Teague v. Lane*[57] that habeas relief is not available to litigants urging a new rule of constitutional law upon the courts. Nevertheless, the national concept of positive Ninth Amendment rights carries with it the possibility that the Ninth Amendment might become a device for relitigation of settled issues of both federal and state constitutional law. That potentially destabilizing effect provides a significant reason to pause before embracing the national concept of positive Ninth Amendment rights.

The state-specific and the national concept of positive Ninth Amendment rights raise questions of their compatibility with our understanding of the supremacy clause, which provides that constitutionally valid federal law displaces any contrary state law, including state constitutional law. The state-specific view poses the more difficult issues.

A simple, albeit too simple, reason the state-specific concept of positive Ninth Amendment rights does not violate the supremacy clause is because the Ninth Amendment incorporates into the federal Constitution state constitutional rights and secures them against federal invasion in the same manner as is done with other federal constitutional rights. But under some circumstances the state-specific theory might create the possibility of conflicts between two federal constitutional rights: one based in state law and the other in federal law. This is a serious problem. Such a view of the Ninth Amendment cannot survive without some mechanism to resolve the inevitable inconsistencies arising between rights specifically enumerated in the federal Constitution and unenumerated federal constitutional rights incorporated from state constitutions. A number of examples may serve to illustrate the scope of this problem.

Suppose that a state constitution provides that fetuses are persons and enjoy all the constitutional rights provided all other persons. Let us also assume that the *Roe v. Wade* decision is still good law.[58] This situation creates a plain conflict between the putative state-specific positive Ninth Amendment rights of the fetus and the Fourteenth Amendment substantive due process rights of the incubatory woman. Which prevails? This is an example of a pure constitutional conflict; we will stipulate that Congress has not attempted to preempt the state constitutional right in any fashion.

Resolution of this hypothetical case, which poses a purely constitutional conflict, requires that one federal constitutional right yield to the other. In such a case of unavoidable conflict the supremacy clause appears to dictate that the right with its substantive source in federal law should prevail. Thus, in the hypothetical example it would appear that the federally sourced right of the incubatory woman would prevail over the state-sourced and state-specific putative Ninth Amendment right of the fetus. But suppose that the U.S. Supreme Court reverses *Roe* in an opinion that also concludes that fetuses are persons entitled to constitutional protection. If a state were to respond by adding to its constitution a guarantee of an absolute right to terminate an unwanted pregnancy it seems clear that, at least in some circumstances, the federally created rights of the fetus would prevail.[59] Such is the inevitable consequence of obedience to the supremacy of federally created rights and obligations.

Now suppose that the Supreme Court has reversed *Roe v. Wade* in an opinion that simply declares that the constitutional right of privacy does not extend to abortion. In response, the people of a state add to their constitution a guarantee of an individual right to terminate unwanted pregnancies. In reply, Congress exercises its power under Section 5 of the Fourteenth Amendment, or perhaps under the commerce clause, to prohibit the states from enforcing such a right, perhaps by legislation that simply forbids all abortions. Although not without doubt, let us stipulate that, in the absence of some paramount constitutional norm, Congress has acted within the legitimate scope of its authority. This constitutes what would normally be a simple instance of preemption: The congressional will would displace the contrary provision of state constitutional law. In light of the theory of state-specific positive Ninth Amendment rights, however, such a conclusion would not readily be available. Indeed, the logic of state-specific positive Ninth Amendment rights would dictate precisely the reverse result; the Ninth Amendment, like the first amendment, would operate to curb the scope of congressional power. But the conflict posed is actually more subtle and requires further examination. Resolution of the matter depends in part on whether Congress has acted pursuant to Section 5 of the Fourteenth Amendment or under the commerce power and, if pursuant to Section 5, whether it possesses the power to define the substance of Fourteenth Amendment rights.

To explore the problem, consider another version of the hypothetical abortion case just posed. The people of a state add to their constitution a guarantee of the individual right to practice private racial discrimination. In response, Congress exercises its power under Section 5 of the Fourteenth Amendment, or under the commerce clause, to prohibit the states from enforcing such a right, perhaps by a comprehensive statute prohibiting virtually all forms of private racial discrimination.

To the extent that Congress has acted upon its power under Section 5 of the Fourteenth Amendment "to enforce, by appropriate legislation," the equal protection guarantee of the Fourteenth Amendment, Congress may have articulated a constitutional norm that would thus create a clear conflict with the Ninth Amendment right to terminate pregnancy, or practice private racial discrimination, derived from the state constitution. In *Katzenbach v. Morgan*[60] the Supreme Court concluded that Congress had power under Section 5 to enact legislation prohibiting state electoral practices that had previously been determined by the Court to comport with the equal protection guarantee. Although *Morgan* certainly suggests that Congress has power to define the *substance* of equal protection that implication was qualified by *Morgan* and subsequent cases. *Morgan* stated that the congressional power did not extend to legislation that might "restrict, abrogate, or dilute" equal protection.[61] Thus it is for the Court to determine when congressional action is in aid of or derogation from the equal protection guarantee, a conclusion underscored by the Court's conclusion in *Metro Broadcasting, Inc. v. Federal Communications Commission* that "benign race-conscious measures mandated by Congress" are compatible with the equal protection guarantee so long as they are substantially related to the achievement of important governmental objectives.[62] Thus, the hypothetical state-specific Ninth

Amendment right to practice private racial discrimination would collide with a federally sourced guarantee of equal protection, specifically instantiated in congressional legislation prohibiting such practices.

The conclusion might well be the same with respect to the hypothetical abortion case, but that conclusion must be hedged by the fact that there is, as yet, no developed law concerning congressional power to prohibit abortions in the name of securing the benefits of equal protection for fetuses. Indeed, a congressional attempt to do so would be deeply contested. In *Oregon v. Mitchell*[63] the Court invalidated federal legislation extending the vote in state elections to eighteen-year-olds, specifically rejecting the argument that Congress could do so as part of its Section 5 power to define the contours of equal protection. The boundaries of congressional power to enforce equal protection by redefining its substance are murky and controversial. There is more latitude for congressional action in matters of racial equity than elsewhere. Thus, in a world of state-specific positive Ninth Amendment rights, the Court would be forced to articulate the extent of congressional power to define equal protection, especially when that definition is pitted against contrary determinations of constitutional content emanating from the states. *Oregon v. Mitchell* limited congressional power under Section 5 to actions remedial of Fourteenth Amendment violations, and may have established a collateral principle that Congress lacks power under Section 5 to preempt state law in areas in which the states have clearly been assigned authority by the Constitution.[64] Racial discrimination and its elimination is not within either category; thus, putative state-specific positive Ninth Amendment rights that attempt to poach on matters of race are clearly destined for nonrecognition. But because the positive dimension of the Ninth Amendment was intended to preserve latitude for state polities to articulate fundamental norms, state-specific positive Ninth Amendment rights should be recognized absent a clear conflict with a federally sourced constitutional right. Thus, the hypothetical abortion case should be resolved in favor of the state-specific Ninth Amendment right, given the hypothesized absence of any federal constitutional principle bringing abortion within the ambit of Fourteenth Amendment protections.

If Congress were to act solely upon its power to regulate commerce a different set of problems emerge. The congressional power to regulate interstate commerce is indisputable, although argument can be raised concerning the scope of that power.[65] Whatever its scope, however, it does not confer upon Congress authority to infringe other constitutional rights in the name of regulating commerce. Congress may not prohibit interstate traffic in books. This condition results from our modern penchant of viewing "rights" as trumping "powers." Accordingly, the scope of congressional power is limited by the scope of individual rights secured elsewhere in the Constitution. If state-specific, positive Ninth Amendment rights are part of the constitutional constellation of individual rights, congressional regulation of commerce ends at the threshold of the Ninth Amendment. By contrast, congressional legislation enforcing the equal protection guarantee, at least with respect to matters of racial equity, directly involves Congress in *interpretation* of an individual rights guarantee contained in the Constitution. At a minimum it provides remedies for violations of this constitutional guarantee, rather than, as is the case with commerce regulation, merely *acting in accordance with powers conferred by the Constitution*. Although this suggests that state-specific, positive Ninth Amendment rights will always trump congressional regulations of interstate commerce, the problem is not that simple.

Suppose that a state establishes in its constitution the right to buy and sell securities traded on national securities markets while in possession of material inside information obtained in the performance of a fiduciary obligation of trust to the corporate issuer of the securities. Does this putative state-specific, positive Ninth Amendment right trump Section 10b of the Securities and Exchange Act of 1934[66] and Rule 10b-5,[67] which, as interpreted, clearly prohibit such practices? If so, then states will be free to evade and obviate all congressional authority over national life, preventing the creation of needed uniform national policies. All that state politicians and citizens need do is insert statutory norms into their state constitutions.[68]

There are at least two reasons why such a result would be inconsistent with the originally intended purpose of the positive dimension of the Ninth Amendment as well as its reconceived purpose in the context of constitutional cy pres.

First, the positive aspect of the Ninth Amendment was designed to preserve state-sourced fundamental liberties but was rooted in an attempt to strike a *balance* between federal power and the individual liberties of citizens whom that power could affect. In the world of the founders, it will be remembered, individual rights were thought of as the absence of governmental powers. Thus, to the founders, although the rights retained by the people were those left over after the federal government had fully exercised its legitimate powers, the point of the reservation was, in part, to make sure that those powers were never stretched to include implied powers. Of course, were we to recognize the principle that rights begin where powers end in the context of the modern bloat of governmental powers, the result would be to strip the positive Ninth Amendment of any constitutional cy pres role, for positive Ninth Amendment rights would, like Tenth Amendment rights, exist only at the grace of a Congress in full possession of a welter of implied powers. In struggling today to interpret the positive Ninth Amendment in a way that would validate the founders' goal of preventing the growth of implied governmental powers (which would inevitably and correspondingly shrink individual rights) while still leaving Congress free to exercise its legitimate powers, it is necessary to consider the broader historical and structural context of the problem. The original Constitution was intended, in part, to create a national marketplace and end state trade practices of preference and exclusion. Because the hypothetical state constitutional provision would effectively balkanize national economic life, recognition of it as a positive Ninth Amendment right is inconsistent with both the originally intended purposes of the Ninth Amendment as well as its reconceived function.

Second, the hypothetical right posed is one with no plausible connection to fundamental individual liberty. Again, although the founding generation considered rights to be the absence of powers and consequently thought that fundamental human rights could be guaranteed by careful circumscriptions upon powers, our divorce of the concepts requires us to relate Ninth Amendment rights to some concept of fundamental human rights. But because the very notion of fundamental rights has been criticized as incoherent by votaries of the political right and left it is incumbent upon one who would invoke fundamental liberties as a guide to defend the utility of the principle.[69]

Theorists of the political right contend that it is unprincipled to distinguish among enumerated constitutional rights, labeling one "fundamental" and another not, thereby rendering the nonfundamental right nonexistent for all practical purposes. To the rightists, it is even more unprincipled to identify fundamental rights that are nowhere specified in the Constitution. Although some leftists justify the division of constitutional rights into fundamental and nonfundamental categories, others maintain that the whole enterprise is incoherent. Professor Jed Rubenfeld, for example, contends that fundamentality cannot be premised on the absence of harm to others, for "there is no such thing as a self-regarding act"; that there is never "any plausible explanation of why one right — and not others — is fundamental"; and that the concept of fundamentality "fail[s] to capture even the very case it wants to explain."[70]

The argument in favor of fundamentality as a principle for categorizing human liberties protected by the Ninth Amendment differs depending upon whether the objective is to identify positive or natural Ninth Amendment rights. Chapter Six contains the argument addressed to natural Ninth Amendment rights. The argument made here concerning positive Ninth Amendment rights is, perhaps surprisingly, a version of the theory Professor Rubenfeld offers to displace fundamental rights thinking.

Rubenfeld contends that conventional fundamental rights analysis begins by asking what the state is trying to forbid and then identifying certain things (e.g., marriage, procreation, child-raising) as so central to some concept of "personhood," whether conceived as autonomy, self-definition, or what have you, that governmental infringements upon them are deemed to trench upon the forbidden ground of fundamental rights. This is hopeless, says Rubenfeld, because every act of autonomous self-definition is theoretically in collision with someone else's similar quest. Thus, termination of pregnancy collides with moral beliefs that abortion is murder; adult consensual homosexual sex collides with someone else's deep conviction that society should abjure and condemn homosexual behavior. There is no easy method by which these competing concepts of autonomous development can be resolved. To cut this Gordian knot Rubenfeld proposes that the focus should be on the degree to which any given law occupies a person's life, in the sense that the autonomous human is forced to serve the state in some capacity that so consumes an individual's life that it amounts to a totalitarian intervention, a conscription of the person as an instrument of the state. "Thus the state both commits an injustice to the individual, who ought to be recognized and treated as a political end" rather than an instrument for the accomplishment of the state's ends, "and threatens the political liberty of the people" by rendering them conscripts in a cultural war waged by the state for its own ends.[71] To be sure, Rubenfeld's test is one of degree, for some governmental regulations impinge but do not consume. Governmental edicts that force me to stop at red lights do not *occupy* my life in the way that a governmental edict forcing me to confine my work to the practice of law would.

Rubenfeld's notion of fundamentality is related to Robert Post's insight that American democracy is perpetually in tension between two polar desires: the desire to construct rules of social organization that regard individuals as autonomous, independent actors (which Post calls "responsive democracy") and the simultaneous desire to construct rules of social organization that treat people as "socially imbedded and dependent" (which Post labels "community").[72] When governments seek to instatiate community in a way that wholly occupies the individual's felt sense of autonomy the intrusion of social rules of community into the sphere of responsive democracy is so thorough that we can feel sure that a "fundamental" right has been infringed. When the rules of responsive democracy so completely insulate individuals from social accountability that the structure of community is imperiled, not only are community values infringed but the very possibility of continued individual autonomy is threatened. The proper function of "fundamental" rights is to identify those circumstances where the power of community has so thoroughly swamped the individual that she has been reduced to a servant of the community and nothing more. This is not to say that either the Constitution in general or the Ninth Amendment in particular has nothing to say about the opposite problem: rampant individuality that endangers the survival of the community. That issue will be addressed in a different context.

A version of this approach can be applied to the problem of selecting which state constitutional rights ought to be treated as state-specific positive Ninth Amendment rights. The judicial task is to separate state constitutional rights that preserve fundamental human liberty against governmental invasion from those rights that seek only to preserve structural arrangements of the state government or to insulate individuals from noninvasive and justifiable governmental regulation. Some judicial good sense is necessary to sort the liberty-bearing norms from the purely administrative ones. There is a world of difference between a state constitutional right to cumulative voting in corporate shareholder elections and a right to be free of governmental selection of the race of one's marriage partner.

It is thus clear that courts need a test that will enable them to identify these "liberty-bearing norms." An unbounded concept of state-specific, positive Ninth Amendment rights would permit the states wholly to frustrate national policies squarely within the legitimate powers of the national government. But the limits to be imposed on recognition of putative, state-specific, positive Ninth Amendment rights should not be so restrictive as to impinge upon the proper structural function of the positive Ninth Amendment: to permit the people, through their state agencies, to limit the ability of any government — state or federal — to invade fundamental individual rights. This inherent paradox requires some device to enable the judiciary to enforce positive Ninth Amendment rights that promote the latter function while denying recognition to those purported positive Ninth Amendment rights that serve the undesirable former function.

It is important to state precisely what any test would be designed to accomplish. It can only be part of a larger inquiry. The positive dimension of the Ninth Amendment states a presumption that state constitutional rights are Ninth Amendment rights, but that presumption can be overcome by a showing that the substance of the state constitutional right asserted as a positive Ninth Amendment right is one that is either in conflict with other parts of the federal Constitution or that preserves some nonfundamental right. With respect to problems of true constitutional conflict, a doctrine of constitutional preemption would operate conclusively to rebut some asserted positive Ninth Amendment rights. As an extreme example, should a state include in its constitution a provision guaranteeing the right of its citizens to "own" people as slaves, the attempt to assert such a "right" as a Ninth Amendment right would be an absurdity, given the preemptive effect of the Thirteenth Amendment. It is only when the asserted positive Ninth Amendment right is not preempted by the federal Constitution or by definitive constitutional case law that any proposed test would operate. It would be, to repeat, a test designed to sift the wheat — fundamental "liberty-bearing" rights — from the chaff.

In the best (or perhaps worst) tradition of the "formulaic" Constitution,[73] I propose a three-part test to accomplish this task. After setting out the skeleton of the test I will examine the components in more detail.

First, is the state constitutional right one that protects "constitutionally fundamental" rights? For this to be meaningful, one must settle upon a definition of fundamentality and a mode of identifying the quality. Boiled down, my argument is that constitutionally fundamental rights are those that prevent governments from converting autonomous individuals into leashed instruments of the state.

Second, would the putative, positive Ninth Amendment right, if recognized as such, substantially infringe upon some other recognized fundamental right, albeit not of constitutional dimension? If so, it would be denied recognition as a Ninth Amendment right. Bear in mind that this inquiry will occur after we have satisfied ourselves that there is no constitutional conflict. The "fundamental" right in tension with the putative Ninth Amendment right will necessarily be one that is not rooted in constitutional guarantees. For example, although there is no *constitutional* right to be free from privately inflicted racial discrimination in public accommo-dations, a state constitutional right such as that at issue in *Reitman v. Mulkey*[74] (California's attempt to secure the private right to sell or rent one's real estate to whomever one pleased) would eviscerate the nonconstitutional but nevertheless fundamental right to be free of such racial discrimination. Here, fundamentality is used in a different sense than with respect to constitutionally fundamental rights. Constitutionally fundamental rights are essentially nega-tive. They restrain governments from appropriating individuality in the service of community. These nonconstitutional fundamen-tal rights are more affirmative. They are conditions that need to be present for the optimal health of individuals and of the community. This does not mean that such "fundamental" rights (perhaps in-cluding basic needs of sustenance) are themselves to be elevated to the pantheon of constitutional fundamental rights, thus imposing affirmative duties upon state governments. It does mean that states may not use the Ninth Amendment to invade their domain.

Finally, if the first two hurdles have been met, is the putative Ninth Amendment right one that simply attempts to secure bene-fits for state residents at the expense of outsiders? Borrowing from dormant commerce clause jurisprudence, one can ask whether the right at issue is facially discriminatory against outsiders (as would be a right secured exclusively to New Jerseyans to dump their garbage in New Jersey) or whether, even if facially neutral it still imposes disproportionate costs on outsiders and confers dispro-portionate benefits on insiders (as would be a right conferred by Ohio to burn unlimited quantities of high-sulfur coal). This would necessarily involve some sophisticated judicial appraisal of legisla-tive motive and actual effects. Based on the dormant commerce clause experience, it may be that courts are not very good at this inquiry. But they still do it and, as I shall argue, they could improve this process by both sharpening and limiting their analysis as ap-plied to claims of positive Ninth Amendment rights.

The desirability of permitting the people, through their state constitutions, to define their fundamental liberties suggests that at least one criterion for any test is that the proposed right qualify as "constitutionally fundamental." The test of constitutional fundamentality is essentially revealed by Post's insight into the tension between democracy and community and by Rubenfeld's description of the individual right to be free of governmental conscription as a purely instrumental servant of the state.

The problem of identifying fundamental rights in a principled fashion has plagued constitutional law for some time. The problem goes back to the origins of U.S. constitutional law and *Calder v. Bull*,[75] in which justices Samuel Chase and James Iredell engaged in their now famous debate over the role of natural law in constitutional interpretation. This prefigured the modern debate over the legitimacy of rights wholly implied from the Constitution, such as the right to privacy articulated in *Griswold v. Connecticut*[76] that was extended to abortion in *Roe v. Wade*.[77]

The murkiness of the debate has not, however, restrained the Court from vigorous attempts to formulate diverse criteria for locating fundamental rights. Justice Harlan Stone sought to justify "exacting judicial scrutiny" with respect to "legislation which restricts those political processes which can ordinarily be expected to bring about repeal of undesirable legislation," specifically including statutes "directed . . . against discrete and insular minorities."[78] Justice Cardozo tried to limit fundamental rights to those "implicit in the concept of ordered liberty."[79] Justice Lewis Powell contended that fundamental rights could be limited to those "explicitly or implicitly guaranteed by the [federal] Constitution" but could not be determined by the "relative societal significance" of the asserted right.[80] Chief Justice William Rehnquist and Justice Antonin Scalia now advocate reliance on history, in the form of the "most specific tradition available."[81] By contrast, the second Justice John Harlan stated that the proper historical inquiry relevant to locating fundamental rights is one that seeks to determine that "what history teaches are the traditions from which [our constitutional principles] developed as well as the traditions from which it broke. That tradition is a living thing."[82] To Harlan, unlike Rehnquist and Scalia, history is a moving picture, not a snapshot frozen in time.

Although some have criticized judicial attempts to locate fundamental rights as essentially standardless, and even defenders of the quest admit it to be an exercise fraught with indeterminacy, the courts have persisted in operating in this milieu because there is a felt sense of the purposes for which the American democratic experiment was designed to accomplish.[83] Philip Bobbitt describes this as "the character, or *ethos*, of the American polity" and devotes a substantial portion of his book *Constitutional Fate* to discussion of this ethical mode of constitutional interpretation. To Bobbitt, the enumerated rights in the "Bill of Rights . . . act[ ] to give us a constitutional motif, a cadence for our rights, so that once heard we can supply the rest on our own."[84]

Although that may be so, the Ninth Amendment supplies a firm constitutional directive that rights that derive their substance from sources located outside the federal Constitution must be treated equally with constitutionally enumerated rights. Accordingly, it would subvert the Ninth Amendment and render it meaningless to limit such rights to those "explicitly or implicitly guaranteed by the [federal] Constitution," excluding the Ninth Amendment.[85] The Ninth Amendment and its command to preserve unenumerated rights should be treated as a repository of explicit or implicit constitutional rights. Defining fundamental rights as those explicitly or implicitly guaranteed in the Constitution does not aid the Ninth Amendment problem. Rather, the purpose of asking whether a putative positive Ninth Amendment right grounded in a state constitution is "fundamental" is to be certain that we do not recognize rights created by state polities that are inimical to either

rights inherent in national citizenship or to the legitimate func-
tioning of national policy, but only those rights that are compatible
with the *ethos* of our nation.

In probing this we could usefully employ the various extant
devices for locating fundamental rights, but in the context of positive Ninth Amendment rights they should not be dispositive. Professor Barnett has argued that "the Ninth Amendment can be
viewed as establishing a general constitutional presumption in
favor of individual liberty."[86] If such a presumption were observed,
the tests currently employed, such as reliance upon history and
tradition, would become evidence bearing upon rebuttal of the
presumption, rather than dispositive in and of itself. Similar to the
enumerated rights, governmental intrusion upon otherwise lawful
individual conduct would be presumed invalid unless found justified by a neutral magistrate. Professor Barnett would place the
burden of justification on the government,[87] for as Stephen Macedo has noted, the Constitution established islands of governmental powers "surrounded by a sea of individual rights[, not] . . .
islands [of individual rights] surrounded by a sea of governmental
powers."[88] The Ninth Amendment is a critical link in preventing
the sea of individual rights from being drained by the engineers of
governmental power.

We need not, however, stop at this rather indeterminate point.
Professor Rubenfeld's insight that fundamentality can be reconceived as the right to be free of governmental constraints that
convert our individual wills into slaves of the state can be usefully
employed to sharpen the analysis. When states establish constitutional individual protection against governmental *usurpation* of
their lives, rather than merely protection against regulations that
limit or prohibit discrete acts that are in no sense critical to the
continued existence of one as an autonomous being, they have
articulated a fundamental right. Thus, for example, a state constitutional provision securing to every competent person the abso-

lute "right to die" — to direct that her caregivers cease providing life-support measures — declares a fundamental right. It is fundamental because the harm it avoids is the real possibility that the state might direct that individuals be kept alive in circumstances substantially dictated by the state: medically supervised confinement to a hospital bed, attached to complicated medical equipment supplying the bodily functions and nutrients necessary for continued mortal existence. By contrast, the fundamentality of a state constitutional provision securing to every healthy person the right to commit suicide is more problematic. To be sure, such a right does cover the "right to die" case, but it also secures a much broader course of conduct. One might contend that the provision simply prevents the state from compelling a person to continue to live, but a governmental prohibition upon suicide, as applied to healthy people, does not work the same occupation of the individual's life as does a similar prohibition in the "right to die" case. The comatose or vegetative patient is forced into an existence virtually every whit of which is prescribed by the state. The physically healthy person, though commanded by the state to stay alive, is not similarly directed into a life of state-prescribed conformity. The difference is one of degree. The fundamental right is the right that prevents government from converting autonomous individuals into leashed instruments of the state.

Application of these principles to the foregoing hypothetical cases is reasonably straightforward. Few would seriously contend that trading securities while in possession of inside information entrusted for corporate purposes is a fundamental right.[89] Even under conventional understandings of fundamental rights, it is hard to imagine this right as one implicit in ordered liberty or essential to a free people. It is hardly part of the most specific tradition available, and if tradition is viewed as a evolving organism, the vector of our traditions suggests that we have repeatedly sought to limit sharp, if not fraudulent, commercial practices that injure society. Nor can this right be thought of as one implicit in, or even emanating from, other enumerated rights. Moreover, applying the concept of fundamentality as freedom from state usurpation of individual autonomy, a prohibition upon inside trading is so minimal a "usurpation" that it is laughable to suggest that inside trading might be a fundamental right.

The case of an asserted state constitutional right to practice private racial discrimination is equally simple. From the conventional perspective of fundamental rights, it would be necessary to probe the history and tradition of immunizing private choice, however odious, from governmental control. But even brief scrutiny of the "traditions from which we broke" would condemn an asserted fundamental right to practice private racial discrimination. Nor could this right be thought of as one linked in some implicit manner to enumerated rights. To the contrary, it is a right that has its legitimacy called into question by the existence of the equality-of-process principle that underlies the equal protection clause. Once again, however, the "antitotalitarian" concept of fundamentality makes resolution of the case relatively easy. A state constitutional provision immunizing private racial discrimination is hardly necessary to preserve individual autonomy from state seizure and control. All that a governmental prohibition upon private racial discrimination does is to forbid a certain act, leaving the individual actor free to pursue her private ends in any number of alternative ways. The state forbids one relatively trivial manifestation of individual will. It does not usurp the totality of individual will for state purposes, nor does it usurp individual will in some critical faculty relevant to autonomous existence.

In conventional fundamental rights analysis, the questions posed by a state constitutional right securing to fetuses a right to be born, or to a woman the right to terminate an unwanted pregnancy, are deeply contested matters. But viewed from the antitotalitarian perspective of fundamentality these issues seem simpler. In the absence of a contrary federal constitutional right that would control the question through the supremacy clause the state created right should be presumed fundamental. A provision securing a woman's choice to end pregnancy is one squarely designed to prevent governments from dictating to a woman that she must conform to a state-prescribed life as a mother. It is no answer to say that her pregnancy was voluntary for, even presuming voluntariness, the issue is whether the state can, by force of law, seize control of a woman's life so thoroughly that she is forced, against her will, to become an instrument of state design by becoming a mother.

A provision securing a fetal right to be born, at least as against *governmental* attempts to deny the right, poses more difficult problems. The harm that this provision seeks to prevent is governmental extinguishment of fetuses. It might be said that this is an occupation of "fetal life" that is so pervasive that it must be regarded as declaratory of a fundamental right, but it might also be said that it is no occupation because the state is not mandating a particular role for fetuses. Governmental permission of abortions in the face of a state constitutional provision guaranteeing fetal life does not seize, occupy, use, or direct fetuses for state purposes in the way that governmental prohibitions of abortion do by forcing a woman to carry her fetus to term. An analogy from property may help. By requiring the destruction of property that harbors disease a government extinguishes but does not use the destroyed property. By requiring that property be devoted to a single governmentally specified purpose (which purpose is utterly valueless to the nominal owner) a government has used and effectively taken the property.[90] Governments that prohibit abortions use and effectively conscript a woman into state service for state purposes. Governments that permit abortions aid the extinguishment but do not use fetuses.

If this distinction is rejected, and the state constitutional right to fetal life is deemed fundamental, in the absence of any other controlling federal constitutional right (such as equal protection) the effect of a regime of state-specific, positive Ninth Amendment rights would be to produce a welter of antagonistic fundamental rights, differing with the variety of judgments made by the various state polities on the issue of abortion. To the extent that arrangement might be thought a deficiency it can be overcome by abandoning the state-specific concept of positive Ninth Amendment rights and substituting the national concept, although that decision carries considerable costs that have been previously outlined.

In any case, a determination that a putative state-specific, positive Ninth Amendment right is fundamental ought not end the inquiry as to whether the claimed right should be recognized as a positive Ninth Amendment right. The second prong of the test is one that would explicitly require judges to balance competing individual and social costs involved by recognizing Ninth Amendment rights. In this calculus, most fundamental rights will likely survive, but some may not.

The positive Ninth Amendment's structural role in the Constitution would be to preserve constitutionally fundamental individual rights from governmental infringement, but the creation of new constitutional rights can produce a reduction in the stock of statutory or common law rights held by other people. For example, if the right to speak freely includes the right to hurl personalized racial insults, there is a corresponding reduction in the auditor's right (albeit perhaps not *constitutionally* fundamental right) to be free of private racial harassment. For this reason, it is important to limit putative positive Ninth Amendment rights to those that do not significantly impair other existing and recognized fundamental rights, whether or not they might be termed "constitutionally fundamental."

Our constitutional tradition increasingly asks us to balance the interests contained in asserted rights. For example, is free speech, at bottom, more *important* than a rape victim's privacy or society's interest in protecting children from exploitation in the creation of child pornography?[91] Is protection from the harm inflicted by racist speech more important than preserving unfettered public discourse?[92] Is the state's interest in eradicating racial discrimination sufficiently compelling to justify the imposition of a racial quota in the allocation of contracts or licenses?[93]

As rights expand they conflict more often. This tendency is exacerbated as we begin to conceive of rights as collective rather than individual entitlements. Thus, the *collective* right of an ethnic group to be free of racial discrimination is pitted against the *individual* right of a racist to freely spout racial invective. The state action doctrine has traditionally served as a device to permit courts partially to avoid resolution of these clashes as a constitutional matter. Thus, in the case of hate speech the collective right to be free of racial discrimination may not be invoked generally, as a constitutional matter, to prevent a *private* actor from hurling racist insults. To curb hate speech governments must act by legislation, and when they do the state action doctrine permits the individual racist to claim that her free speech rights are thereby invaded. But the state action doctrine has partially broken down, thus permitting, for example, plausible claims that the state has acted to deny equal protection by its failure to prohibit hate speech. Legislatures have also sought to protect collective rights by statute, thus forcing the courts increasingly to confront competing claims of entitlement. Regardless of the fate of the Ninth Amendment as a living aspect of constitutional law, the judicial task inevitably includes the responsibility of weighing rights against one another. This portion of the proposed test for recognition of positive Ninth Amendment rights is but another aspect of that role.

This is not to suggest that courts should have free rein to assess the relative importance of all manner of claimed rights. The judicial function I propose with respect to the weighing of rights to determine whether or not to recognize a claimed positive Ninth Amendment right is considerably more limited. This balancing process should operate only when the source of the right in collision with the claimed Ninth Amendment right is also located outside of the federal Constitution. If its source is congressional legislation, there is no reason automatically to prefer Congress' judgment to that of the states, especially because the positive dimension of the Ninth Amendment expresses an original preference for the state decision. Of course, if the source of a right in conflict with a claimed positive Ninth Amendment right is the Constitution, the federally sourced right would prevail.

To implement this proposed balancing courts would be required to assess the fundamentality of the right that would assertedly be infringed by a claimed positive Ninth Amendment right. If the right claimed to be infringed is found to be fundamental, it would then be necessary to determine the degree to which it will be infringed by the putative positive Ninth Amendment right. Only if the infringement is so substantial as to eviscerate the infringed right should the putative positive Ninth Amendment right be denied recognition. The justification for demanding a showing of near obliteration of the infringed right before denying constitutional recognition as a positive Ninth Amendment right to any given fundamental state constitutional right lies partly in the fact that the infringed right will never be "constitutionally fundamental," and certainly not otherwise protected by the federal Constitution. In addition, the positive dimension of the Ninth Amendment presumes that fundamental state constitutional rights are entitled to recognition as positive Ninth Amendment rights.

Let us again suppose the following circumstances: (1) a reversal of *Roe v. Wade* via an opinion that merely declares abortion to be unprotected by the right to privacy, (2) a state constitutional provision guaranteeing fetal life by prohibiting all abortions, and (3) a federal statute, enacted pursuant to Section 5 of the Fourteenth

Amendment, that prohibits the states from denying abortions. Let us further assume, though the conclusion is a quite contestable one, that the state constitutional provision guarantees a fundamental right. We have already seen that a state constitutional guarantee of the abortion right would be constitutionally fundamental. Thus, the the hypothesized federal statute must instantiate a right that is fundamental if not constitutionally fundamental. A court faced with this case must now decide whether recognition of the state constitutional provision protecting fetuses as a positive Ninth Amendment right would operate to eviscerate the (possibly non-constitutional) fundamental right pitted in opposition to it. The answer is obvious; of course it would.

The mirror-image case is only slightly more difficult. Assume that, instead, the state constitutional provision guarantees the abortion right and the federal statute is one protecting fetuses by prohibiting all abortions. Let us also assume away all difficulties surrounding congressional power to enact the statute under Section 5 of the Fourteenth Amendment and make the further stipulation that the federal statute is preservative of a fundamental human liberty, but is not expressive of a constitutionally fundamental right. Again, a court presented with this case must decide whether recognition of the state-sourced abortion right as a Ninth Amendment right would eviscerate the statutory fundamental right of fetal life. Unlike the prior example, recognition in this instance would not wholly obliterate the statutory right. The state-sourced right is one that permits but does not require invasion of the competing right. In the prior example, the state-sourced putative Ninth Amendment right is one that requires, indeed mandates, a complete preclusion of the competing right.

Across a wide range of issues, courts would be required to weigh constitutionally fundamental state constitutional rights against the effects they would produce on nonconstitutionally fundamental rights should the state-sourced right be recognized as a positive

Ninth Amendment right. Although the task would be difficult, it would be rendered easier by the presumption that state-sourced constitutionally fundamental rights would be recognized as Ninth Amendment rights unless they would obliterate, rather than simply restrict, nonconstitutionally fundamental rights.

In essence the task imposed upon courts here would be to make the judgment of what constitutes the democratic community. Robert Post has noted that "lawmaker[s] who must fashion law to create forms of social order . . . will face a constant choice whether to design legal doctrine to sustain the common, socially imbedded identities of citizens, or instead to design them so as to protect the space for autonomous citizens independently to create their own social arrangements."[94] As with physicians, the first rule of judges should be to do no harm. When faced with these conflicts, courts ought to be sure that the claimed positive Ninth Amendment right is, indeed, constitutionally fundamental to the autonomous being and, second, that the forms of community (family, church, school, to name only a few) are not substantially endangered or eroded by recognition of the asserted new right.

Finally, in order to control the possible abuse of using state constitutions as a device to frustrate legitimate national policies, it would be necessary to refuse to recognize claimed positive Ninth Amendment rights that are, in essence, attempts by a state to capture some perceived benefit for its citizens while leaving the cost of providing the benefit to be borne by out-of-staters. The third leg of the proposed test to filter legitimate state-sourced positive Ninth Amendment rights from the pretenders to that status is one designed to prevent this kind of economic or social balkanization that the original Constitution was intended to prevent.[95]

The problem is a pervasive one, consisting of each political jurisdiction in a polity seeking to better itself at the expense of its neighbors. Small units of government will be tempted to adopt policies that produce benefits for their constituents paid for by residents of other jurisdictions. Similarly, large-scale units of government will be susceptible to factional alliances arranged to capture the machinery of government in order to deliver benefits to the faction's members, the costs of which will be borne by citizens not affiliated with the dominant faction. Moreover, small units of government will not incur some costs, like national defense, because their benefit is so sufficiently dissipated over the entire polity that it makes little economic sense for a single jurisdiction to incur all of the costs of provision of a benefit that will be freely enjoyed by others. Thus, there clearly is reason to tinker with the jurisdictional authority of political units in order to make the boundaries of such authority congruent with the full costs and benefits of the decisions made by the political unit. Dissonance results in externalities, and politicians shrewdly exploit these opportunities to capture "free" benefits by imposing their costs on others. It is a form of political arbitrage, although, unlike economic arbitrage, it serves less to achieve market equilibrium than to distort and pervert both allocations of public resources and the democratic process itself. Economists call the phenomenon "rent-seeking" and observe that the pursuit of these rents results in mammoth inefficiencies.

Borrowing from dormant commerce clause jurisprudence, it is possible to address this issue by a series of inquiries. First, is the right at issue one that is facially designed to capture benefits for local residents at the expense of outsiders? If so, it must fail. A state constitutional right preserving New Jersey lands for New Jersey waste by excluding garbage generated elsewhere would certainly not meet this test.[96] Second, is the right at issue facially neutral, but nevertheless one that imposes a disproportionate share of its costs on outsiders and vests a disproportionate share of its benefits with insiders? This claimed right, too, must fail. Thus, were Arizona to make it a matter of constitutional right to have trains of no longer than seventy freight cars traverse the state, it would not be recognized as a positive Ninth Amendment right on this ground as well as for failure to demonstrate the fundamental nature of the right involved.[97]

To make the point more concrete, suppose that Nevada's constitution secured the right of its citizens to possess and view child pornography in the privacy of their homes. Also assume that Congress has used its commerce power to prohibit the interstate movement of such materials and has prohibited the production of child pornography. A Nevadan is then prosecuted in federal court because he accepted shipment by mail of child pornography that all parties concede he intends to view and possess solely within his own home. The Nevadan contends that the prosecution is barred by a Nevada-specific positive Ninth Amendment right, even though we concede that this right is not part of his federally protected privacy rights.[98]

Let us assume, although I do not for one moment think it to be the case, that the right to possess child pornography in one's home is a constitutionally fundamental right and does not eliminate the fundamental right of children to be free of the physical and psychological burdens imposed upon them attendant to the creation of pornography. Assuming that Nevada has a statute that bars Nevadans from producing child pornography within Nevada, the asserted right, although facially neutral, certainly seems to impose the social costs of the protected liberty on non-Nevadans. As a result, it does not acquire Ninth Amendment status. But what if Nevada has no such statute? The problem, at least under the third prong of the proposed test, becomes much tougher. The decision must ultimately rest on an empirical assessment of the in-state and out-of-state impact of the social costs of producing child pornography. Courts will necessarily be forced to rely, to some degree, on social scientific (but not exclusively economic) studies to assess this empirical impact in order to reach decision.[99] A court will be required to ask and answer how much demand for child pornography comes from Nevada, how much of the social costs of its production are borne exclusively by Nevadans, and whether there is a sufficient disparity in favor of Nevadans to merit invocation of this third prong to invalidate the claimed right. These questions are difficult to answer because their resolution depends on reliable empirical data that may not be readily available. When the empirical data leave resolution uncertain, courts ought to be free to probe legislative motive. If the record or the circumstances reveal that the motive in creating the state constitutional right was to capture benefits at the cost of outsiders, courts should not hesitate to refuse to recognize the right as a Ninth Amendment right. Although it is arguable that such problems have not been handled adeptly in the dormant commerce clause area,[100] there is no reason why courts cannot require, with respect to the Ninth Amendment, that state constitutional rights be shown to be free of either impermissible motive or effect. In any case, this inquiry would occur only after the asserted positive Ninth Amendment right had already overcome the first two hurdles.

An analytical process of the sort described would result in the recognition of additional fundamental human liberties selected by the citizens of the various states, but with minimal impact on the differing judgments of neighboring states, and with minimal disturbance to the values of the federal system sought to be preserved by the supremacy clause. Moreover, this analytical approach to positive Ninth Amendment rights would not "disparage" unenumerated rights by recognizing that when putative positive Ninth Amendment rights are placed in conflict with enumerated constitutional rights or constitutionally instantiated values of federal union they must yield to the entrenched federal principle. This result is necessitated by the delicate balance of interests demanded of a truly dual, co-equal, partnership in a federal system. Courts can reasonably be asked to make the delicate judgments this test requires. The interstices and intersections of federal and state power require sensitive judgment, and a keen appreciation of the value to human liberty of the structural architecture of federalism will help courts with the job. Without judicial attention, the framework of federalism as an aid to human liberty and community betterment will rust and eventually collapse. The positive dimension of the Ninth Amendment is a textual reminder to do the necessary maintenance to avoid this disaster. However difficult these judgments may prove to be, this inquiry is preferable to the alternative: the total disavowal of unenumerated rights, with the attendant consequence that Congress will continue freely to ignore legitimate state barriers to the imposition of its authority upon the liberty of individuals.

SIX

The Natural Law Component

Natural law both frightens and fascinates us. We fear it because we suspect that "you can invoke natural law to support anything you want."[1] We are fascinated with it because it holds the promise of providing a normative reference point that reconciles the ageless conundrum of free choice (to which moral responsibility can be attached) in a causally determined universe (from which individual moral responsibility appears to be absent). If there is some plausible way of ascribing normative significance to the determinate events of our existence, we have located a standard by which the nominal free choice of an actor within that constrained and determined world can be judged. Even more importantly, this standard is one that also operates to supervene governmental rules that contravene the normative natural order. We fear that this quest is illusory, that there is no such discoverable standard, and that all attempts to locate one must degenerate into either unprincipled assertions of personal preference or statements at such a high order of abstraction that they are "uselessly vague."[2]

The duality of this preoccupation with natural law has been a part of U.S. constitutional law since its inception. Constitutional scholars and judges have employed principles of natural law as a device to amplify, supplement, or simply fill the interstices of the written law of the Constitution,[3] yet the legitimacy of natural law as an aspect of constitutional law has been assailed on two major fronts. It is contended that there is no textual or historical warrant for reading such a principle into the Constitution.[4] If by some feat of intellectual legerdemain it is possible to do so, it is still claimed to be impossible to locate principles of natural law that can serve as rules of decision in any particular case without resorting to one's personal preferences about the issues in question.

But, as we have seen, natural law has a connection to the Ninth Amendment. The founding generation's fear that an incomplete and imperfect enumeration of rights would endanger the continuing vitality of unenumerated rights was rooted in recognition that there were certain "natural" or "inalienable" rights that occupied a prepolitical position of advantage. The founding generation may have had multiple and differing concepts of the manner in which natural rights and a written Constitution would interact.

As demonstrated in Chapter Two, there is ample evidence that some political actors in the founding generation relied upon unwritten concepts of natural law as the authority for judicial invalidation of legislative actions that were thought to be contrary to these principles of natural law. At the same time, there is contrary evidence that the founding generation regarded natural law in a far more constrained fashion than the early cases might suggest. As Professor Philip Hamburger has suggested, natural rights "were understood to be subject to natural law,"[5] meaning that natural rights were bounded by the natural obligation to use them only in a fashion that would not injure others, an idea memorialized in the hoary common law maxim, *sic utere tuo, ut alienum non laedas.*[6] Somewhat more controversial is Hamburger's contention that the founding generation thought that natural rights were preserved only to the extent that they were expressly guaranteed by written constitutions. Of course, with respect to the Ninth Amendment this position solves nothing, inasmuch as the Ninth Amendment was apparently intended in part as a device to retain under the constitutional umbrella natural rights that were not so expressly guaranteed. In any case, there was undoubtedly an expectation on the part of the founding generation that the positive law would reflect the precepts of natural law and, to the extent it did so, incompatibility between the two regimes would melt away. These views do not lead to the conclusion that there is no room in constitutional adjudication for natural law. If the founders had, indeed, exiled natural law from the Constitution it would be correct to claim, as does Hamburger, that to the founding generation "[a] failure of a constitution to reflect natural law was a ground for altering or abandoning the constitution rather than for making a claim in court."[7]

The Ninth Amendment is, however, the sticky wicket. There it is, in all its embarrassing nakedness, exhorting us not to forget that the Constitution also protects unenumerated retained rights. Although late eighteenth-century Americans no doubt relied upon natural law as a prudential and moral guide, and some feared or denied that the Constitution protected natural rights at all,[8] others of the generation relied upon the awkward, Janus-faced, Ninth Amendment to preserve natural rights in U.S. constitutional law.

But what *is* natural law? Discussion of the natural law dimension of the Ninth Amendment can hardly be very sensible without some understanding of the concept. Unfortunately and, perhaps predictably, the concept of natural law is sufficiently plastic to render natural law impervious to any single description. The usual starting point for definition of natural law is the assertion that natural laws are those that are morally valid. Implicit in this formulation is the assumption that positive law is an imperfect expression of morality. It is not altogether clear whether natural lawyers contend that positive law can *never* fully capture morality or whether the failings of positive law are simply the product of human imperfection. In either case, the natural lawyer's starting point is the assumed cleavage between positive law and morality. To this version of the natural lawyer, whom I will style the "natural purist," the only thing that can be "law" is that which is morally valid.

Unlike the positivist, who thinks that law is simply the backed-by-force command of the sovereign, or perhaps those commands of the sovereign that are socially accepted, the natural purist cannot conceive of a law that is legally valid but morally wrong.

The natural purist necessarily assumes that there is some objective validity to the moral principles that determine law. If the unjust law is not law, the concept of justice must have some determinate meaning; otherwise, there is neither law nor justice, but anarchy. Theologians such as Thomas Aquinas found the source of determinate justice and moral validity in divine will. The will of a creator of all temporal existence was necessarily of eternal duration and binding upon humans. Our task was to apprehend this will; when done imperfectly the result was unjust law, the product of a human will at variance with the divine command. Of course, the theological approach assumed that there was such a thing as a correct human apprehension of divine will, and not simply a variety of unverifiable opinions on the subject. In the thirteenth century that assumption went largely unchallenged. The interpretation of God's will supplied by ecclesiastical bureaucrats was widely, if not universally, accepted as authoritative. Today, of course, any such assumption would be riddled with the shrapnel of moral skepticism and promptly reduced to intellectual rubble.

But there are other possible sources of objective validity for the natural purist. The earliest Western concepts of natural law were an attempt to mediate an essential duality of the human condition: "Human beings are apart from nature and a part of it. As *human* beings, we are uniquely capable of reflecting on our experience and formulating laws of our own governance. . . . As human *beings*, we are subject to nature's laws." Thus, the Greeks posited that there was "a unitary normative natural order immanent in the cosmos, to which human beings adhere in both their aspects."[9] From this point of view, events determined by the causal order of nature are normatively prescribed and events created by the human agency of free will also fulfill the cosmic plan. But when the human faculty of free will, manifested through positive law, conflicts with the normative order of the universe, things fall out of kilter and "law" is no longer law. A fanciful illustration of the principle is an imaginary law prohibiting persons from touching the ground while walking. The conflict is obvious. The natural law of gravity may not be contravened by a human edict to the contrary. Indeed, a legendary example of the principle is the familiar tale of King Canute demonstrating to his subjects that he lacked the power to command the tide to stop its ascent of the beach upon which he sat. Unfortunately, most such conflicts are not so simple. A positive law that prohibits homosexuality, or one that permits homosexuality, may be attacked as inconsistent with the normative natural order. For that matter, laws prohibiting murder are not necessarily in conformity with the natural order. Even a cursory glimpse at the natural world reveals many instances of deliberate intraspecies killing.

It is thus not surprising that the theologians used the Greeks' structure of natural law but displaced nature with the Christian God. Natural law thus became a divine law of eternal duration, "immanent in the creation, accessible to and binding on human beings." But as natural law wandered ever farther from its theological home, it became a device "used to identify whatever was deemed fundamental — that is, certain and non-negotiable." As a consequence "natural law was converted into natural rights, which meant only that the rights in question were self-evident."[10] As the self-evident nature of almost any proposition increasingly comes to be doubted there is a corresponding increase in the skepticism with which any claim of natural right is greeted.

The evolution of natural law thought reveals that early theories of natural law were distinctly ontological. They sought to explain the nature of being and, in particular, to explain how it is that human beings can be simultaneously part of the natural order and free moral actors. By contrast, most modern theories of natural law are distinctly deontological. They seek to explain the nature of obligation and, in particular, explain the reasons why we can be obligated to obey law. In so doing, modern natural law emphasizes the moral component of law, insisting that for "law" to be law it must correspond to the prepolitical demands of morality. In contrast, the dominant mode of contemporary legal thought, legal positivism, holds that "it is no sense a necessary truth that laws reproduce or satisfy certain demands of morality."[11] The problem with almost all modern deontological theories of natural law is that they are unable to convince us that there is an objectively valid moral order, or at least one that we can identify.[12] Ontological theories of natural law are no more convincing, at least when they begin to describe the particular normative natural order they claim exists.

Western society is deeply divided between moral skeptics and moral realists. Moral skeptics assert that there are no certain moral judgments. One person's belief that abortion is murder is no more morally valid than the next person's belief that abortion is a simple removal of some annoying cell tissue. Similarly, in a world of moral skepticism no one can say that homosexuality is a moral abomination or, by contrast, that governmental attempts to suppress homosexuality are a moral abomination.

By contrast, moral realists assert that there are reasonably certain moral judgments. The task of moral judgment is not easy but is possible. Some moral claims, say the moral realists, are clearly superior to others. The moral justification for a parent's killing of her child because she was momentarily bothersome is less persuasive than the justification offered by that same parent for the killing of her child suffering an agonizing and incurably fatal illness. But why is this so, if it is so? Some moral realists—I will call them "moral absolutists"—might deny that there is any moral difference between the two killings. But even to the moral absolutists, there are distinctions to be drawn and categories to be defined. A moral absolutist may defend a principle — say, the immorality of taking another's life — with total and complete consistency but the moral absolutist is still left with the problem of explaining why that principle is entitled to respect. The nonabsolute moral realist has a similarly difficult task. She must establish either that the principle involved is objectively valid or defend an exception to a general moral principle as well as defending the validity of the general moral principle. If the taking of life is immoral, is it because life is sacred? Is that conclusion rooted in one's sense of divine command? How is the epistemological problem of ascertaining divine will to be solved? If the taking of life (at least in certain circumstances) is immoral because it is nearly universally condemned, how can it be said that this is an objectively valid principle? Isn't it, instead, a principle the validity of which is authenticated merely by majoritarian sentiment?

Whether the fact that we live in a world dominated by moral skepticism in which the answers of the moral realists are not necessarily convincing is deplorable or cause for rejoicing is a judgment that need not be made here, but it is a fact with considerable implications for any attempt to incorporate natural law into constitutional adjudication. The problem is not the moral skepticism of our times; that is more of a symptom than a cause. The problem is that we are no longer able to agree upon even the fundamental suppositions of our existence.

There was a time in our past when our principal mechanism for regulating and adjusting social relationships was not formal declarations of law, but widely shared cultural customs and traditions. In that now distant day, law and custom were roughly coterminous and law simply mimicked the real force for controlling social behavior — the cultural ethos.[13] This was a time in which belief in natural law was easy because, if only as a matter of description, law appeared to be inextricably tied to seemingly self-evident propositions about social organization. But the political, scientific, technological, economic, theological, and social revolutions of the last two centuries have broken that linkage between law and cultural ethos. Without a shared core of cultural values we have attempted, instead, to govern our behavior with law, and ever more law. At the same time, our concept of law has become increasingly positivistic because its connection to self-evident cultural propositions has been severed.[14] Professor Grant Gilmore captured the problem well when he observed:

> Law reflects but in no sense determines the moral worth of a society. The values of a reasonably just society will reflect themselves in a reasonably just law. The better the society, the less law there will be. In Heaven there will be no law, and the lion will lie down with the lamb. The values of an unjust society will reflect themselves in an unjust law. The worse the society, the more law there will be. In Hell, there will be nothing but law, and due process will be meticulously observed.[15]

There are several implications in this for natural law. First, natural law has its most powerful claim to legitimacy in a society with a commonly shared set of values that are thought transcendent to temporal deviance. If our society is lacking that fundamental condition, the role of natural law is necessarily attenuated, but possibly not totally extinguished. Even in a society lacking a common set of values there are likely to be some propositions that are overwhelmingly, if not universally, accepted. In the presumably rare instance when such norms are contravened by legislatures it is appropriate for courts to enforce the culturally shared principle of natural law to curb the usurpation of the legislature.[16]

Second, the present time, characterized by deep divisions concerning the proper relationship between moral values and the polity, is one in which natural law is implicitly asked to hibernate. Hibernation is not death, however, and it is appropriate to preserve the mechanisms by which natural law can contribute to our fundamental law at some future time. It would be an arrogant act for our generation to expunge natural law from the Constitution. It would be equally arrogant to give to natural law a place in contemporary constitutional adjudication that is larger than will be supported by the cultural foundations of our time. In one sense that cynical positivist, Oliver Wendell Holmes, Jr., a man "savage, harsh, and cruel, a bitter and lifelong pessimist,"[17] had it right when he observed that "the first requirement of a sound body of law is that it should correspond with the actual feelings and demands of the community, whether right or wrong."[18] Natural law cannot be forced on an unwilling and disbelieving community; rather, it is the inevitable outgrowth of a community that shares deeply the same unverifiable assumptions about the natural world or the forms of social organization.

If it is reasonably clear that natural rights inhere in culturally shared understandings of individual practices that are so basic and fundamental to human liberty that it is beyond cavil that governments lack the legitimate moral authority to prohibit them, it is reasonable to ask why we should do anything other than let legislatures articulate our current understanding of natural rights. On this view statutory law will fairly reflect the moral consensus that seems to constitute our contemporary understanding of natural law. This position is of course one that would render extinct the natural law component of the Ninth Amendment, for there would be no occasion for the judiciary to define natural Ninth Amendment rights. There are several responses to this position, but none so devastating that we can safely consign the entire task of defining natural Ninth Amendment rights to the virtually unreviewable domain of the judiciary.

First, it is not at all clear that legislatures actually capture the sense of the community. There are multiple reasons why legislative decisions will not reliably represent an aggregation of the disparate preferences of the represented community. Public choice theorists have demonstrated that, in fact, legislatures are frequently captured by small elements of the polity that seek to enlist the power of the state to extract economic or social gains from other, less skillful or less organized, portions of the community. On some issues legislators adhere to personal views that may differ from their constituents' views. Loyalty to political parties, "logrolling," and other aspects of coalition building or group dynamics produce legislative action at variance from the underlying desires of the represented people. Indeed, the very possibility of legislative preference aggregation may be chimerical. Kenneth Arrow's "Impossibility Theorem"[19] purports to establish the inherent indeterminacy of any group decisional process accurately capturing the individual preferences of the group and has been relied upon by one of the foremost constitutional thinkers of our times to conclude that it is doubtful whether "*any* process could even hope to 'reflect' any such thing as the will of the majority."[20] All of these difficulties combine to suggest that many, if not most, statutes do not represent shared cultural understandings of basic norms, but instead represent the fragmentary desires of various individuals or pressure groups that have captured public machinery for their parochial ends.

Second, like all holders of power and privilege legislators have an inherent incentive to justify their possession of power. To do this, legislators legislate. It is their function, and they perform it despite the absence of need for their services. Legislators manufacture problems as much as they identify problems. It is thus not at all clear that legislation represents the shared sentiments of the people so much as it does the perceptions of the legislators that something needs to be done in order to satisfy themselves that they are worthy possessors of power.

Third, in the sophisticated world of modern electoral politics, representatives are representative in name only. To be elected, they must be wealthy or possess exceptional skill at raising money, have a flair for publicity, possess or hire organizational talent, and be perceived as free of most of the foibles with which ordinary humans are afflicted. Moreover, once elected, and particularly in the case of members of Congress, they remove themselves from their geographic and cultural surroundings to an artificial hot-house culture that bears little relationship to the lives of their constituents. It is not long before North Dakotans and Oregonians become, instead, suburban Virginians or Georgetown urbanites, mingling with others similarly caught up in the exotica of political intrigue at the seat of government. Meanwhile, the folks back home borrow dollars to plant wheat, watch the weather anxiously, calculate the futures markets to determine when to sell, and hope that the crop comes in. Or they struggle daily to get the kids off to school, themselves to work, and to somehow do the laundry, buy the groceries, and have dinner ready at a reasonable hour. Legislators have lives, too, but they operate in a distinctly more privileged environment. The result is that legislators begin to substitute their preferences, formed in part by their experiences in the elite political culture, for those of their constituents. Even if legislators sincerely desire to do otherwise, the removal (culturally, geographically, and structurally, through such insulating devices as political staff) poses considerable problems of information transmission from the governed to the governor.

Finally, even if none of the foregoing problems are present, public tastes change and legislation does not always reflect those changing tastes. Once enacted, laws remain until there is sufficient clamor for their removal. But laws that no longer reflect current public preferences are often unenforced, thereby removing some of the pressure that might otherwise develop to cause their repeal. The very existence of unenforced laws poses several dangers. Some people will be inhibited from taking action in violation of the law. Those not so inhibited will learn that conformity to law is a selective exercise. The unenforced law remains available for selective, or random, or sporadic, enforcement by governmental officials. Thus, by the time the Court in *Griswold* struck down Connecticut's prohibition of the use of contraceptives it was evident to everyone that the law was completely incongruent with the public mores of Connecticut.

From all of this we might conclude that the judicially enforceable natural law function of the Ninth Amendment is simply to rid the statute books of cultural relics, those laws that instantiate moral principles once dominant but now no longer accepted. This would be too narrow a concept, though, because it is not realistic to suppose that even the most recently enacted statute is one that reliably aggregates the moral preferences of the polity. Moreover, even when legislatures do so, there remains the possibility that some polities will possess moral preferences sufficiently divergent from the overwhelming preferences of the entire national community that their localized judgments should not be permitted to exist. Assume for the moment that the Thirteenth Amendment's prohibition upon slavery did not exist. If a state were to enact legislation enslaving African-Americans, and that legislation accurately reflected the moral sentiments of the state polity, it is self-evident that the legislation would be profoundly repugnant to the overwhelmingly shared moral sentiments of the national community. Morally, it could not stand; legally, it would not. Admittedly, there may be few such cases, but when they occur the natural law component of the Ninth Amendment should be available as a corrective device.

Several necessary implications follow from the conception of a judicially cognizable natural law component of the Ninth Amendment. The idea of retained natural rights implies some set of pre-political entitlements never ceded to the national government. Whatever they may be the federal government has no warrant for invading them. Consequently, natural Ninth Amendment rights must be of national scope and dimension, operating uniformly across the country to disable the federal government from acting to seize those unenumerated natural rights. In their national uniformity natural Ninth Amendment rights are thus quite unlike positive Ninth Amendment rights, which should properly assume a state-specific dimension. Both types should act against the federal government, but natural Ninth Amendment rights should be national in application while positive Ninth Amendment rights should be localized.

Another implication follows from the notion that natural retained rights are some set of prepolitical entitlements. The incorporation doctrine employs the Fourteenth Amendment's due process clause — "nor shall any state deprive any person of life, liberty, or property, without due process of law" — to make applicable to the states most of the guarantees of the Bill of Rights. The essential theory is that the Fourteenth Amendment's due process clause incorporates those constitutional guarantees that embody "principle[s] of justice so rooted in the tradition and conscience of our people as to be ranked as fundamental" and "implicit in the concept of ordered liberty."[21] However imprecise this standard may be it is difficult to imagine that a constitutional guarantee of the unenumerated fundamental rights of the people is insufficiently rooted in our tradition and collective conscience that it could be said with a straight face that such rights are not implicit in the concept of ordered liberty. As indicated in Chapter One, the list of unenumerated rights accorded constitutional protection is long and impressive. Moreover, the tradition of referring to sources, practices, and understandings outside of constitutional text is a long-standing, if sometimes controversial, one. The problem is not that unenumerated natural rights lack sufficient fundamentality to be incorporated into the Fourteenth Amendment's due process clause and thereby impinge upon state governments; rather, the problem is that we fear the open-endedness of the inquiry, the possibility that democratically elected legislatures will be casually turfed out by judges imposing their peculiar individual moral tastes in the guise of constitutional adjudication.

This possibility is not imaginary, especially when one admits that the natural rights retained by the Ninth Amendment are those that, from time to time, are removed from the arena of legitimate governmental regulation by assertion of overwhelming societal moral preferences. Despite the logic of prepolitical retained rights, the fact is that there is probably no such thing. Indeed, there is no set of historical circumstances relevant to European colonization and settlement in North America that can fairly be said to be prepolitical. We must face the reality that natural Ninth Amendment rights are contingent, and once we do so, we seem to be admitting the possibility that judicial enforcement of such rights is a whimsical undertaking.

There are several answers to this dilemma. The fact that natural Ninth Amendment rights may be contingent upon the existence of widely shared moral sentiments within the polity does not necessarily mean that the judiciary is any less qualified than the legislature to apprehend faithfully those sentiments. As noted, the reliability of legislative judgments concerning the moral preferences of the community is highly questionable. Unlike legislatures, which are prone to "act upon expediency rather than take the long view," the judiciary possesses an institutional capability for reflective assessment of "the enduring values of a society." There will always be the exceptional individual judge who displays little wisdom, but as an *institution* the judiciary is probably better able to assess which moral principles are so deeply rooted and widely shared that they should be vindicated at the expense of contrary legislative judgments. This is so not so much because judges have "the leisure, the training, and the insulation to follow the ways of the scholar" as it is due to the legislative propensity to accentuate immediate objectives at the expense of abstract values and to pay inadequate attention to the many culturally diverse segments of the polity. The end result, of course, is that legislatures are *institutionally* incapable of a reliably accurate assessment of the moral preferences of the community. This is not to say that the judiciary will perform infallibly but it is to say that the judiciary *must also* perform.[22]

Justice Robert Jackson once observed that "we are not final because we are infallible, but we are infallible only because we are final."[23] The inherent fallibility of judges and legislators as the prophets of natural Ninth Amendment rights leads to the need for an iterative dialogue between courts and legislatures whenever the subject is the content or scope of natural Ninth Amendment rights. There are several devices by which this can be accomplished; each will be briefly introduced here and discussed in more detail later.

The Canadian Charter of Rights and Freedoms contains a legislative override provision, sometimes referred to as the "notwithstanding clause." The override provision permits a simple majority of any provincial legislature or the federal Parliament expressly to declare that legislation will take effect despite the fact that the statute is repugnant to certain guarantees of the Charter of Rights.[24] In fashioning natural Ninth Amendment rights the Supreme Court could recognize that its judgments are provisional and expressly permit Congress to override its judgments so long as it does so unambiguously and unequivocally. A variation on this theme would be to assign to the congressional override an additional provisional quality, so that the congressional override would bind the Court unless the Court was strongly convinced that its original judgment was the better assessment of the status of the right in question. This structure would require each actor to make its judgments openly and to endure the criticism implicit in taking a position directly contrary to another branch of government equally bound to observe the Constitution. Of course there are defects. Friction between the branches might well increase. The fact that some constitutional judgments of the Court would be susceptible to congressional override might undermine the Court's authoritativeness in other aspects of constitutional adjudication. Even the creation of the doctrine might seem especially like a judicially enacted constitutional amendment. As we shall see, none of these obstacles are of sufficient magnitude to reject the idea.

Alternatively, the Court could recognize that the provisional nature of its judgments concerning the identity and scope of natural Ninth Amendment rights justifies elimination of the usual rule of stare decisis with respect to natural Ninth Amendment rights. Freed from the obligation to obey precedent the Court would be able more easily to change its mind if it realizes that its earlier recognition of a natural Ninth Amendment right was inappropriate. The Court already recognizes that, because of the difficulty of altering constitutional law, the doctrine of stare decisis is at its weakest with respect to constitutional decisions. This alternative is simply an extension of that principle. But this, too, has its drawbacks. If precedent is of no value here, why should it be obeyed elsewhere? Even if we are able to justify the distinction, as I think we are able to, the spectacle of the Court reversing itself when it misjudges popular values may carry with it the destabilizing message that popular opinion counts, or should count, decisively in other areas of constitutional law. These objections, although real, are not necessarily fatal.

Another possibility would be to treat natural Ninth Amendment rights as constitutional rights that may be declared by the Supreme Court but may not be enforced by any of the remedies usually available to judges. There are other constitutional rights that are effectively incapable of judicial vindication but this alternative would create the ungainly spectacle of the Court announcing the existence of new constitutional rights that are unattainable. Natural Ninth Amendment rights would have many of the same qualities as the Emperor's clothes or, to invoke a more contemporary metaphor, would be as practically available to the public as new cars displayed in Kiev showrooms are to the Ukrainian people. But the existence of statutes invasive of these unvindicated rights would create pressure upon legislatures to repeal the offending statutes. Presumably, if the Court had correctly divined the moral sentiments of the community, that pressure would be of considerable force. In a sense, the Court's function with respect to natural Ninth Amendment rights would be to focus the attention of legislatures upon specific issues where legislative preferences and popular moral preferences have badly diverged.

Yet another possibility would be to treat the natural law component of the Ninth Amendment as merely an aid to construction of the specifically enumerated rights. This is Laurence Tribe's view of the proper role of the Ninth Amendment. It would employ the Ninth Amendment as a rule of construction to legitimate expansive interpretations of the scope of the enumerated powers. In essence, it would operate to continue the development of constitutional recognition of unenumerated rights under the rubric of due process or equal protection. The problem with this approach is not so much that it denigrates unenumerated rights, because the Ninth Amendment as rule of construction would simply assimilate those rights to other parts of the Constitution. Rather, the problem is that this approach by itself provides insufficient guidance for how we determine the substance of unenumerated rights. Professor Tribe's approach to this latter problem is to acknowledge that the application of open-ended guarantees, such as due process, to specific issues necessarily involves a choice of values. The relevance of the Ninth Amendment as a rule of construction to this choice is that the Ninth Amendment offers support for application of the open-ended constitutional guarantee at a relatively high level of generality. Thus, for example, if due process implies a substantive liberty interest in procreative choice (as *Griswold* concluded) the Ninth Amendment supplies a constructional principle that suggests that the liberty interest ought to be interpreted in a sufficiently general manner that would encompass most matters of consensual sexual choice. Although this is a valuable approach, it suffers from several defects. First, it relies entirely upon the judiciary to make these highly subjective judgments about the appropriate level of generality to read into any given open-ended enumerated right. To the extent that this exercise is simply natural law under a different name it fails to employ the iterative relationship between courts and legislatures that might better capture the moral consensus of the community. Second, it continues to rely upon the fiction that unenumerated rights really are not; they are simply attributes of grand constitutional generalities like due process. When that aspect of Tribe's approach is coupled with its exclusive reliance upon the judiciary, it becomes reasonably clear that the deeply contested nature of unenumerated rights is unlikely to be removed. Although there is no guarantee that an iterative approach would end all controversy surrounding the project of identifying and enforcing unenumerated rights, it would increase the institutional pressures to select for constitutional recognition only those unenumerated rights around which the polity can coalesce.

A final iterative possibility would be to adopt some version of the Canadian Charter's justification provision. Section 1 of the Canadian Charter provides that most of the individual liberties guaranteed by the Charter are "subject only to such reasonable limits as may be demonstrably justified in a free and democratic society."[25] The Supreme Court of Canada has developed a body of law detailing the conditions that must be met in order to demonstrate that any given governmental infringement of a Charter right is indeed justified. The U.S. Supreme Court is free to create analogous doctrine limited to the category of natural Ninth Amendment rights. This is an approach by which the judiciary would accord unusual deference to legislative choices that impinge upon what the Court would regard as an unenumerated natural right. The rationale for doing so is the recognition that the Court is not certain to gauge the moral sentiments of the community more accurately than legislatures. The rationale for requiring governments to justify their infringement of natural Ninth Amendment rights (the existence and scope of which would be determined by the Court) is our belief that legislatures also are prone to error in stating the moral sentiments of the national community.

The level of justification required might vary with the legislative body in question. States could be held to stiffer levels of proof than Congress to justify their infringements, on the theory that local legislatures are less likely than the national legislature to capture the prevailing national moral consensus.

The level of justification might also vary with the nature of the natural Ninth Amendment right determined by the Court. My colleague David Faigman has suggested that the evidentiary burden to be borne by governments in justifying prima facie infringements of constitutional liberties ought to increase as the Constitution is more deeply implicated. He has proposed that we might usefully label nominal infringements of the Constitution as marginal infringements, consequential, central, or core infringements.[26] Of course, for this methodology to be useful it is necessary to possess some principled way of distinguishing between constitutional infringements. But even without a developed constitutional abacus to calculate the degree of constitutional infringement involved in any given case it is possible for the Court to make some broad distinctions between unenumerated natural rights that are relatively trivial (such as the right to sleep until noon) and those that are relatively profound (such as the right to marry a person of a different race). It is true that people may disagree over whether any given unenumerated right is trivial or profound but, within broad limits, it is probably possible to determine which unenumerated rights resonate harmoniously with the moral chords of society and which are slightly off-key. When the Court is least certain that it has identified a natural Ninth Amendment right with widely shared moral underpinnings it could easily characterize the right as marginal or consequential and thus impose a relatively light evidentiary burden upon governments seeking to establish that their statutes or regulations permissibly burden the right.

These devices would create a structural framework within which a public dialogue concerning the content and scope of natural Ninth Amendment rights could emerge. But their utility is dependent upon a demonstration that, as an initial matter, courts may be relied upon to identify natural Ninth Amendment rights with some plausible degree of principle. If the judicial process by which natural Ninth Amendment rights are declared, even provisionally, is entirely capricious, the product of unconstrained and individualized judicial whim, it is presumptively illegitimate. The problem is to describe a method by which these fundamental rights can be identified in a fashion that is tied to some principle other than the moral predilections of the deciding judge. There are multiple indicators of the conventional cultural understanding that forms the basis for contemporary natural rights. I will examine briefly the potential sources from which we might conclude that there exists a sufficiently widely shared cultural understanding to support recognition of unenumerated natural rights as aspects of the natural rights retained by the Ninth Amendment.

One can look to the Constitution and derive from the nature of the guarantees of that document principles that suggest that a given unenumerated right is within the ambit of those principles. This is essentially the approach taken by Justice Douglas in *Griswold v. Connecticut*,[27] in which the right of privacy was located in the penumbra of certain relevant enumerated rights. Professor Charles Black also takes this approach by emphasizing the importance of construing any portion of the Constitution by reference to the structural relationships created by the entire document.[28] Justice Douglas's penumbral approach has been widely ridiculed but it is surely correct that any recitation of general principles and guarantees designed to endure necessarily implies some specific entitlements that may not be readily apparent in the general language of the text. "Ideas have consequences" may be a moderately trite aphorism but in the context of generalized constitutional guarantees it is another way of stating that the explicit provisions of the Constitution carry with them some thematic principles that we ignore at our peril.

One can also consult the Constitution to determine whether any given claimed unenumerated natural right is consistent with the enumerated rights. Determination that any given claimed natural Ninth Amendment right is consistent with the enumerated rights might result in a presumption of the validity of the putative unenumerated natural Ninth Amendment right. The burden would then rest with the government to overcome that presumption by demonstrating the existence of governmental interests that are sufficiently powerful to legitimate the exercise of governmental force upon presumptively reserved rights. The effect of this exercise would certainly be to treat unenumerated rights on a par with enumerated rights, but would not totally foreclose governments from legislative initiatives that can be justified.

Randy Barnett and Bernard Siegan have advanced some version of this argument. Barnett suggests that we "adopt a justificatory *presumption of liberty* that puts the burden on government to show that any interference with the exercise of the rights retained by the people is justified." He adds that "liberty does not mean license to do whatever one wishes" and contends that "the common law . . . defines the boundaries within which one may do as one wishes. . . . Provided that one is acting rightfully [in terms of the common law] . . . government must justify any interference with such conduct." Barnett defends the common law as the instantiation of natural rights, "the means of giving these otherwise abstract [natural] rights a conventionally established, specific content." The problem with reliance upon the common law is that it is a highly organic system that has been so radically altered by legislation that it is no longer, if it ever was, a reliable indicator of natural rights that would trigger the justificatory presumption urged by Barnett. Moreover, if I am correct that the nature of contemporary natural rights inheres in the *current* cultural ethos, Barnett's justificatory presumption would never arise, for current positive law would act as the device to define the boundaries of liberty and it is, of course, the validity of precisely that law that is the question to be decided.[29]

Bernard Siegan has proposed that governments be required to justify *all* legislation. According to Siegan, governments should "have the burden of persuading a court . . . that the legislation serves important governmental objectives; . . . that the restraint imposed by government is substantially related to achievement of those objectives, that is, . . . the fit between ends and means must be close; and . . . that a similar result cannot be obtained by less drastic means."[30] Siegan's position is one that derives considerable support from the original structure of the Constitution, a document that created a central government of carefully circumscribed powers. Given the limited grant of powers to the central government and the reservation of all rights (intended in part as a device to limit the growth by implication of the limited powers of government) it is entirely reasonable to place upon the government, rather than on the citizen, the burden of justifying the validity of its conduct. If the modern meaning of the natural law dimension of the Ninth Amendment is to be found by bringing constitutional cy pres to bear upon it, Siegan's test may be reasonably adapted to the furtherance of that goal.

Siegan's test does not mean that courts will invalidate all legislative initiatives impinging upon matters that have previously escaped regulation. In examining the justification offered by the government for any given legislation, courts ought to give considerable weight to the needs of the entire community, presumably expressed in the legislation under scrutiny. Mary Ann Glendon has properly excoriated our tendency to speak of rights with "exaggerated absoluteness, . . . hyperindividualism, and . . . silence with respect to personal, civic, and collective responsibilities." Glendon contends that "our stark, simple rights dialect puts a damper on the processes of public justification, communication, and deliberation upon which the continuing vitality of a democratic regime depends . . . [and] contributes to the erosion of the habits, practices, and attitudes of respect for others that are the ultimate and surest guarantors of human rights."[31] When confronted with challenges to legislation, and in the course of applying Siegan's test, it is entirely proper to uphold legislation that substantially serves some pressing public need, and does so in a fashion that impinges upon liberty in a fashion proportionate to the public benefits obtainable only through the legislation.

This would be an approach similar to that taken by the Supreme Court of Canada in deciding when legislative infringements of rights guaranteed under the Charter of Rights and Freedoms are "demonstrably justified in a free and democratic society."[32] Charter rights may be justifiably infringed if the "impugned state action has an objective of *pressing and substantial concern* in a free and democratic society."[33] In *Regina v. Oakes*,[34] the Supreme Court of Canada established the following test for justification of legislative invasions of Charter rights:

> First, the measures adopted must be carefully designed to achieve the objective in question. . . . [T]hey must be rationally connected to the objective. Second, the means, even if rationally connected to the objective, . . . should impair 'as little as possible' the right or freedom in question. . . . Third,

there must be a proportionality between the effects of the measures which are responsible for limiting the Charter right or freedom, and the objective which has been identified as of 'sufficient importance'.[35]

The Canadian Supreme Court has begun to develop a fairly elaborate jurisprudence that refines these elements in a way that permits a great deal of latitude for legislative judgments to encroach upon expressly declared fundamental rights. I do not propose anything as sweeping as the Canadian doctrine permitting impingement upon constitutional liberties. Rather, I propose that an American version of the *Oakes* test could be useful in the quite limited circumstance of deciding whether any given law can be said to infringe a claimed natural Ninth Amendment right.

The European Court of Human Rights employs a similar analysis. Article 8, section 1 of the European Convention on Human Rights guarantees "respect for . . . private life" but section 2 permits governments to interfere with that right when it is "necessary" to do so "in the interests of national security, public safety, . . . economic well-being of the country, . . . prevention of disorder or crime, . . . protection of health or morals, or for the protection of the rights and freedoms of others."[36] In *Dudgeon v. United Kingdom*,[37] the European Court interpreted "necessary" to mean (1) the existence of some pressing social need and (2) the presence of proportionality between the restriction imposed by the challenged legislation and the legitimate aims sought to be accomplished by the legislation. Again, a U.S. version of this test could prove quite useful in analyzing whether any given statute, administrative practice, or executive action is invasive of a claimed natural Ninth Amendment right.

The Canadian or European justification tests could easily be combined with Professor Faigman's notion of marginal, consequential, central, and core infringements of constitutional guarantees. Faigman's refinement is to tinker with the evidentiary burden upon governments to justify their intrusions, based on the degree to which the governmental infringement implicates the constitutional values at issue. Governments would be required to shoulder a greater justificatory burden as the moral consensus concerning any given natural Ninth Amendment right becomes firmer.

To be sure, employment of some version of the Canadian, European, or Professor Siegan's approach does not define affirmatively the content of natural Ninth Amendment rights. All of these approaches assume that the statute in question is invalid absent some justification, and proceed to describe the necessary justification. The initial problem with natural Ninth Amendment rights is to define them with sufficient clarity that we can know when a colorable natural Ninth Amendment claim has been stated. Unless there is some threshold definition of natural Ninth Amendment rights every statute would be susceptible to a claim of constitutional invalidity under the natural rights dimension of the Ninth Amendment. The Ninth Amendment would become, as Justice Holmes once derided the equal protection clause, "the usual last resort of constitutional arguments."[38]

If natural Ninth Amendment rights are connected to reasonable inferences that can be drawn from the written Constitution, the threshold of validity for asserted natural Ninth Amendment rights might well be a demonstration by the challenger to the constitutionality of a statute that the asserted natural Ninth Amendment right is not inconsistent with the Constitution's enumerated rights and that it is logically implied by the enumerated rights. Thus, for example, one might plausibly claim that the abortion right is a colorable natural Ninth Amendment right because it is not inconsistent with the Constitution's enumerated rights (at least so long as fetuses are continued to be regarded as constitutional nonpersons) and the right to personal freedom from being forced to become an instrument of state policy is implied by the entire panorama of enumerated rights. If there is a theme that unifies the enumerated rights it is that individuals should be free from state coercion and dominion over those choices and beliefs that lie at the heart of our unique personality. But there may be other sources for determining the threshold content of natural Ninth Amendment rights, the quantum of entitlement that would trigger a requirement of justification on the part of the state to uphold the validity of any given statute against a claim of infringement upon natural Ninth Amendment rights.

The history and traditions of our national experience ought also to be consulted, not to divine the "most specific tradition available,"[39] but to determine "the balance which our Nation, built upon postulates of respect for the liberty of the individual, has struck between that liberty and the demands of organized society. . . . [It] is the balance struck by this country, having regard to what history teaches are the traditions from which it developed as well as the traditions from which it broke. That tradition is a living thing."[40] Our history and traditions are dynamic rather than static. They are not snapshots, frozen in time, in our family photo album; rather, they consist of a continuously running motion picture, to which new frames are added every moment of our existence.

It is a mistake to think, as Chief Justice Rehnquist and Justice Scalia do, that we can consult some static and specific referent to derive meaning from history and tradition. Indeed, modest reflection upon the possible referents that could be used illustrate the problem. Neither the absence nor presence of positive law bearing upon a particular claimed right can be dispositive. It is difficult to attribute meaning to the absence of law, and a long pattern of unconstitutional regulation only establishes a continuing legislative contempt for our fundamental law.[41] "Moreover, historical traditions, like rights themselves, exist at various levels of generality."[42] Nor is it easy to identify how we measure specificity when examining history and tradition. It is not clear whether this specificity refers to positive law or social attitudes and, if the latter, what device is appropriate to detect social attitudes. If there is no specific tradition available to tell us whether women desiring to abort are required to notify their husbands of their intent to do so, where do we turn for the most relevant specific tradition? Do we look to more general traditions concerning women's reproductive freedom, to traditions concerning fetuses, or to traditions concerning a husband's control of his wife? Justice Scalia asserts that we must rely on the most specific tradition available, but he has no guidance for us here.

When consulting the garbled text of history and tradition, it is inevitable that choices must be made concerning the relevant evidence. Rather than pretending that there are readily identifiable static and specific referents we ought, instead, look at the vectors of history — the rate, direction, and nature of change in our cultural ethos. A static perspective upon history and tradition would suggest that we have an entrenched practice of denying women the same measure of personal autonomy we have accorded men. Thus, for example, a statute that conditions availability of abortion upon the woman's proof that she has notified her husband of her intent to abort might be considered consistent with history and tradition. But if the vector of our history and tradition is consulted, one would be forced to admit that it points to ever increasing recognition of the fundamental equality between the sexes as autonomous individuals. From this perspective, the same statute would seem to be at odds with a dynamic concept of our history and tradition. Because our contemporary concept of natural rights is one that relies on a shared cultural ethos, it is all the more important to choose the vectors of history rather than the tombstones of history to guide us in locating natural enumerated rights.

From this we might extend our criteria for recognition of the threshold content of natural Ninth Amendment rights. In addition to demanding consistency with enumerated rights and some logical nexus with the themes that inform the enumerated rights, we might also require that any claimed natural Ninth Amendment right be consistent with our dynamic history and traditions. After all, the goal is to identify those unenumerated rights that are so firmly established in our collective moral taxonomy that they can be labeled "natural." The Court that ignores the vectors of history in doing so runs the risk that it will take the pulse of a national corpse instead of the living organism. The Court that treats the vectors of history as mere guidelines for the future runs the risk that it will engage in predicting the natural moral values of some future polity but not the one that exists today. These major errors are the same — the denial of the validity of the moral sentiments of the polity — but the process by which they are reached differs slightly. The first is simply the failure to recognize change. The second is the failure to recognize that change has not occurred to the extent it might be expected to in some indeterminate future. With respect to unenumerated rights, the Court's task should not be to "lead[ ] a Volk who will be 'tested by following,' and whose very 'belief in themselves' is mystically bound up in their 'understanding' of a Court that 'speak[s] before all others for their constitutional ideals,' "[43] but to apprehend the moral consensus that attaches to the polity at the moment it must reach decision. Of course there must be some margin for error, but the Court plunges itself into the cauldron of politics when it renders judgments that push the envelope of tolerable error.

This process of divining natural rights is one that carries a great deal of risk, for the Court is not always certain to make the correct judgment that any given claimed natural right is sufficiently well-grounded in our cultural ethos to constitute such a right. Indeed, when the Court recognizes the existence of an unenumerated right, and that recognition becomes a bitter political issue, it is almost certain to have erred. Thus, the Court was correct to recognize the unenumerated natural right of married couples to use contraceptives,[44] but quite possibly wrong to have recognized the right to terminate pregnancy as an unenumerated aspect of liberty substantively protected by the due process clause.[45] This is not to suggest that *Roe v. Wade* was necessarily wrongly decided as a matter of constitutional law. It is to suggest that the Court was wrong to treat the right at issue as an aspect of substantive due process. The Court would have done better to ground the right to terminate pregnancy in the equal protection clause. What is less clear is whether the abortion right might have acquired more perceived legitimacy had it been squarely recognized as an unenumerated natural right. Although it is entirely possible that the Court in *Roe* was simply reading the vectors of history a bit too aggressively it may also be that the error, if error it was, would have been more adeptly corrected by some version of the override power, weak *stare decisis*, or justified infringement.

The present result of the Court's twenty-year odyssey with abortion is that, with broad limits, governments do have the ability to circumscribe the abortion right. An override power would be only a slightly greater encroachment upon abortion. Moreover, the Court has reached its present position by a "reliance upon stare decisis [that] can best be described as contrived." If retrenchment with respect to unenumerated natural rights is necessary when the Court misjudges the national moral consensus, it would be better to do so by owning up to the inapplicability of the normal rules of stare decisis to unenumerated natural rights than to undercut stare decisis generally. The present constitutional status of abortion is in fact very much like a Canadian Charter right that may be justifiably infringed. The "undue burden" test, which requires courts to determine whether any given governmental regulation of abortion "has the purpose or effect of placing a substantial obstacle in the path of a woman seeking an abortion of a nonviable fetus," is a test that frankly admits that governmental infringements of unenumerated constitutional rights are indeed justifiable. Indeed, the

Court noted that "the undue burden standard is the appropriate means of reconciling the State's interest [in preserving fetuses as potential human lives] with the woman's constitutionally protected liberty [in terminating pregnancy]." It should hardly be surprising that in the same opinion the Court relied on the Ninth Amendment for partial support of the constitutional legitimacy of a woman's right to terminate her pregnancy.[46]

There is, however, no certainty that the Court is the correct institution to make these judgments. If natural rights in our time come down to a judgment about the current cultural understanding of the nature of such rights, why are not democratically elected legislators more qualified than judges to make this determination?[47] In addition to my earlier responses to this problem, another answer may be that, given the evident constitutional bias toward making the government an island of powers in a sea of rights, it is appropriate not to vest too much trust in the organ that wields those powers — the legislature. But if doubt persists on this point, it might be appropriate to consider further some judicially created version of the power given to Canadian legislatures, both national and provincial, to override certain constitutional guarantees. In fashioning natural rights under the Ninth Amendment, the Court might treat the rights thus established as only provisionally created, pending some definitive, explicit, and unequivocal repudiation by Congress.

This is an iterative scheme that is much like the current relationship between Court and Congress with respect to the dormant, or negative, commerce clause. The current understanding of congressional power over interstate commerce is that it is plenary, encompassing even the power to confer regulatory authority upon the states that would otherwise be struck down by the courts as an unconstitutional burden upon interstate commerce. In effect, the Court's judgment that the commerce clause forbids any given state regulation of commerce is provisional, and may be overridden by a subsequent congressional judgment that the states should be free to exercise the forbidden power. Indeed, U.S. constitutional law contains several other examples of a judicially created override power — sometimes vested in Congress, sometimes vested in the states — that effectively render the constitutional judgments of the Court provisional.[48]

The Court could limit the extent of any override power it might create. It might very well conclude that only Congress should possess an override power, on the grounds that natural Ninth Amendment rights reflect, or ought to reflect, a national moral consensus. Thus, in some future time if the nation as a whole should conclude that it is morally intolerable to inflict official governmental discrimination upon people based upon their sexual orientation, and should the political community of any given state prefer the maintenance of such official discrimination, the national moral consensus would presumably prevail in the form of an absence of congressional action to override the Court. The Court might also require that any override by Congress of its natural Ninth Amendment judgments must be done unambiguously and unequivocally. This would require that the congressional decision to substitute its moral judgments for that of the Court would not be hidden from public view. Presumably, the benefit of this would be that, on any given contested issue of natural Ninth Amendment rights, public institutions would be forced to engage in some open and searching inquiry about the moral consensus of our society.

Another variation upon the override power would be to treat the congressional override as equally provisional as the Court's natural Ninth Amendment judgments. Thus, the congressional override would not be binding upon the Court. In the rare event that the Court was strongly convinced that its original judgment was the better assessment of the status of the right in question it would be free to insist that its view must prevail. This variation would raise the possibility of open conflict between Court and Congress. Presumably neither institution would relish the combat and instances of confrontation would be rare. If both actors were truly committed to the idea that, with respect to unenumerated natural rights, the essence of the task is to divine the moral sentiments of the nation, it is hard to imagine that such deeply felt disagreements would occur with any frequency.

The defects of this scheme are not so substantial as to reject the idea. The Court and Congress function without undue friction today in all the various areas in which the Court has created some analogue to the override power. The fact that only the constitutional judgments of the Court pertaining to unenumerated natural rights would be susceptible to congressional override is not likely to undermine the Court's authoritativeness in other aspects of constitutional adjudication. It is the murkiness of unenumerated natural rights that justifies the Court's deference to other institutional readers of the public moral pulse. Those considerations are simply not present, or at least not as strongly implicated, in other areas of constitutional law. So long as the Court is clear about what it is doing, there is no reason to fear the creation of another (albeit explicit) override power would lead to ever-increasing demands for a broad congressional power of constitutional override.

Nor is there any reason to think that the creation of an override power for unenumerated natural rights would require explicit constitutional amendment. For many years after John Marshall's opinion in *Gibbons v. Ogden*[49] it was a staple of U.S. constitutional law that the commerce clause conferred some zone of exclusive authority upon Congress. Thus, although Congress could "adopt" state law and thereby make it federal, it could not "delegate" its exclusive legislative authority to the states.[50] When this doctrine was dissolved, to be replaced by the notion that congressional power over commerce was plenary and inclusive of the power to validate state laws that would otherwise be impermissible burdens on interstate commerce, the Court effected the transformation, including the recognition of an effective congressional override power, without aid of formal amendment. There is no reason to think that the Court lacks the authority to create similar doctrine in the case of unenumerated natural Ninth Amendment rights.

Another mechanism by which to respond to the doubt that courts are the appropriate vehicle to enforce unenumerated rights might be a judicially created doctrine that such rights are subject to a much weaker version of stare decisis than is generally applicable to constitutional doctrine. This would, of course, make it easier for the Court to retreat from the recognition of new natural rights when it becomes obvious that there is no cultural ethos supporting the right. It is already recognized that stare decisis "is not an inexorable command; rather, it 'is a principle of policy and not a mechanical formula of adherence to the latest decision.' "[51] The Court has described this principle as "particularly true in constitutional cases, because in such cases 'correction through legislative action is practically impossible.' "[52] Moreover, the Court has indicated that stare decisis applies most weakly "when the decision believed erroneous is the *application* of a constitutional principle rather than an interpretation of the principle itself."[53] When it comes to the identification of natural Ninth Amendment rights surely the Court is squarely engaged in the application of constitutional principles.

Ordinarily, stare decisis "is the preferred course because it promotes the evenhanded, predictable, and consistent development of legal principles, fosters reliance on judicial decisions, and contributes to the actual and perceived integrity of the judicial process."[54] It may be that "in most matters it is more important that the applicable rule of law be settled than it be settled right,"[55] but the question of whether or not to recognize the constitutional existence of a claimed natural Ninth Amendment right is surely one of the exceptional matters. In matters of natural law, where the only pragmatic measure of correctness is the congruence of natural law and overwhelmingly shared societal moral preference, there is almost no warrant for settling the question at the expense of accuracy, for the inaccurate settlement will produce no settlement at all. The argument for stare decisis in matters of natural Ninth Amendment rights is stronger were the Court to create an override power, for then an iterative process by which moral and legal consensus might be reached would be established. But absent such a device the Court needs to be free to react to its own errors. In the garden of natural law the judicial gardener cannot be expected to recognize unerringly the difference between desirable flowers and noxious weeds. As sprouts they are similar to one another; the judicial gardener may need some license later to weed and prune.

In a sense, the weak version of stare decisis and the judicially created version of Canada's override power seem to fly in the face of the Ninth Amendment's textual injunction not to *disparage* the unenumerated rights, because I do not make any suggestion that these doctrines would apply to enumerated rights. There are several defenses that can be offered in response to this objection.

The natural law tradition within U.S. fundamental law is a conflicted one. It is a theme that runs through our discourse about fundamental rights from European colonization until the present. At the same time there is a contrapuntal theme that accompanies the melody of natural law; a theme that questions the legitimacy of reliance upon unwritten sources of fundamental law and, to the extent natural law is admitted as having any legitimacy, one that confines the operation of natural law to the realm of legislative politics. In this view, the proper place for natural law is to shape public opinion and, in turn, to influence the policy choices of elected representatives. Thus, Philip Hamburger has argued that Americans of the founding generation "assumed that individuals retained only such natural rights as were reserved by a constitution or, much less securely, were left unimpeded by their other civil laws." Of course, Hamburger also admits that eighteenth-century

Americans thought that "civil law should reflect natural law. . . . Americans asserted that the people . . . should protect their natural liberty by establishing government and should formulate their constitutions and laws to reflect natural law." But, in Hamburger's view, this does not mean that natural law was incorporated into constitutional law. Rather, "natural law typically was assumed to be the reasoning on the basis of which individuals adopted constitutions and a means by which the people could measure the adequacy of their constitutions. A failure of a constitution to reflect natural law was a ground for altering or abandoning the constitution rather than for making a claim in court." The essence of the contrapuntal theme is that natural law is merely "a prudential or moral guide" rather than a separate, independent facet of fundamental law.[56]

The contrapuntal view of the role of natural law in U.S. constitutional law is accommodated by the iterative scheme proposed. A court identifying natural Ninth Amendment rights would be required to recognize that natural law is, indeed, a prudential or moral guide, albeit one invited into the Constitution by the Ninth Amendment. That recognition, in turn, would operate to temper the otherwise virtually unreviewable authority of the Supreme Court to pronounce new such rights. By relying upon the deliberative processes of the legislative and judicial branches of government to identify natural Ninth Amendment rights, any right that emerges is far more likely to reflect the prudential and moral guidance that Hamburger claims was the true essence of natural law at the time of constitutional coalescence. Similarly, weak stare decisis or a doctrine of justified infringement are each far more likely to provide the Court with the room to maneuver that is essential to the prudential mode of constitutional adjudication. These iterative devices provide a decent accommodation to the Constitution's invitation to rely upon natural law and to the historical and pragmatic reluctance to do so.

If this defense is attacked as one that rests primarily on the dubious ground of pragmatism, I can only recall the reminder of Justice Robert Jackson that the Supreme Court, as well as being a court of law, is also a branch of government. Governments do not operate well without a healthy dose of the pragmatic. If the art of politics is the possible, the art of constitutional law is the combination of the possible and the principled. Given the skepticism, if not downright antagonism, with which discussion of the legitimacy of natural rights is greeted, the framework I propose for locating natural Ninth Amendment rights is one that is designed to capture the principles of natural law as well as make the medicine of natural law slide a bit easier down the throats of orthodox positivists. It is neither easy to reconstruct natural law in a positivistic world nor to sell the product to a skeptical audience. This is a tentative attempt in that direction.

SEVEN

Stewards of the Constitution

So why is the Ninth Amendment needed? The foregoing may be an interesting exercise in imagining a different method for apprehension of unenumerated rights, but what is its utility to constitutional law? Specifically, why can we not protect unenumerated rights adequately by the due process clause, the fundamental rights prong of equal protection analysis, and assimilation to other textual guarantees of the Constitution? What benefits for constitutional law are derived by creating an elaborate new body of Ninth Amendment jurisprudence? And if there are any benefits, are they not outweighed by the destabilizing effects of this radical new doctrine? These are reasonable objections, or at least questions. Any advocate of the new and untested necessarily labors under a burden of proving the efficacy of the new, for there seems to be a human tendency to presume that the status quo is preferable. As the homely adage puts it, "If it ain't broke, don't fix it." Although constitutional adjudicators and expositors speak with greater elegance, at least in public, there is no reason to think that the legal mind is less freighted with mental inertia than any other. Thus, although much of the case for reconceiving the Ninth Amendment has been embedded in the argument thus far, it is time to sum up the evidence.

First, is a reconceived Ninth Amendment possible? Its implementation would entail a number of problems. For example, would courts immediately assimilate to the Ninth Amendment all the existing unenumerated rights ancillary to other parts of the Constitution? If they did not, there would exist two separate tiers of unenumerated rights with different doctrinal roots and differing degrees of immutability attached to their existence. That is a situation that is incoherent, but no more incoherent than many other illogical quirks in the existing design of constitutional law. If courts did assimilate all preexisting unenumerated rights to the Ninth Amendment, they would be rejecting implicitly the prior methodology that led to recognition of rights such as voting, privacy, access to trials, and the presumption of innocence as attributes of other parts of the Constitution. Moreover, to the extent that these rights were to be regarded as natural Ninth Amendment rights they would become susceptible to alteration by means of the legislative override, weak stare decisis, or some version of the justified infringement power. Courts would be forced to confront the question of whether to facilitate mutability of some unenumerated rights but not others. It might be that voting, or the presumption of innocence, are so deeply ingrained and morally accepted (at least in principle) that their status as natural Ninth Amendment rights would be more firmly fixed than, say, the right to physician-assisted suicide. The Court would be forced to articulate why it makes such a distinction, and in that articulation would be exposed the degree of real consensus that surrounds any given claimed natural Ninth Amendment right.

There would be considerable overlap between positive Ninth Amendment rights and natural Ninth Amendment rights, but this should not prove overly troublesome. For example, California's constitution expressly protects the right of privacy, and that right might well receive recognition as a state-specific positive Ninth Amendment right. At the same time, privacy might be regarded as a natural Ninth Amendment right. If so, neither Congress nor any of the states would be free to infringe the natural privacy right until and unless that right was altered by one of the iterative processes previously discussed. But even after such alteration neither Congress nor California would be free to infringe upon the California-specific privacy right. By contrast, if California were to eliminate its privacy right at a time when privacy was recognized as a natural Ninth Amendment right California would not be able to infringe the natural dimension of privacy until and unless that right had been validly altered. This scheme is not conceptually difficult, bears many similarities to the present-day relationship between federal and state constitutional law, and is thus unlikely to pose much difficulty in administration.

These are mere technical problems of adjusting to a new way of thinking about unenumerated constitutional rights. The more fundamental issue is whether we ought to expend the energy to fashion a new discourse about unenumerated constitutional rights. What benefits accrue, and are they worth the effort?

A Ninth Amendment reconceived through the lens of constitutional cy pres would be more faithful to constitutional text than the present understanding of the amendment. The received wisdom of the Ninth Amendment treats it as duplicative of the Tenth Amendment, merely a hortatory truism that all is retained that was not surrendered to government. But that is not what the Ninth Amendment seems to say, and to regard it as the Tenth Amendment in a different linguistic suit is to dismiss the founding generation as inept draftsmen and hopelessly muddled thinkers. The prevailing interpretation is one that sneers at text, rather than taking seriously the constitutional interpreter's obligation both to start with text and ultimately to deliver constitutional interpretations that at least do no violence to text.

By contrast, the reconceived reading of the Ninth Amendment pays attention to what the founding generation actually stated. By granting constitutional recognition to unwritten rights retained by the people and simultaneously declaring that those unwritten rights were not to be denied or disparaged by enumeration of other rights, the founding generation imbedded in the Constitution a principle of providing constitutional protection to human liberties with no apparent textual linkage to the Constitution. If we now are willing to act on that principle, as we plainly are given the second coming of substantive due process, it behooves us to use as our warrant for the venture the constitutional guarantee that is textually best suited for the purpose. The Ninth Amendment provides the best textual justification for recognition of unenumerated rights.

We need not rely on text alone. Indeed, we should not stop with text, not simply because text may at some level be inherently indeterminate, but because the task of faithful constitutional stewardship is one that requires us to harmonize the disparate aids to constitutional interpretation. It is important to divine what we can about the intentions of the generation that bequeathed us the Ninth Amendment. Careful examination of those intentions reveals that the founding generation's objective in creating the Ninth Amendment may well have been singular — to better protect human liberties from the jealous encroachments of government — but the mechanism selected, the Ninth Amendment, embodied two quite different means to the end of preservation of human liberty. The Ninth Amendment was designed to prevent the accretion of central governmental powers by implication, but it was also designed to insure against the possibility that the enumerated rights of the Constitution would come to be regarded as a definitive, and exclusive, itemization of human liberties. Our present understanding of the Ninth Amendment is one that does justice to neither of these means and, as a consequence, fails utterly to accomplish the intended objective of preserving individual rights from governmental invasion. The reconceived Ninth Amendment responds directly to these intended means for preserving liberty, and thus would use the Ninth Amendment as an active vehicle to police the use and abuse of governmental power.

A resurrected Ninth Amendment would also remove the present doctrinal arbitrariness of treating some implied fundamental rights as aspects of the equal protection clause and others as aspects of substantive due process. The right to vote is, by and large, wholly implied. So, too, is the right of privacy. Why is the right to vote commonly analyzed as one of the fundamental rights protected by equal protection while claims of privacy are treated as aspects of due process? Although it is true that there is not, or at least should not be, any significant legal consequence to the different sliver of text to which the implied fundamental right is assimilated, there is no logical coherence to a doctrine that seems to ground itself in the Constitution in an almost whimsical fashion. Recognition that the Ninth Amendment is the textual foundation for all implied constitutional rights would greatly simplify matters. There would be no need to tinker with other doctrinal frameworks to accommodate the awkward ghost of unwritten rights. The ghost would have her own constitutional bedchamber, and the Court could set about keeping it tidy.

The pedigree of unenumerated rights would improve. The association with discredited notions of substantive due process would disappear, or at least abate. Unenumerated rights that are also implied from some other constitutional guarantee would gain an additional measure of respect. For example, in a world of a reconceived Ninth Amendment the right of the public to attend criminal trials would derive with equal force from the first amendment's guarantees of free speech and press as well as the Ninth Amendment. In short, constitutional doctrine would become more straightforward. At last we could be honest. Truth has many virtues and among them are clarity of thought and peace of mind.

Truth in the constitutional manufacture of implied fundamental rights would make it easier to recognize squarely that we treat implied fundamental rights (to say nothing of the enumerated rights) as subject to infringement when the governmental justification is high enough. We already have a de facto version of Canada's explicit constitutional recognition of legislative power sufficient to justify infringements of constitutional liberties; we just pretend that we do not countenance governmental invasions of the Constitution. Our current mode of justifying constitutional infringements is to balance the asserted interests of governments against the individual interest in protection at the definitional stage. When we conclude that the governmental interests are sufficiently substantial we declare that the particular constitutional right in question has not been infringed. Thus, for example, the Court was able to opine that imprisonment for burning a draft card to protest the Vietnam War did not infringe David O'Brien's right to speak freely.[1] This is nonsense. Of course O'Brien's right of free expression was infringed; the question was whether the government was justified in doing so. When we stop asking the real questions and instead engage in euphemistic assertions that we are deciding something else, eventually we delude even ourselves. Euphemisms are the cancers of thought, left untreated they will metastatize and overwhelm a formerly healthy system. An honest statement of the epistemological, moral, and political problems that are presented by constitutional protection of unwritten rights would help us to develop those rights in a way that will preserve both liberty and democracy. Prevarication will end in failure.

Recognition of positive Ninth Amendment rights would permit states to increase the quantum of liberty protected against governmental invasion. True, that can be and is being done now by interpreting state constitutions more generously than the federal Constitution, but an expansive rights-preservative reading of state constitutions does nothing to prevent Congress from reversing those state judgments. The positive Ninth Amendment would brake Congress as well. The immediate reaction of a U.S. constitutional lawyer to this suggestion is likely to be that it is nonsense, or heretical, or just plain lunacy. Steeped in the brew of federal supremacy, U.S. constitutional interpreters have made of the supremacy clause a mantra that operates to obscure judgment about the way in which the original structural allocations of power between federal and state governments might be adapted to reflect historical conditions and our present circumstances. There is no magic to any particular allocation of power between governments in a federal system but there is an inherent danger to liberty when that allocation becomes grossly imbalanced. The positive component of the reconceived Ninth Amendment is an attempt to reorient ourselves in a way that prevents governmental oppression from the center while simultaneously prohibiting states from oppressing their own people.

Natural Ninth Amendment rights would permit the Court to make provisional judgments about which human liberties are so basic that neither the states nor the federal government should be permitted to invade them. Under the current situation, once the Court has embarked upon the quest of identifying and protecting any given unenumerated right it finds it politically difficult, if not impossible, to modify or depart from its self-adopted course. By contrast, the iterative relationship envisioned between Court, Congress, and the states with respect to natural Ninth Amendment rights would insure a political dialogue on the level of constitutional politics. Recently, Professor Bruce Ackerman and others have begun to write about the need for distinguishing between ordinary political discourse and those transcendent moments when the polity engages seriously the meaning of constitutional values. An iterative methodology for locating unenumerated natural rights would force us, as a people, to reflect upon the constitutional choices we make. In the reflection we might wrench ourselves out of our ordinary concerns and focus more clearly upon what kind of people we wish to be.

In any case, natural law has a long association with American ideas of fundamental law, both prior to, during, and after the Revolution. When the intellectual background of the colonial, revolutionary, and post-revolutionary periods are recalled, it is difficult to dismiss the influence of natural law in the creation of the Ninth Amendment. Indeed, Roger Sherman's draft of the Bill of Rights expressly declared that "the people have certain natural rights which are retained by them when they enter into Society."[2] Randy Barnett has accurately described this as "reflect[ing] the sentiment that came to be expressed in the ninth [amendment]."[3] The tradition of judicial enforcement of natural rights as part of the fundamental law, thereby voiding contrary legislation, is equally long but considerably more controversial. The Ninth Amendment was thus intended, in part, to instantiate the natural law tradition. It was also designed to preserve, as against federal legislative invasion, rights secured under state constitutions and was thought to be a device by which the expansion of federal legislative powers by implication could be prevented. There is thus a reasonable warrant in the original intentions of the founders to treat the Ninth Amendment as a source of judicially enforceable natural rights.

Even if one were to suppose that the only intended function of the Ninth Amendment was to guard against the extension of federal power by implication, there is good reason to treat the Ninth Amendment today as a source of individual rights that trump legislative powers. The battle against extending federal power has been hopelessly lost. If the Ninth Amendment is to perform anything close to its originally intended function it is necessary to employ some form of constitutional cy pres to accomplish that object. Thus, even if we grant for the sake of argument that the sole function of the Ninth Amendment was to prevent bloat of the powers delegated to Congress, the framers' reason for selecting that purpose was that they regarded it as the most effective way of preserving the natural rights that they had never ceded to the government they created. Because, on this view, the framers labored under the misconception that rights were simply the absence of powers, it is crucial, now that we know that rights can trump powers and that the Ninth Amendment has failed of its original purpose, to recreate the framers' vision by preserving directly the natural rights the framers sought to preserve indirectly.

It is not easy to do this in a world filled with skepticism about whether there is any such thing as natural law. Yet, the problem of defining and locating natural rights in a principled fashion is not hopeless. Natural rights do exist in our positivistic world. In a sense, like Justice Potter Stewart, we know them when we see them. Natural rights inhere in the widely shared cultural ethos. There may be relatively few instances of such rights that are also abrogated by legislative majorities, but they do occur. On those occasions, it is appropriate for courts to enforce the natural rights dimension of the Ninth Amendment. If there are doubts about the wisdom of courts acting in this manner, there are several devices available to us to temper this judicial action. We could make judicial recognition of such rights subject to legislative revision or susceptible to review without the restraining affect of stare decisis. We could admit openly that governmental infringements of unenumerated rights are sometimes justified and set about establishing the criteria for such justification.

We live in a time of legal positivism and moral skepticism but it may not always be so. A small but increasing number of observers have begun to realize that "the Cartesian-Newtonian conception of the universe as a machine filled with separate objects" whose relationships are governed by principles of linear causality fails adequately to describe observable phenomena.[4] Instead, many westerners are discovering "that the Eastern conceptions of related duality—stressing dynamism, rhythm, balance, and harmony—describe an organic, holistic world that more closely approximates observable phenomena than the Cartesian-Newtonian view."[5] In this emerging world-view opposites are no longer warring "thesis" and "antithesis" but paired complements. "Light does not struggle with dark for ultimate supremacy; rather, there would be no understanding of either concept without its complementary twin. The focus is no longer upon either aspect of a diad, but upon the *relationship* between them."[6]

The organizing principle of a worldview centered on relationships between connected phenomena is one of maintaining "dynamic balance."[7] The implications of this worldview may not be fully appreciated as yet, but if it does begin to describe for us the meaning of our existence it may well lead to a state of affairs where we sense a greater number of "certainties." Should that come to pass, the ontological versions of natural law will walk the legal landscape again. We would be arrogant custodians of our fundamental law to expel natural law entirely from our discourse. Natural law deserves a role in our fundamental law. In our present world, its role is deservedly small, but it should not be shunned as a pariah.

We are custodians of a constitutional trust. Just as aboriginal Americans regarded the land as something they did not possess, but simply husbanded for their grandchildren's grandchildren, so are we charged with a responsibility to cultivate our constitutional understanding with care. We must make sense of it for our time, but we must not do so in a fashion that renders it less usable for the future. Nor should we do so in a fashion that ignores the tradition from which our sense of fundamental liberties is derived. In constitutional interpretation we face the very same dilemma that confronts the natural lawyer. We are free actors, but at the same time we are imprisoned by a normative order not of our making. How well we deal with this dilemma is the measure of our stewardship of the Constitution.

Notes and Index

NOTES

Chapter One: The Symbolic Constitution

1. William O. Douglas, *An Almanac of Liberty* 5 (Garden City, N.Y.: Doubleday, 1954).

2. These and other unenumerated rights are collected, together with the relevant supporting citations, by Walter F. Murphy, James E. Fleming, and William F. Harris, II, *American Constitutional Interpretation* 1083–84 (Mineola, N.Y.: Foundation Press, 1986).

3. See generally, A. E. Dick Howard, *The Road from Runnymede: Magna Carta and Constitutionalism in America* 298–315 (Charlottesville, Va.: University Press of Virginia, 1968).

4. *Id.* at 303–4.

5. *Jones v. Robbins*, 74 Mass. (8 Gray) 329, 342–43 (1857). The author of the opinion was Chief Justice Lemuel Shaw, one of the most highly regarded antebellum judges. See, e.g., Leonard W. Levy, *The Law of the Commonwealth and Chief Justice Shaw* (New York: Oxford University Press, 1957).

6. 17 U.S. (4 Wheat.) 518, 581–82 (1819).

7. *Hurtado v. California*, 110 U.S. 516, 531–32 (1884).

8. *Twining v. New Jersey*, 211 U.S. 78 (1908), quote at 106.

9. *Palko v. Connecticut*, 302 U.S. 319, 325–26 (1937).

10. *Calder v. Bull*, 3 U.S. (3 Dall.) 386, 388 (1798).

11. *Id.* at 399.

12. *Meachum v. Fanno*, 427 U.S. 215, 230 (1976) (Stevens, J., dissenting).

13. *Smith v. Organization of Foster Families*, 431 U.S. 816, 845 (1977), citing *Moore v. East Cleveland*, 431 U.S. 494, 503 (1977).

14. See, e.g., Philip Bobbitt, *Constitutional Fate* 25–38 (New York: Oxford University Press, 1982), which discusses Justice Black's use of textual arguments.

15. Alex Kozinski, "It Is a Constitution We Are Expounding," 1987 *Utah L. Rev.* 977, 981, 984.

16. Bobbitt, *supra* note 14, at 3–8; quotes at 7 and 94.

17. The closest the Court has come to reliance upon the Ninth Amendment was *Richmond Newspapers, Inc. v. Virginia*, 448 U.S. 555, 579n.15 (1980), in which the plurality invoked the Ninth Amendment as a partial basis for its opinion. The most famous judicial use of the Ninth Amendment was Justice Goldberg's reliance upon the amendment to support the existence of a constitutional right of privacy. See *Griswold v. Connecticut*, 381 U.S. 479 (1965). Justice William O. Douglas authored the Court's opinion, in which he dared not venture as far as Justice Goldberg, preferring merely to include the Ninth Amendment among the provisions of the Bill of Rights, which have "penumbras formed by emanations from [such] guarantees." *Id.* at 484.

Only seven Supreme Court cases prior to *Griswold* dealt in any fashion with the Ninth Amendment: *Roth v. United States*, 354 U.S. 476, 492 (1957); *Woods v. Cloyd W. Miller Co.*, 333 U.S. 138, 144 (1948); *United Public Workers v. Mitchell*, 330 U.S. 75, 94–95 (1947); *Tennessee Elec. Power Co. v. TVA*, 306 U.S. 118, 143–44 (1939); *Ashwander v. TVA*, 297 U.S. 288, 330–31 (1936); *Scott v. Sandford*, 60 U.S. (19 How.) 393, 511 (1857) (Campbell, J., concurring); *Lessee of Livingston v. Moore*, 32 U.S. (7 Pet.) 470, 551 (1833) (in which the Court's reference to the "ninth article of amendment" is unclear and may refer to the ninth proposed amendment, which is the Seventh Amendment enacted).

18. *Griswold v. Connecticut*, 381 U.S. 479, 491 (1965) (Goldberg, J., concurring).

19. See Laurence H. Tribe and Michael C. Dorf, *On Reading the Constitution* 54 (Cambridge, Mass.: Harvard University Press, 1991).

20. The Nomination of Robert H. Bork to be Associate Justice of the Supreme Court of the United States, Hearings before the Comm. on the Judiciary, United States Senate, 100th Cong., 1st Sess. 249 (1988).

21. See Raoul Berger, "The Ninth Amendment," 66 *Cornell L. Rev.* 1, 9 (1980); Leslie Dunbar, "James Madison and the Ninth Amendment," 42 *Va. L. Rev.* 627, 641 (1956); and Raoul Berger, "The Ninth Amendment: The Beckoning Mirage," 42 *Rutgers L. Rev.* 951, 966–73 (1990).

22. *Webster's New International Dictionary of the English Language* 750 (2d ed. 1944).

23. See, e.g., Lawrence Sager, "You Can Raise the First, Hide Behind the Fourth, and Plead the Fifth, But What on Earth Can You Do With the Ninth Amendment?" 64 *Chi.-Kent L. Rev.* 239, 252 (1988).

24. The "hard-nut-to-crack" metaphor is Sotirios Barber's. See Sotirios Barber, "The Ninth Amendment: Inkblot or Another Hard Nut to Crack?" 64 *Chi.-Kent L. Rev.* 67 (1988).

25. See generally, Sanford Levinson, *Constitutional Faith* (Princeton, N.J.: Princeton University Press, 1988).

Chapter Two: The Political Context of the Founding Generation

1. This point and many of those in the immediately succeeding paragraphs concerning the utility of history to constitutional interpretation are derived from H. Jefferson Powell, "Rules for Orginalists," 73 *Va. L. Rev.* 659 (1987).

2. 163 U.S. 537 (1896).

3. See generally, Forrest McDonald, *Novus Ordo Seclorum: The Intellectual Origins of the Constitution* (Lawrence: University Press of Kansas, 1985); Bernard Bailyn, *The Ideological Origins of the American Revolution* (Cambridge, Mass.: Belknap Press, 1967); Gordon S. Wood, *The Creation of the American Republic, 1776–1787* (Chapel Hill: University of North Carolina Press, 1969); Jack P. Greene, *The Intellectual Heritage of the Constitutional Era* (Philadelphia: Library Company of Philadelphia, 1986).

4. Greene, *supra* note 3, at 56.

5. McDonald, *supra* note 3, at 224. See also James Q. Whitman, "Why Did the Revolutionary Lawyers Confuse Custom and Reason?" 58 *U. Chi. L. Rev.* 1321, 1323 (1991): "For generations, [we] have debated whether the legal thinking of the American Revolutionaries was "about" custom or "about" deductive natural law. . . . Both . . . interpretation[s] attribute much more coherence and intelligibility to revolutionary era legal writings than those writings possess. Revolutionary era lawyers unreflectively conflated reason and custom—which means that, in many respects, we

can never draw definitive conclusions about constitutional interpretation from their writings."

6. See, e.g., Robert H. Bork, *The Tempting of America* (New York: Free Press, 1990). For the view that the original intent of the framers was that their intent would not bind future generations, see H. Jefferson Powell, "The Original Understanding of Original Intent," 98 *Harv. L. Rev.* 885 (1985).

7. Calvin R. Massey, "Federalism and Fundamental Rights: The Ninth Amendment," 38 *Hastings L. J.* 305, 319–20 (1987).

8. Suzanna Sherry, The Founders' Unwritten Constitution, 54 *U. Chi. L. Rev.* 1127, 1129 (1987).

9. See generally, Helen K. Michael, "The Role of Natural Law in Early American Constitutionalism: Did the Founders Contemplate Judicial Enforcement of 'Unwritten' Individual Rights?" 69 *N.C. L. Rev.* 421 (1991).

10. Philip Hamburger, "Natural Rights, Natural Law, and American Constitutions," 102 *Yale L. J.* 907, 956 (1993).

11. Edward S. Corwin, "The 'Higher Law' Background of American Constitutional Law," 42 *Harv. L. Rev.* 365, 394, 395 (1928).

12. McDonald, *supra* note 3, at 59.

13. 8 Co. 113b, 77 Eng. Rep. 646 (K.B. 1610).

14. *Id.* at 118a, 77 Eng. Rep. at 652.

15. Professor Plucknett contended that the case states a theory of fundamental law. See Theodore Plucknett, "Bonham's Case and Judicial Review," 40 *Harv. L. Rev.* 30 (1926); Theodore Plucknett, *Concise History of the Common Law* 337 (Boston: Little, Brown, 5th ed., 1956). Professor Thorne asserted that the case supports only a theory of strict statutory construction. See Samuel Thorne, "Dr. Bonham's Case," 54 *L.Q. Rev.* 543, 548–52 (1938).

16. Corwin, *supra* note 11, at 370, 372.

17. A. E. Dick Howard, *The Road from Runnymede* 122 (Charlottesville: University Press of Virginia, 1968). Coke could be maddeningly inconsistent. In the Fourth Part of his *Institutes* he opines that "the power and jurisdiction of . . . Parliament . . . is so transcendent and absolute . . . it cannot be confined either for causes or persons within any bounds." Edward Coke, *Fourth Part of the Institutes of the Laws of England* 36 (London,

1681). But this statement is followed by examples of its "boundless" exercise, most of which amount to Parliament's ability to alter the common or statutory law of the realm. Coke cites one case — the attainder of Thomas Cromwell, Earl of Essex, during the reign of Henry VIII — in which Henry's judges, much pressed by the King, expressed the view that Parliament could attaint without giving the subject any opportunity to respond to the charge. Of this, Coke says that "their opinion was according to law, yet might they have made a better answer, for [by] . . . Mag[na] Car[ta] . . . no man ought to be condemned without answer." *Id.* at 38. The reader is left wondering whether Coke thought Parliament exceeded its authority or if the judges simply erred. Even if Coke's view of parliamentary power in his *Institutes* is irreconcilable with his view in *Bonham's Case,* the most telling fact is that colonial Americans relied on *Bonham's Case,* not the *Institutes,* to proclaim the legitimacy of a judicial check upon parliamentary power.

18. Quincy's *Massachusetts Reports* 51 (1761) and appendixes 395–552, of which 469–85 are especially germane. See also Maurice H. Smith, *The Writs of Assistance Case* (Berkeley: University of California Press, 1978), quote at 471. Otis expressly invoked the authority of *Bonham's Case; id.* at 474.

19. 10 Adams, *Life and Works* 248 (C. F. Adams, ed. 1850), quoted in Corwin, *supra* note 11, at 398.

20. Corwin, *supra* note 11, at 398.

21. *Id.* at 399.

22. Quincy's *Massachusetts Reports* 527–28n.28.

23. Corwin, *supra* note 11, at 399 n.108.

24. *Id.* at 395–404.

25. McDonald, *supra* note 3, at 60.

26. John Locke, *Two Treatises of Government,* Bk. 2, secs. 221–22, at 430 (Peter Laslett, ed., Cambridge, England: Cambridge University Press, 1967). Peter Laslett's edition is the definitive work, containing his invaluable introduction, but I will also provide parenthetical citations to Locke's book and section numbers, in order to aid the reader in finding cited material in other editions of Locke's works.

27. *Id.,* Bk. 2, sec. 77, at 336–37.

28. Strictly speaking, there was "no contract as such, only a network of forced exchanges designed to leave everyone better off than before." Richard A. Epstein, *Takings: Private Property and the Power of Eminent Domain* 11 (Cambridge, Mass.: Harvard University Press, 1985).

29. Corwin, *supra* note 11, at 396.

30. Locke, *supra* note 26, Bk. 2, sec. 134, at 374.

31. Michael, *supra* note 9, at 436.

32. Corwin, *supra* note 11, at 400. Text is from the Massachusetts Circular Letter of 1768.

33. Emerich Vattel, *The Law of Nations* 15 (John Chitty trans., Philadelphia: T. & J. W. Johnson, 7th Amer. ed., 1849). See also *id.*, Bk. I, chs. 3 and 4, at 8–22, which discusses generally the limits upon the authority of the prince and the legislature.

34. Samuel Pufendorf, *The Law of Nature and Nations* 1068–72, 1105–11 (C. W. and W. A. Oldfather trans., New York: Oceana Publications, 1964); 2 Jean Jacques Burlamaqui, *The Principles of Natural and Politic Law* 37 (Thomas Nugent, trans., 5th ed., Cambridge, Mass.: University Press, 1807).

35. Hugo Grotius, *The Law of War and Peace*, Bk. I, ch. III, sec. VIII(1) and ch. IV, sec. VII(2), at 103–4, 149 (F. Kelsey, trans., New York: Oceana Publications, 1964).

36. Michael, *supra* note 9, at 432.

37. See David L. Jacobsen, ed., *The English Libertarian Heritage from the Writings of John Trenchard and Thomas Gordon* (Indianapolis: Bobbs-Merril, 1965). *Cato's Letters* were written about 1720. See generally Alice M. Baldwin, *The New England Clergy and the American Revolution* (Durham, N.C.: Duke University Press, 1928); Edmund Morgan, "The Puritan Ethic and the American Revolution," 24 *William & Mary Q.* 3 (1967). See McDonald, *supra* note 3, at 54–55; Greene, *supra* note 3, at 45–52. Perhaps the most vigorous champion of the influence of the Scottish Enlightenment upon U.S. political thought has been Garry Wills. See Garry Wills, *Inventing America: Jefferson's Declaration of Independence* (Garden City, N.Y.: Doubleday, 1978). Some scholars sharply dispute the influence that Wills attributes to the Scottish Enlightenment. See, e.g., Harry Jaffa, "Inventing the Past: Garry Wills's Inventing America and the Pa-

thology of Ideological Scholarship," 33 *St. John's L. Rev.* 3 (1981); Ronald Hamowy, "Jefferson and the Scottish Enlightenment: A Critique of Garry Wills's *Inventing America: Thomas Jefferson's Declaration of Independence*," 36 *William & Mary Q.* 503 (1979).

38. *Trenchard and Gordon,* Jacobsen, ed., *supra* note 37, at 128 (Gordon, Letter No. 62, Jan 20, 1721). *Id.* at 121 (Trenchard, Letter No. 60, Jan. 6, 1721). See Wood, *supra* note 3, at 291–92. Jacobsen, ed., *supra* note 46, at 121 (Trenchard, Letter No. 60, Jan. 6, 1721). See Wood, *supra* note 3, at 292.

39. Corwin, *supra* note 11, at 396.

40. See, e.g., Wills, *supra* note 37, at 228; McDonald, *supra* note 3, at 87–89; Wood, *supra* note 3, at 118; Bailyn, *supra* note 3, at 303.

41. McDonald, *supra* note 3, at 54.

42. Wood, *supra* note 3, at 301–2.

43. Paine's tract is partially reprinted in Joseph Lewis, *Thomas Paine: Author of the Declaration of Independence* 55–80 (New York: Freethought Press, 1947), quotes at 59, 70.

44. *Calvin's Case,* 7 Co. 1, 4b, 12a; 77 Eng. Rep. 377, 392 (K.B. 1609).

45. *Prohibitions del Roy,* 7 Co. 63, 77 Eng. Rep. 1342, 1343 (K.B. 1609). This is, of course, one of the celebrated moments in legal history: Coke's temerity in telling James I to his face that he lacked sufficient "artificial reason and judgment" to decide matters of law. Coke was not breaking new ground; he was squarely in the tradition of such earlier English lawyers as Sir John Fortescue, Henry IV's Chief Justice. In his renowned work, *De Laudibus Legum Angliae* (Praises of the Laws of England), he instructs the imaginary prince that he will "not need to explore the mysteries of the law of England by long study . . . ; [or] to investigate precise points of the law, . . . but these should be left to your judges, . . . [since] the experience of [law] necessary for judges is scarcely attainable in the labours of twenty years." John Fortescue, *De Laudibus Legum Angliae* 23–25 (ch. 8) (S. B. Chrimes trans. and ed., Cambridge: Cambridge University Press, 1949).

46. McDonald, *supra* note 3, at 59.

47. See 5 Pennsylvania Declaration of Rights and Constitution of 1776 in Francis N. Thorpe, ed., *The Federal and State Constitutions, Colonial Charters, and Other Organic Laws of the States, Territories, and Colonies Now*

or Heretofore Forming the United States of America 3812 (Washington, D.C.: U.S. Government Printing Office, 1909). According to Stephen Presser, "[O]f all the state constitutions [adopted in the revolutionary period], Pennsylvania's was the purest application of revolutionary political theory to government." Stephen B. Presser and Jamil S. Zainaldin, *Law and Jurisprudence in American History* 115 (St. Paul: West Publishing, 2d ed. 1989). Gordon Wood has declared that Pennsylvania's was "the most radical constitution of the Revolution." Wood, *supra* note 3, at 85.

48. 5 Thorpe, *supra* note 47 at 3086–87, sect. 19; and 3088, sect. 23 of Pennsylvania Constitution of 1776.

49. Stephen B. Presser, *The Original Misunderstanding: The English, the Americans, and the Dialectic of Federalist Jurisprudence* 28 (footnote omitted) (Durham, N.C.: Carolina Academic Press, 1991).

50. McDonald, *supra* note 3, at 85.

51. Presser, *supra* note 49, at 30, 55.

52. Wood, *supra* note 3, at 454–55.

53. There is general agreement that the list includes the following eight cases:

a. *Josiah Philips's Case* (Va. 1778), described in 1 St. George Tucker, *Blackstone's Commentaries with Notes of Reference to the Constitution and Laws of the Federal Government of the United States and of the Commonwealth of Virginia* Appendix 293 (1803) [hereinafter Tucker's *Blackstone*]; William Winslow Crosskey, *Politics and the Constitution in the History of the United States*, vol. 2, 944–48 (Chicago: University of Chicago Press, 1953); Charles G. Haines, *The American Doctrine of Judicial Supremacy* 89–92 (New York: Russell & Russell, 1959); William P. Trent, 1 *Am. Hist. Rev.* 444 (1896); Jesse Turner, *A Phantom Precedent*, 48 *Amer. L. Rev.* 321 (1914).

b. *Holmes v. Walton* (N.J. 1780), described in Crosskey, *supra*, at 948–52; Haines, *supra*, at 92–95; Austin Scott, "Holmes v. Walton: The New Jersey Precedent," 4 *Am. Hist. Rev.* 456 (1899).

c. *Commonwealth v. Caton*, 8 Va. (4 Call) 5 (1782), described in Crosskey, *supra*, at 952–61; Haines, *supra*, at 95–98.

d. *Rutgers v. Waddington* (N.Y. City Mayor's Ct. 1784), reprinted in Julius Goebel, Jr. *The Law Practice of Alexander Hamilton: Documents and Commentary* 393 (New York: Columbia University Press, 1964); described in Crosskey, *supra*, at 962–65; Haines, *supra*, at 98–104; Sherry, *supra* note 8, at 1136–38; Henry B. Dawson, *The Case of Elizabeth Rutgers versus Joshua Waddington*, with a historical introduction (Morrisania, N.Y., 1866).

e. *Trevett v. Weeden* (R.I. 1786), described in James Mitchell Varnum, *The Case, Trevett v. Weeden: On Information and Complaint, for refusing* Paper Bills *in Payment for* Butcher's Meat, *in Market, at Par with* Specie (Providence, R.I.: James Carter, 1787); Crosskey, *supra*, at 965–68; Haines, *supra*, at 105–12; Charles Warren, "Earliest Cases of Judicial Review of State Legislation by Federal Courts," 32 *Yale L. J.* 16 (1922); Sherry, *supra* note 8, at 1138–41.

f. *Symsbury's Case*, 1 Kirby 444 (Conn. Super. Ct. 1785), described in Crosskey, *supra*, at 961; Haines, *supra*, at 104.

g. *Bayard v. Singleton*, 1 Martin 42 (N.C. 1787), described in Crosskey, *supra*, at 971–74; Haines, *supra*, at 112–20.

h. *The "Ten-Pound Act" Cases* (N.H. 1786), described in Crosskey, *supra*, at 969–71.

There is a ninth case, described by Haines as "a Massachusetts precedent," which is probably spurious. See Haines, *supra*, at 120–21; Crosskey, *supra*, at 961–62.

Perhaps the leading advocate of the position that the American instances of judicial review in the 1780s are false precedents was William Winslow Crosskey. See Crosskey, *supra*, at 938–75; Michael, *supra* note 9, at 448–57. For the opposite view, see Sherry, *supra* note 8, at 1134–46.

54. Crosskey, *supra* note 53, at 944–45, quoting the Virginia legislation; see also Haines, *supra* note 53, at 90.

55. Haines, *supra* note 53, at 91n.6.

56. 1 Tucker's *Blackstone*, Appendix 293 (1803). In agreement with Tucker is Trent, *supra* note 53, at 453. Cf. Edward Corwin, *The Doctrine of Judicial Review* 71 (Princeton: Princeton University Press, 1914), for discussion of the case as a "myth."

57. 7 Thorpe, *supra* note 47, at 3812; 10 William Swindler, ed., *Sources and Documents of United States Constitutions* 48 (Dobbs Ferry, N.Y.: Oceana Publications, 1979).

Section 8 of the 1776 Virginia Constitution provided that "in all capital
... prosecutions a man hath a right to demand the cause and nature of his
accusation, to be confronted with the accusers and witnesses, to call for
evidence in his favor, and to a speedy trial by an impartial jury of twelve
men of his vicinage, without whose unanimous consent he cannot be
found guilty." 7 Thorpe, *supra* note 47, at 3813; 10 Swindler, *supra* note
57, at 49 (Va. Const. of 1776, sec. 8). The legislative attaint of Philips
would certainly seem to contradict these guarantees, although it seems
possible, though implausible, that the provisions of this section could have
been observed with the issue of fact for jury decision being limited to
whether the legislative attaint applied to Philips.

58. See Crosskey, *supra* note 53, at 945; Turner, *supra* note 53, at 342.

59. See 3 Jonathon Elliot, ed., *The Debates in the Several State Conventions on the adoption of the Federal Constitution* 66–67, 140, 193, 222–23,
236, 298–99, 324, 450 Philadelphia: J. B. Lippincott, 1836) [hereinafter
Elliot's *Debates*].

60. Crosskey, *supra* note 53, at 947 (emphasis in original).

61. 3 Elliot's *Debates* at 140, 236, 299.

62. See Haines, *supra* note 53, at 91–92; Andrew C. McLaughlin, *The
Courts, The Constitution and Parties* 48 (Chicago: University of Chicago
Press, 1912). McLaughlin asserted that contemporary observers may have
regarded the case as one "in which the court asserted its independent right
to interpret the constitution." That this may have been due to what Crosskey derisively described as the "oral tradition and the transient memories
of judges and lawyers" does not diminish its effect. The oral tradition and
transient memories reflect the current importance of past events. The
importance of *Philips's Case* lies not so much in what actually transpired as
in what the immediately following generation thought happened.

63. Crosskey, *supra* note 53, at 948, quoting 1 Zephaniah Swift, *System of
the Laws of the State of Connecticut* 1 (Windham, Conn.: John Byrne, 1795).

64. See 1 Tucker's *Blackstone* at App. 357.

65. Crosskey, *supra* note 53, at 950.

66. Scott, *supra* note 53, at 458.

67. See generally, Whitman, *supra* note 5.

68. Votes and Proceedings of N.J. Assembly 52 (Dec. 8, 1780), quoted
in Haines, *supra* note 53, at 93.

69. See 3 Jared Sparks, *The Life of Gouverneur Morris, with Selections from his Correspondence and Miscellaneous Papers* 438 (Boston: Gray & Bowen, 1832), quoted and discussed in Crosskey, *supra* note 53, at 951–52.

70. Crosskey, *supra* note 53, at 952.

71. *Id.* at 952–53; Haines, *supra* note 53, at 95–97. The relevant provision of the Virginia Constitution vested the pardon power in the Governor "except where . . . the law shall otherwise particularly direct; in which cases, no . . . pardon shall be granted, but by resolve of the House of Delegates." 7 Thorpe, *supra* note 47, at 3817.

The conclusion is debatable, given the clear constitutional reference to the House of Delegates. It is possible that the court was influenced in its decision by the fact that the House of Delegates apparently thought it necessary to secure the Senate's approval, or the Delegates would not have forwarded the pardon to the Senate for action. See Crosskey, *supra* note 53, at 955.

72. 8 Va. (4 Call) 5, 20 (1782), quoted in Crosskey, *supra* note 53, at 953 (emphasis in original report of the case).

73. 8 Va. (4 Call) 5, 7 (1782), quoted in Haines, *supra* note 53, at 96.

74. See generally, Edmund S. Morgan, *Inventing the People* 239–45 (New York: W. W. Norton, 1988).

75. See Crosskey, *supra* note 53, at 962–63; Haines, *supra* note 53, at 98–99.

76. The court imitated Blackstone almost verbatim in declaring that, if the legislature "think fit positively to declare a law, there is no power which can control them." Dawson, *supra* note 53, at 40, quoted in Haines, *supra* note 53, at 99. See also 1 William Blackstone, *Commentaries on the Laws of England* 91 (1765): "[I]f the Parliament will positively enact a thing to be done which is unreasonable, I know of no power that can control it."

77. Crosskey, *supra* note 53, at 964.

78. See Sherry, *supra* note 8, at 1138. See also Goebel, *supra* note 53, at 400, 404.

79. See Crosskey, *supra* note 53, at 964–65.

80. See Varnum, *supra* note 53, at iv, xxi, quoted in Haines, *supra* note 53, at 105–6.

81. Crosskey, *supra* note 53, at 966, 967.

82. *Id.* at 967, quoting the records of the Rhode Island legislature: "Whatever might have been the opinion of the Judges, they spoke by their records, which admitted of no addition or diminution."

83. *Id.* at 965–66, quote at 968.

84. *Id.* at 971.

85. Haines, *supra* note 53, at 113 (footnote omitted).

86. 1 Martin 42, 45 (N.C. 1787).

87. See Sherry, *supra* note 8, at 1143.

88. Crosskey, *supra* note 53, at 972–73.

89. James Whitman argues that this haphazardness was characteristic of the mingled discourse of the age, one in which distinctions were not made between custom and reason, or between natural law and positive law. See Whitman, *supra* note 5.

90. See Crosskey, *supra* note 53, at 944–74; Michael, *supra* note 9, at 455–57.

91. 10 Adams, *Life and Works* 248 (C.F. Adams, ed., 1850), quoted in Corwin, *supra* note 11, at 398.

92. 1 Bay 93 (S.C. 1789), quotes at 96.

93. 1 Va. 23 (1793), quotes at 31 (Nelson, J.), 40 (Roane, J.) (emphasis added). Speaking in similar tone were Judges Henry, Tyler, and Tucker. See *id.* at 65–66, which states that "the law is unconstitutional . . . and this opinion I form . . . from honest reason, common sense, and the great letter of a Free Constitution."

94. 1 Bay 252 (S.C. 1792), quotes at 254.

95. 1 N.H. 199 (1818), quote at 211.

96. Haines, *supra* note 53, at 168, quoting Dupy v. Wickwire, 1 D. Chipman 237–39 (Vt. 1814). See Haines, *supra* note 53, at 148–70 for discussion of these cases.

97. Haines, *supra* note 53, at 169 (footnote omitted).

98. 5 U.S. (1 Cranch) 137 (1803).

99. 2 U.S. (2 Dall.) 409 (1792). Though the justices decided the case in their various capacities as circuit judges, they did not write opinions. Alexander Dallas's report is of their letters to President Washington, explaining their refusal to decide. See also Max Farrand, "The First Hayburn Case, 1792," 13 *Am. Hist. Rev.* 281 (1908); 1 Charles Warren, *The Supreme*

Court in American History 69–80 (Boston: Little, Brown, 1922); Haines, *supra* note 53, at 173–79.

100. 1 Warren, *supra* note 99, at 69.

101. Act of March 23, 1792, ch. 11, sec. 2, 1 Stat. 243, 244 (repealed by Act of Feb. 28, 1793, ch. 17, sec. 1, 1 Stat. 324).

102. 2 U.S. (2 Dall.) at 411. To similar effect is *Vanhorne's Lessee v. Dorrance*, 2 U.S. (2 Dall.) 304 (C.C. Pa. 1795), in which Justice Paterson, riding circuit, charged a jury "that there can be no doubt, that every Act of the Legislature, repugnant to the Constitution, is absolutely void." *Id.* at 309. Justice Paterson made it quite clear that this judicial power applied only to statutes offending the written Constitution. *Id.* at 308–10.

103. 2 U.S. (2 Dall.) 419 (1793).

104. 3 U.S. (3 Dall.) 378 (1798).

105. Judiciary Act of 1789, ch. 20, sec. 13, 1 Stat. 73, 80.

106. David P. Currie, *The Constitution in the Supreme Court: The First Hundred Years, 1789–1888* 22 (Chicago: University of Chicago Press, 1985.

107. 3 U.S. (3 Dall.) 171 (1796).

108. Currie, *supra* note 106, at 33. Justice Chase alone mentioned the issue, by saying that he did not need to address it because he found the statute constitutional. 3 U.S. (3 Dall.) at 175.

109. Sherry, *supra* note 8, at 1169–70.

110. 5 U.S. (1 Cranch) at 162–63.

111. Judiciary Act of 1789, ch. 20, sec. 13, 1 Stat. 73, 81.

112. 10 U.S. (6 Cranch) 87 (1810).

113. The acreage in question consisted of most of present-day Alabama and Mississippi.

114. Currie, *supra* note 106, at 130.

115. 10 U.S. (6 Cranch) at 139.

116. *Id.* at 143.

117. 3 U.S. (3 Dall.) 386 (1798), quote at 388. Some devout positivists, like John Ely, contend that Chase did not mean by this passage to embrace unwritten fundamental law as a judicially enforceable limit on legislation. See John Hart Ely, *Democracy and Distrust: A Theory of Judicial Review* 210–11 (Cambridge, Mass.: Harvard University Press, 1980). Other skeptics of

natural law, such as David Currie, are convinced that Chase did, indeed, endorse natural law as a limiting principle. See Currie, *supra* note 106, at 46.

118. Charles Haines, for example, described Marshall's opinion in *Marbury v. Madison* as having "asserted Coke's theory of judicial supremacy." Haines, *supra* note 53, at 202.

119. *Calder v. Bull*, 3 U.S. (3 Dall.) 386, 398–99 (1798).

120. Michael, *supra* note 9, at 457.

121. Massey, *supra* note 7, at 315.

122. Calvin R. Massey, "The Anti-Federalist Ninth Amendment and Its Implications for State Constitutional Law," 1990 *Wis. L. Rev.* 1229, 1265 (1990). The metaphor is Stephen Macedo's. See Stephen Macedo, *The New Right v. the Constitution* 32 (Washington, D.C.: Cato Institute, rev. ed., 1987).

Chapter Three: Dual Paths to a Single End

1. The metaphor of Constitution as image belongs to William Conklin. See William E. Conklin, *Images of a Constitution* (Toronto: University of Toronto Press, 1989).

2. See generally, Gordon S. Wood, *The Creation of the American Republic, 1776–1787* 393–429 (Chapel Hill: University of North Carolina Press, 1969); Forrest McDonald, *Novus Ordo Seclorum: The Intellectual Origins of the Constitution* 143–83 (Lawrence: University Press of Kansas, 1985); Richard B. Morris, *Witnesses at the Creation* 120–78 (New York: Holt, Rinehart & Winston, 1985).

3. See Herbert J. Storing, *What the Anti-Federalists Were For,* 24–32 (Chicago: University of Chicago Press, 1981), for a most thoughtful survey of the Antifederalists' view of the need for a stronger central government. Storing argues that the Antifederalists were divided on this point, but even those who accepted the need for a stronger central government did so only with respect to limited purposes, such as national defense.

4. "The financial condition was chaos," claimed historian Albert Beveridge. See 1 Albert J. Beveridge, *The Life of John Marshall* 295 (Boston: Houghton, Mifflin, 1916). Each state issued its own paper currency, which

was virtually worthless and unacceptable outside the state of issuance. Interstate commerce was predictably stifled by the lack of a common currency. States commonly imposed tariffs on goods imported into the state regardless of their origin in some other American state. See generally, *id.* at 295–311.

5. In *Federalist* No. 10 Madison explored the means of controlling self-interested factions that, when constituting a majority of the polity, threaten "to sacrifice to its ruling passion or interest both the public good and the rights of other citizens." Max Beloff, ed., *Federalist* No. 10, at 44 (J. Madison) (Oxford: Basil Blackwell, 2d ed., 1987) [hereinafter *Federalist*]. Madison argued that, in small communities, the dangers of faction were heightened because "[a] common passion or interest will . . . be felt by a majority of the whole . . . [leaving] nothing to check the inducements to sacrifice the [minority]." *Id.* at 45. But, in a large, diverse community — the "extended republic" — the dangers of faction will be diminished by reason of the "greater variety of parties and interests . . . [which] make it less probable that a majority of the whole will have a common motive to invade the rights of other citizens." *Id.* at 47; see also at 41–48. Madison's view was in stark contrast to that of Montesquieu, who believed that republics could only survive in small, homogeneous, societies. See Baron de Montesquieu, *The Spirit of the Laws*, Bk. VIII, ch. 16, at 124 (Anne M. Cohler, Basia Carolyn Miller, & Harold Samuel Stone trans & eds., Cambridge: Cambridge University Press, 1989).

6. *Federalist* No. 46, at 240 and 242 (J. Madison).

7. See, e.g., *Federalist* No. 45, at 236, quote at 237–38 (J. Madison).

8. Arthur E. Wilmarth, Jr., "The Original Purpose of the Bill of Rights: James Madison and the Founders' Search for a Workable Balance Between Federal and State Power," 26 *Amer. Crim. L. Rev.* 1261, 1272, 1273 (1989).

9. *Federalist* No. 46, at 239 (J. Madison).

10. 2 Max Farrand, ed., *The Records of the Federal Convention of 1787* 588 (New Haven: Yale University Press, 1937), see George Mason speech of Sept. 12, 1787.

11. On August 20, 1787, Pinckney proposed that a number of rights provisions be added to the Constitution. On September 12 the Conven-

tion rejected a motion by Gerry to draft a bill of rights. On September 14 the Convention rejected a motion offered by Pinckney and Gerry to add a proviso guaranteeing freedom of the press. See Farrand, *supra* note 10, at 340–42, 588, 617–18; quote at 618.

12. Wilmarth, *supra* note 8, at 1276. See also Storing, *supra* note 3, at 64–70 ("[T]he legacy of the Anti-Federalists was the Bill of Rights."). *Id.* at 65.

13. *Id.*, at 15–23, for Storing's discussion of the Anti-Federalist "belief that there was an inherent connection between the states and the preservation of human liberty. . . [since] states . . . are the natural homes of individual liberty." *Id.* at 15.

14. Wilmarth, *supra* note 8, at 1281; Storing, *supra* note 3, at 24–37, for discussion of the qualified acceptance by the Antifederalists of a stronger central government.

15. 3 Jonathan Elliott, ed., *The Debates in the Several State Conventions on the Adoption of the Federal Constitution* 271 (Philadelphia: J. B. Lippincott, 1836) [hereinafter Elliot's *Debates*]; see especially George Mason speech of June 11, 1788 in the Virginia convention; also Bernard Schwartz, ed., *The Bill of Rights: A Documentary History*, vol. 2, 793 (New York: Chelsea House, 1971).

16. See Schwartz, *supra* note 15, at 665–66 (Pennsylvania); 712 (Massachusetts); 732 (Maryland); 757 (South Carolina); 760 (New Hampshire); 842 (Virginia); 911–12 (New York); 968 (North Carolina).

17. 3 Elliott's *Debates*, at 410, 445 (Patrick Henry, Virginia Ratifying Convention, June 14, 1788).

18. 5 Herbert J. Storing, ed., *The Complete Anti-Federalist* 176–79 (Chicago: University of Chicago Press, 1981) (Feb. 20, 1788); quotes at 176 and 177.

19. "Letters from the Federal Farmer," in 2 *id.* at 324 (Letter of Jan. 20, 1788).

20. 2 Merrill Jensen, ed., *The Documentary History of the Ratification of the Constitution* 167 (Madison: State Historical Society of Wisconsin, 1976) (James Wilson, Speech in the State House Yard, Oct. 6, 1787).

21. 3 Elliott's *Debates* at 194 (George Nicholas, Virginia Ratifying Convention, June 10, 1788). One reason this condition prevailed in England

was the lack of acceptance there of a power of judicial review to invalidate legislation contradictory to principles of fundamental law. But, as Chapter Two indicates, by the decade of the 1780s American judicial review power, based upon written and unwritten expressions of fundamental law, was in a lively flux quite uncharacteristic of England.

22. 2 Jensen, *supra* note 20, at 167–68 (James Wilson, Speech in the State House Yard, Oct. 6, 1787).

23. Thomas McAffee, "The Original Meaning of the Ninth Amendment," 90 *Colum. L. Rev.* 1215, 1231 (1990).

24. 2 Jensen, *supra* note 20, 167–68 (James Wilson, Speech in the State House Yard, Oct. 6, 1787).

25. 2 Elliott's *Debates* 436 (James Wilson, Pennsylvania Ratifying Convention, Nov. 28, 1787).

26. 4 Elliott's *Debates* 167 (James Iredell, North Carolina Ratifying Convention, July 28, 1788).

27. 3 Elliott's *Debates* 620 (James Madison, Virginia Ratifying Convention, June 24, 1788).

28. *Federalist* No. 84 at 439–40 (Alexander Hamilton).

29. 2 Elliott's *Debates* 151, 153 (Charles Jarvis, Massachusetts Ratification Convention, Feb. 4, 1788).

30. 3 Elliott's *Debates* 318 (Patrick Henry, Virginia Ratification Convention, June 12, 1788).

31. U.S. Const., art. III, sec. 2; art. I, sec. 9.

32. 2 Jensen, *supra* note 20, 425, 427 (Robert Whitehill, Pennsylvania Ratification Convention, Nov. 30, 1787).

33. Leonard W. Levy, *Original Intent and the Framers' Constitution* 160 (New York: Macmillan, 1988).

34. 2 Storing, *supra* note 18, at 324 (Letter XVI of "The Federal Farmer," Jan. 20, 1788).

35. 3 Elliott's *Debates* 661 (Virginia); 4 Elliott's *Debates* 246 (North Carolina). The North Carolina proposal was actually made after Congress had proposed the Bill of Rights to the states, but it clearly reflects the identical concerns that motivated the earlier Virginia proposal.

36. 1 Elliott's *Debates* 327. The New York proposal was virtually identical to the third article of Rhode Island's declaration of rights, quote at 336.

37. 4 Elliott's *Debates* 167 (James Iredell, North Carolina ratification convention, July 28, 1788).

38. 1 Annals of Congress 435 (J. Gales & W. Seaton ed. 1836) (remarks of James Madison on June 8, 1789); 2 Schwartz, *supra* note 15, at 1027.

39. 1 Annals of Congress at 439.

40. *Id.* at 435.

41. *Id.*

42. *Id.* at 439.

43. 2 Schwartz, *supra* note 15, at 1043.

44. Leslie Dunbar, "James Madison and the Ninth Amendment," 42 *Va. L. Rev.* 627, 632 (1956).

45. 1 Annals of Congress 731–32. Benson was a prominent Poughkeepsie, New York, lawyer whose political fortunes had skyrocketed with the successful Revolution. He had also been the law office teacher to James Kent, the future New York judge, chancellor, law professor, and author of *Commentaries on American Law*, "the most influential American law book of the antebellum period." John H. Langbein, "Chancellor Kent and the History of Legal Literature," 93 *Colum. L. Rev.* 547, 548 (1993). See also *id.* at 553.

46. *Id.* at 732.

47. 2 Schwartz, *supra* note 15, at 1190 (Letter of James Madison to George Washington, Dec. 5, 1789).

48. *Id.* at 1188 (Letter of Hardin Burnley to James Madison, Nov. 28, 1789).

49. Wilmarth, *supra* note 11, at 1302 (emphasis in original). In Burnley's letter to Madison he stated that "if the house should agree to the resolution for rejecting the two last [the ninth and tenth amendments] I am of opinion that it will bring the whole into hazzard again, as some who have been decided friends to the [enumerated bill of rights] think it would be unwise to adopt them without the [ninth and tenth amendments]." 2 Schwartz, *supra* note 15, at 1188 (Letter from Hardin Burnley to James Madison, Nov. 28, 1789).

50. 2 Schwartz, *supra* note 15, at 1190 (Letter of James Madison to George Washington, Dec. 5, 1789).

51. *Id.* at 1190; 2 Gaillard Hunt, ed., *The Writings of James Madison* 432

(New York: G. P. Putnam's Sons, 1904) (letter from Madison to George Washington, dated Dec. 5, 1789, discussing Randolph's objections). See Randy Barnett, "Reconceiving the Ninth Amendment," 74 *Cornell L. Rev.* 1, 15–16 (1988).

52. See 1 Annals of Congress, *supra* note 49, at 790; 2 Schwartz, *supra* note 15, at 1118 (House of Representatives debates of Aug. 18, 1789). Though the debates provide no certain reason for the change, the phrase was probably added to underscore the theme that "ultimate authority . . . resides in the people alone" and that "[t]he federal and state governments are in fact but different agents and trustees of the people." *Federalist* No. 46, at 239 (J. Madison).

53. 3 Joseph Story, *Commentaries on the Constitution of the United States* 752 (Boston: Hilliard, Gray, 1833) (emphasis added). John Calhoun stated that the powers reserved by the Tenth Amendment "are divided into two distinct classes—those delegated by the people of the several States to their separate State governments, and those which they still retain—not having delegated them to either government." John C. Calhoun, "A Discourse on the Constitution and Government of the United States," reprinted in Ross Lence, ed., *Union and Liberty: The Political Philosophy of John C. Calhoun* 104 (Indianapolis: Liberty Fund, 1992).

54. See also Wilmarth, *supra* note 11, at 1302: "[T]he ninth and tenth amendments were intended to operate in tandem to protect the unenumerated rights of the people and the unenumerated powers of the states against federal encroachment."

55. *Id.*

56. 2 Schwartz, *supra* note 15, at 1191 (letter from Edmund Randolph to George Washington, dated Dec. 6, 1789).

57. 1 Farrand, *supra* note 10, at 492.

58. 2 Annals of Cong. at 1899, 1901 (statement of Rep. Madison). See also Randy E. Barnett, "Unenumerated Constitutional Rights and the Rule of Law," 14 *Harv. J.L. & Pub. Pol'y* 615, 635–39 (1991); David N. Mayer, "The Natural Rights Basis of the Ninth Amendment: A Reply to Professor McAffee," 16 *S. Ill. U. L. J.* 313, 318 (1992).

59. 2 Annals of Congress at 1899 (statement of Rep. Madison).

60. It is true that Story's nominal political affiliation was with the Jeffer-

sonian Democratic Republicans when President Madison appointed him to the Supreme Court, but Jefferson warned Madison that Story was a Federalist in disguise (a "pseudo-republican" and a "tory"), as indeed Story ultimately proved to be. See 11 Paul Leicester Ford, ed., *Works of Thomas Jefferson* 150–52 (New York: G.P. Putnam's Sons, 1905) (Letter from Jefferson to James Madison, Oct. 15, 1810); R. Kent Newmyer, *Supreme Court Justice Joseph Story: Statesman of the Old Republic* 70 (Chapel Hill: University of North Carolina Press, 1985); Dumas Malone, *Jefferson and His Time: The Sage of Monticello* 67 (Boston: Little, Brown, 1981); 3 Story, *supra* note 53, at 751–52 (1833); Thomas McAffee, "The Original Meaning of the Ninth Amendment," 90 *Colum. L. Rev.* 1215, 1311–13 (1990).

61. Thomas M. Cooley, *The General Principles of Constitutional Law in the United States of America* 36–37 (Andrew C. McLaughlin, ed., Boston: Little, Brown, 3rd ed, 1898) (emphasis added).

62. Peter S. Du Ponceau, *A Brief View of the Constitution of the United States* 44–45 (Philadelphia: E. G. Dorsey, 1834).

63. Abel P. Upshur, *A Brief Enquiry into the True Nature and Character of Our Federal Government* 99 (Petersburg, Va.: Edmund and Julian Ruffin, 1840).

64. 17 U.S. (4 Wheat.) 316 (1819), quote at 406.

65. Thomas McAffee, *supra* note 60, at 1215, 1300n.325, 1306–7 (1990) (emphasis added).

66. 79 U.S. (12 Wall.) 457 (1871), quotes at 535 and 534.

67. *United States v. Carmack*, 329 U.S. 230, 241–42 (1946).

68. See Jesse Dukeminier and James Krier, *Property* 1142 (Boston: Little, Brown, 3rd ed., 1993).

69. See the constitutions of Alabama (1819), in 1 Francis N. Thorpe, Ed., *The Federal and State Constitutions, Colonial Charters, and Other Organic Laws of the States, Territories, and Colonies Now or Heretofore Forming the United States of America* 98 (Washington, D.C.: U.S. Government Printing Office, 1909); Arkansas (1836), *id.* at 270–71; California (1849), *id.* at 392; Colorado (1876), *id.* at 478; Florida (1885), 2 *id.* at 734; Georgia (1865), *id.* at 811; Iowa (1846), *id.* at 1125; Kansas (1855), *id.* at 1181; Louisiana (1868), 3 *id.* at 1450; Maine (1819), *id.* at 1649; Maryland (1851), *id.* at 1716; Minnesota (1857), 4 *id.* at 1993; Mississippi (1868), *id.*

at 2071; Missouri (1875), *id.* at 2232; Montana (1889), *id.* at 2304; Nebraska (1866–1867), *id.* at 2351; Nevada (1864), *id.* at 2404; New Jersey (1844), 5 *id.* at 2600; North Carolina (1868), *id.* at 2803; Ohio (1851), *id.* at 2915; Oregon (1857), *id.* at 3000; Rhode Island (1842), 6 *id.* at 3224; South Carolina (1868), *id.* at 3285; Virginia (1870), 7 *id.* at 3875; Washington (1889), *id.* at 3975; Wyoming (1889), *id.* at 4120.

70. See the constitutions of Kansas (1855), 2 *id.* at 1181; Nebraska (1866–67), 4 *id.* at 2351; North Carolina (1868), 5 *id.* at 2803; Ohio (1851), 5 *id.* at 2915; and South Carolina (1868), 6 *id.* at 3285.

71. 17 U.S. (4 Wheat.) 316 (1819).

72. *Dred Scott v. Sandford*, 60 U.S. (19 How.) 393 (1857); quote at 511 (Campbell, J., concurring).

73. 330 U.S. 75 (1947).

74. *Id.* at 94.

75. *Id.* at 95–96.

76. See Randy E. Barnett, Reconceiving the Ninth Amendment, 74 *Cornell L. Rev.* 1, 6–7 (1988).

77. Randy Barnett first made this argument; see *id.* at 7.

78. The same dubious construction was placed upon the Ninth Amendment in several other cases decided by the Court roughly contemporaneously with *Mitchell.* See *Ashwander v. TVA*, 297 US. 288, 330–31 (1936); *Tennessee Electric Power Co. v. TVA*, 306 U.S. 118, 143–44 (1939); *Woods v. Cloyd W. Miller Co.*, 333 U.S. 138, 144 (1948); *Roth v. United States*, 354 U.S. 476, 492–93 (1957).

79. 381 U.S. 479 (1965).

80. 330 U.S. 75 (1947).

81. 448 U.S. 555 (1980).

82. *Id.* at 580, 579n.15, and 580.

83. 112 S. Ct. 2791 (1992).

84. 410 U.S. 113 (1973).

85. *Planned Parenthood v. Casey*, 112 S. Ct. 2791, 2805 (1992).

Chapter Four: Constitutional Cy Pres

1. Joseph B. James, *The Framing of the Fourteenth Amendment* 180 (Urbana: University of Illinois Press, 1956). Representative Jonathan Bing-

ham, the architect of the privileges and immunities clause, expressly declared that "the privileges and immunities of citizens of the United States as contradistinguished from the citizens of a State, are chiefly defined in the first eight amendments to the Constitution of the United States." Cong. Globe, 42nd Cong., 1st Sess., Appendix at 85 (1871). Bingham also pointed to the privileges and immunities clause of Article IV as his model. Cong. Globe, 39th Cong., 1st Sess. part 2, at 1033–34 (1866). In *Corfield v. Coryell*, 6 Fed. Cases 546, 551 (No. 3230) (C.C.E.D. Pa. 1825), Justice Washington, on circuit duty, determined that the Article IV clause protected privileges "which are, in their very nature fundamental; which belong, of right, to the citizens of all free governments." Senator Howard relied directly on *Corfield v. Coryell* to define the content of the Fourteenth Amendment's privileges and immunities and added that "to these . . . should be added the personal rights guarantied and secured by the first eight amendments of the Constitution." Cong. Globe, 39th Cong., 1st Sess., part 3, at 2765 (1866).

For contrary views of the Fourteenth Amendment's origins, see Raoul Berger, *Government by Judiciary* (Cambridge, Mass.: Harvard University Press, 1977); Charles Fairman, "Does the Fourteenth Amendment Incorporate the Bill of Rights?" 2 *Stan. L. Rev.* 5 (1949).

2. 83 U.S. (16 Wall.) 36 (1873).

3. Lucile Lomen, "Privileges and Immunities under the Fourteenth Amendment," 18 *Wash. L. R.* 120, 124 (1943).

4. *Corfield v. Coryell*, 6 Fed. Cases 546, 551 (No, 32230) (C.C.E.D.Pa 1825).

5. *San Antonio Ind. School Dist. v. Rodriguez*, 411 U.S. 1, 33–34 (1973).

6. 2 U.S. (2 Dall. 419 (1793).

7. See Calvin R. Massey, "State Sovereignty and the Tenth and Eleventh Amendments," 56 *U. Chi. L. Rev.* 61, 111–13 (1989).

8. Treaty of Amity, Commerce and Navigation, Nov. 19, 1794, 8 Stat. 116.

9. Massey, *supra* note 7, at 135–36 (footnotes omitted).

10. 134 U.S. 1 (1890).

11. *Griswold v. Connecticut*, 381 U.S. 479, 529 (1965) (Stewart, J., dissenting).

12. I do not mean to imply that Bradley's interpretation of the Eleventh Amendment in Hans v. Louisiana was the *best* way to recapture the original intentions surrounding the Eleventh Amendment. I have argued that the Eleventh Amendment ought to be construed merely as erecting a party-based barrier to the exercise of federal jurisdiction and that the Tenth Amendment ought to be the independent source of the principle of state sovereign immunity from suit in federal court. See Massey, *supra* note 7, at 61. What the Supreme Court has *actually* done is to employ a version of constitutional *cy pres* with respect to the Eleventh Amendment.

13. 347 U.S. 483 (1954).

14. See Alexander Bickel, "The Original Understanding and the Segregation Decision," 69 *Harv. L. Rev.* 1, 58 (1955) ("[S]ection 1 of the fourteenth amendment . . . as originally understood, was [not] meant to apply [to] segregation."). See also Raoul Berger, *Government by Judiciary: The Transformation of the Fourteenth Amendment* 117–33 (Cambridge: Harvard University Press, 1977).

15. Berger, *supra* note 14, at 125; see also *id.* at 123–28.

16. See, e.g., Herbert Wechsler, "Toward Neutral Principles of Constitutional Law," 73 *Harv. L. Rev.* 1 (1959).

17. See Robert H. Bork, *The Tempting of America* 81–82 (New York: Free Press, 1990).

18. Mark Tushnet, "Following the Rules Laid Down: A Critique of Interpretivism and Neutral Principles," 96 *Harv. L. Rev.* 781, 800–801 (1983).

19. Bickel, *supra* note 14, at 56 and 60.

20. This is the subject of Calvin R. Massey, "The Anti-Federalist Ninth Amendment and Its Implications for State Constitutional Law," 1990 *Wisc. L. Rev.* 1229.

21. Laurence Tribe and Michael Dorf, *On Reading the Constitution*, 54, 111, 110 (Cambridge, Mass.: Harvard University Press 1991) (emphasis in original).

22. Justice Joseph Story, the most influential antebellum constitutional commentator interpreted the phrase "or to the people" in precisely this fashion, to mean that "what is not conferred [to the national government] is withheld, and belongs to the state authorities, *if invested by their constitu-*

tions of government respectively in them; and if not so invested, it is retained by the people, as a part of their residuary sovereignty." 3 Joseph Story, *Commentaries on the Constitution of the United States* 752 (1833) (emphasis added).

23. Massey, *supra* note 20, at 1241.

24. See Randy Barnett, ed., *The Rights Retained by the People* 351 (Fairfax, Va.: George Mason University Press 1989).

25. Randy Barnett, James Madison's Ninth Amendment, in *id.* at 7n.16.

26. Tribe and Dorf, *supra* note 21, at 110, 54, and 111 (emphasis in original).

27. Alex Kozinski, "It Is a Constitution We Are Expounding," 1987 *Utah L. Rev.* 977, 984.

28. See, e.g., David C. Williams, "Civic Republicanism and the Citizen Militia: The Terrifying Second Amendment," 101 *Yale L. J.* 551 (1991); Robert J. Cottrol and Raymond T. Diamond, "The Second Amendment: Toward an Afro-Americanist Reconsideration," 80 *Geo. L. J.* 309 (1991); Sanford Levinson, "The Embarrassing Second Amendment," 99 *Yale L. J.* 637 (1989). For an extensive collection of materials germane to the second amendment see generally, Robert J. Cottrol, ed., *Gun Control and the Constitution: Sources and Explorations on the Second Amendment* (Hamden, Conn.: Garland Publishing, 1993) (3 vols.).

Chapter Five: The Positive Law Component

1. Edmund S. Morgan, ed., *Prologue to Revolution: Sources and Documents on the Stamp Act Crisis* 136 (Chapel Hill: University of North Carolina Press, 1959), quoting William Pitt the Elder.

2. Edmund S. Morgan, *Inventing the People: The Rise of Popular Sovereignty in England and America* 239–40 (New York: W. W. Norton, 1988).

3. *Id.* at 242, quote at 243.

4. See generally, Forrest McDonald, *Novus Ordo Seclorum: The Intellectual Origins of the Constitution* 9–55 (Lawrence: University of Kansas Press, 1985); Hannis Taylor, *The Origin and Growth of the American Constitution* 230–43 (Boston: Houghton, Mifflin, 1911); Thomas J. Curry, *The First Freedoms* 64, 66 (New York: Oxford University Press, 1986). See also 1

William Blackstone, *Commentaries on the Laws of England* 63–64, 104–5, 123–24 (1765). Among the important statutory sources of the "rights of Englishmen" were the Magna Carta (1215), the Petition of Right (1628), the Habeas Corpus Act (1679), the Declaration of Rights (1689), the Toleration Act (1689), the Mutiny Act (1689), and the Settlement Act (1701).

5. Oliver Ellsworth, for example, trusted "for the preservation of his rights to the State Govts. From these alone he could derive the greatest happiness he expects in this life." 1 Max Farrand, ed., *The Records of the Federal Convention of 1787*, at 492 (New Haven: Yale University Press, 1937). In recommending against inclusion of a Bill of Rights in the federal Constitution, Roger Sherman declared, "The State Declaration of Rights are not repealed by this Constitution; and being in force are sufficient." 2 *id.* at 588. James Wilson asserted in 1791 that "our [colonial] assemblies were chosen by ourselves: they were the guardians of our rights, the objects of our confidence, and the anchor of our political hopes." 1 Works of James Wilson 292 (Robert G. McCloskey, ed., Cambridge, Mass.: Harvard University Press, 1967).

6. 1 Annals of Congress 454 (Joseph Gales and W. Seaton eds., 1789).

7. 5 Gaillard Hunt, ed., *The Writings of James Madison* 389 (New York: G. P. Putnam's Sons, 1904).

8. 1 Annals of Congress 454. This distinction was not peculiar to the *American* founding generation. Blackstone also recognized the difference between natural and positive rights. See 1 Blackstone, *supra* note 4, at 42–44, 121–22. Indeed its roots can be traced to Aristotle. See Russell Caplan, "The History and Meaning of the Ninth Amendment," 69 *Va. L. Rev.* 223, 237n.55.

9. 1 Annals of Congress at 457.

10. 5 Hunt, *supra* note 7, at 273.

11. 1 Annals of Congress 450, 456.

12. *Id.* at 454.

13. *Id.* at 455.

14. *Id.* at 455.

15. See Caplan, *supra* note 8, at 254.

16. As noted earlier, Madison feared that enumeration of rights "would

disparage those rights which were not placed in that enumeration; and it might follow, by implication, that those rights which were not singled out, were intended to be assigned into the hands of the General Government, and were consequently insecure." 1 Annals of Congress 456. This inference could be "guarded against" by the Ninth Amendment. *Id.* The fact that Madison had the same fear with respect to state bills of rights, see 5 Hunt, *supra* note 7, at 390, indicates that he appreciated that certain of these rights were "natural, . . . retained by the people," *id.* at 389n.1, and were properly beyond the powers of government.

17. Caplan, *supra* note 8, at 228.

18. Hearings Before the Committee on the Judiciary, United States Senate, 100th Congress, First Session, on the Nomination of Robert H. Bork to be Associate Justice of the Supreme Court of the United States, at 249 (emphasis added).

19. For a most perceptive look at these issues, see Robert C. Post, "Between Democracy and Community: The Legal Constitution of Social Form," in *NOMOS: Democratic Community*, edited by John W. Chapman and Ian Shapiro, 163–90 (New York: New York University Press, 1993).

20. Oliver Wendell Holmes, Jr., *The Common Law* 1 (Boston: Little, Brown, 1881).

21. See, e.g., McDonald, *supra* note 4, who contends that the founding generation subscribed to both multiple and contradictory political philosophies.

22. See Calvin R. Massey, "Federalism and Fundamental Rights: The Ninth Amendment," 38 *Hastings L. J.* 305, 312–23 (1987).

23. See Randy Barnett, "Reconceiving the Ninth Amendment," 74 *Cornell L. Rev.* 1, 27n.88 (1988) and accompanying text.

24. An egregious example of the aridity of this methodology of constitutional interpretation may be seen by examining an episode in Canadian constitutional law. Section 24 of the Constitution Act, 1867 (U.K. 30 & 31 Vict. c. 3), provides that "qualified Persons" may be appointed to the Senate. In 1928, the Supreme Court of Canada unanimously concluded that the word "persons" did not include women because it was unthinkable that the drafters of the 1867 Act could have meant for it to do so. No attempt was made to search for any more contemporary meaning. See

Reference as to the Meaning of the Word "Persons" in Section 24 of the British North America Act, 1867, [1928] S.C.R. 276. On appeal, the Judicial Committee of the Privy Council reversed, contending that the historicist method was inconclusive and would produce results redolent "of days more barbarous than ours." Edwards v. Attorney General for Canada, [1930] A.C. 124, 128. Instead, Lord Sankey declared Canada's basic constitutional document to be "a living tree capable of growth and expansion within its natural limits." *Id.* at 136.

25. *Coyle v. Smith,* 221 U.S. 559, 566 (1911), quoting from the act admitting Tennessee into the Union in 1796.

26. Letter of Edmund Pendleton to Richard Henry Lee, dated June 14, 1788, in 2 David John Mays, ed., *Letters and Papers of Edmund Pendleton* 533 (Charlottesville: University Press of Virginia, 1967), cited in H. Jefferson Powell, "Rules for Originalists," 73 *Va. L. Rev.* 659, 670n.28 (1987).

27. See H. Jefferson Powell, "The Original Understanding of Original Intent," 98 *Harv. L. Rev.* 885 (1985).

28. 2 Max Farrand, ed., *The Records of the Federal Convention of 1787* 137 (New Haven: Yale University Press, 1937); 4 *id.* at 32–38.

29. See, e.g., *Stanford v. Kentucky,* 492 U.S. 361 (1989), which upholds the constitutional validity of executions of juveniles as young as age 16.

30. On the virtues of decentralized federalism, see Deborah Jones Merritt, "The Guarantee Clause and State Autonomy: Federalism for a Third Century," 88 *Colum. L. Rev.* 1, 3–10 (1988); Michael McConnell, "Federalism: Evaluating the Founders' Design," 54 *U. Chi. L. Rev.* 1484, 1491–1511 (1987).

31. 304 U.S. 64 (1938).

32. *Ravin v. State,* 537 P.2d 494, 504, 511 (Alaska 1975).

33. For example, Californians adopted ballot Proposition 115 on June 5, 1990. The measure amends the California Constitution to require that, in criminal cases, most relevant guarantees of the California Declaration of Rights shall be interpreted identically to the appropriate analogue in the federal Bill of Rights.

The adequate and independent state grounds doctrine preserves the states' freedom to chart state constitutional guarantees at variance from federal guarantees. See *Michigan v. Long,* 463 U.S. 1032 (1983); *Pruneyard*

Shopping Center v. Robins, 447 U.S. 74, 81 (1980), in which it states that a state is free "to adopt in its own Constitution individual liberties more expansive than those conferred by the Federal Constitution."

34. See *Erie Railroad Co. v. Tompkins*, 304 U.S. 64 (1983); *Fidelity Union Trust Co. v. Field*, 311 U.S. 169 (1940); *Six Companies of California v. Joint Highway Dist. No. 13*, 311 U.S. 180 (1940). When the state rule is uncertain, federal courts have greater flexibility in announcing what they believe to be the state law. See, e.g., *Commissioner v. Estate of Bosch*, 387 U.S. 456 (1967).

35. See *Michigan v. Long*, 463 U.S. 1032 (1983).

36. Other aspects of the federal Constitution may limit a state's ability to alter or remove certain guarantees of human liberty from the state constitution and the Ninth Amendment. Former Oregon Supreme Court Justice Hans Linde has suggested that although the federal Constitution's guarantee clause, U.S. Const., art. IV, sec. 4, is not justiciable in federal court, *Luther v. Borden*, 48 U.S. (7 How.) 1 (1849), it may be justiciable in state courts. Further, it may operate to prevent certain substantive alterations of state constitutions. See Hans Linde, "When Is Initiative Lawmaking not 'Republican Government'?" 17 *Hastings Const. L. Q.* 159 (1989).

37. See, e.g., John Hart Ely, *Democracy and Distrust: A Theory of Judicial Review* 37 (Cambridge, Mass.: Harvard University Press, 1980); Raoul Berger, "The Ninth Amendment," 66 *Cornell L. Rev.* 1, 23–24 (1980); Caplan, *supra* note 8, at 264. But see Norman Redlich, Are There "Certain Rights . . . Retained by the People?" 37 *N.Y.U. L. Rev.* 787, 806 (1962); Massey, *supra* note 22, at 309–19, 322–31; Barnett, *supra* note 23, at 9–11, 14–21, 30–42. The Ninth Amendment has never been expressly incorporated into the Fourteenth Amendment's due process clause, and thus is not currently applicable to the states through that familiar medium. Presumably the rule of *Barron v. Baltimore*, 32 U.S. (7 Pet.) 243 (1833), currently applies to the Ninth Amendment.

38. John Marshall's definitive conclusion to this effect is contained in *Barron v. Baltimore*, 32 U.S. (7 Pet.) 243 (1833).

39. Judge Bork, for example, regards the Ninth Amendment as analogous to "an amendment that says 'Congress shall make no' and then there

is an ink blot and you cannot read the rest of it." Bork Hearings, *supra* note 18, at 249.

40. Caplan, *supra* note 8, at 261–62 (footnote omitted).

41. See *Griswold v. Connecticut*, 381 U.S. 479 (1965); *Roe v. Wade*, 410 U.S. 113 (1973).

42. Massey, *supra* note 22, at 327.

43. See *Murray's Lessee v. Hoboken Land & Improvement Co.*, 59 U.S. (18 How.) 272, 276 (1855), which states, "the words 'due process of law' were undoubtedly intended to convey the same meaning as the words 'by the law of the land,' in Magna Charta"; see also Edward S. Corwin, "The 'Higher Law' Background of American Constitutional Law" (pt. 2), 42 *Harv. L. Rev.* 365, 378 (1929).

44. 109 S. Ct. 633 (1989).

45. W. Va. Const., Art. X, sec. 1, quoted in Allegheny Pittsburgh, 109 S. Ct. at 635.

46. 109 S. Ct. at 638.

47. See Note, "The Rule of Law and the States: A New Interpretation of the Guarantee Clause," 93 *Yale L. J.* 561 (1984); Massey, *supra* note 22, at 328–29.

48. 465 U.S. 89 (1984).

49. See *California v. Greenwood*, 486 U.S. 35 (1988).

50. 469 U.S. 528 (1985); quote at 552.

51. *Id.* at 550–54; quote at 554.

52. See *South Carolina v. Baker*, 485 U.S. 505 (1988) for discussion on exclusion and singular treatment; *New York v. United States*, 112 S. Ct. 2408 (1992) for discussion on commandeering of the state legislative process; *Gregory v. Ashcroft*, 111 S. Ct. 2395 (1991) for discussion on plain statement rule.

53. Calvin R. Massey, "State Sovereignty and the Tenth and Eleventh Amendments," 56 *U. Chi. L. Rev.* 61, 75 (1989); quote at 75.

54. The adequate and independent state grounds doctrine has generally been thought to be constitutionally compelled since *Murdock v. Memphis*, 87 U.S. (20 Wall.) 590 (1874). That conclusion is certainly not explicit in Murdock. Rather, it is a case that merely raises doubts about the power of Congress to enable the federal courts to review and decide issues of state

law independent of the state courts. *Id.* at 626, 633. See also Laurence Tribe, *American Constitutional Law* 380 (Mineola, N.Y.: Foundation Press, 2d. ed. 1988). Murdock has a "constitutional resonance" that prevents Congress from authorizing the Supreme Court to review pure state law issues. The state-specific view of positive Ninth Amendment rights would validate the result in Murdock and provide further support to the constitutional structural principle preservative of state sovereignty by suggesting that the adequate and independent state grounds doctrine is constitutionally required.

55. Massey, *supra* note 53, at 74.

56. See, e.g., *Smith v. State*, 510 P.2d 793 (Alaska, 1973); *People v. Krivda*, 5 Cal. 3d 357, 486 P. 2d 1262 (1971), vacated and remanded for determination of whether ruling was based on the federal or California constitution, 409 U.S. 33 (1972), reinstated and based on California and U.S. constitutions, 8 Cal. 3d 623, 504 P. 2d 457 (1973), cert. denied, 412 U.S. 919 (1973); *State v. Tanaka*, 67 Haw. 658, 701 P. 2d 1274 (Hawaii, 1985); *New Jersey v. Hempele*, 120 N.J. 182, 576 A. 2d 793 (New Jersey, 1990); *Washington v. Boland*, 115 Wash. 2d 571, 800 P. 2d 1112 (Washington, 1990).

57. 489 U.S. 288 (1989).

58. 410 U.S. 113 (1973).At least the "essential holding" of Roe is still good law. *Planned Parenthood of Southeastern Pennsylvania v. Casey*, 112 S. Ct. 2791, 2804 (1992).

59. The qualifier is necessary because the state-action doctrine would presumably operate to limit application of the newly identified constitutional right of fetal personhood to those instances where the state, rather than some purely private actor, was acting to deprive fetuses of life. But because the hypothesized state constitution would guarantee a right to terminate pregnancy difficult issues of state action would be posed by that very state act. See, e.g., *Reitman v. Mulkey*, 387 U.S. 369 (1967).

60. 384 U.S. 641 (1966).

61. *Id.* at 651 n.10.

62. 497 U.S. 547 (1990); quote at 564.

63. 400 U.S. 112 (1970).

64. This does not mean that there is a generalized "state sovereignty" exception to congressional enforcement powers under section 5 of the

Fourteenth Amendment. Indeed, the Supreme Court has rejected the argument that the Tenth Amendment limits congressional enforcement power under Section 5. See *City of Rome v. United States*, 446 U.S. 156 (1980); *EEOC v. Wyoming*, 460 U.S. 226 (1983). *Oregon v. Mitchell* stands for the more limited proposition that when the Constitution explicitly assigns authority to the states, as it generally does with respect to voting qualifications for nonfederal elections, Congress may not use its Section 5 enforcement powers except to remedy a Fourteenth Amendment violation.

65. See, e.g., Richard Epstein, "The Proper Scope of the Commerce Power," 73 *Va. L. Rev.* 1387 (1987).

66. 15 U.S.C. sec. 78j(b).

67. 17 C.F.R. sec. 240.10b-5 (1976).

68. I make no contention that state statutes are in any way insulated from federal preemption by virtue of the Ninth Amendment.

69. For a discussion of rights by the political right, see Robert H. Bork, *The Tempting of America* 261–65 (New York: Free Press, 1990); for a discussion by the political left, see Jed Rubenfeld, "The Right of Privacy," 102 *Harv. L. Rev.* 737 (1989).

70. Jed Rubenfeld, "Usings," 102 *Yale L. J.* 1077, 1099, 1103, 1104 (1993). See also Jed Rubenfeld, "The Right of Privacy," 102 *Harv. L. Rev.* 737, 756–61 (1989).

71. Rubenfeld, *supra* note 70, "Usings," at 1142.

72. See Post, *supra* note 19, at 164.

73. See generally, Robert Nagel, "The Formulaic Constitution," 84 *Mich. L. Rev.* 165 (1985).

74. 387 U.S. 369 (1967).

75. 3 U.S. (3 Dall.) 386 (1798).

76. 381 U.S. 479 (1965).

77. 410 U.S. 113 (1973).

78. *United States v. Carolene Products Co.*, 304 U.S. 144, 152n.4 (1938).

79. *Palko v. Connecticut*, 302 U.S. 319, 324 (1937).

80. *San Antonio Independent School Dist. v. Rodriguez*, 411 U.S. 1, 33 (1973).

81. *Michael H. v. Gerald D.*, 109 S. Ct. 2333, 2344n.6 (1989).

82. *Poe v. Ullman*, 367 U.S. 497, 543 (1961) (Harlan, J., dissenting).

83. For a discussion on the lack of standards for fundamental rights, see Robert H. Bork, *supra* note 69, at 261–65; for a discussion of indeterminacy, see, for example, Sanford Levinson, *Constitutional Faith* 191 (Princeton: Princeton University Press, 1988), in which he states that "there is nothing unsayable in the language of the Constitution"; Michael Perry, *Morality, Politics, and Law* 149 (New York: Oxford University Press, 1988), in which he states that "the fundamental aspirations signified by the Constitution . . . are highly indeterminate"; Paul Brest, "The Fundamental Rights Controversy: The Essential Contradictions of Normative Scholarship," 90 *Yale L. J.* 1063, 1065, 1097 (1981), in which he states that "the legitimacy of judicial review . . . [to locate fundamental rights] is essentially incoherent and unresolvable . . . [since] no defensible criteria exist . . . to assess theories of judicial review."

84. Philip Bobbitt, *Constitutional Fate* 93–242 (New York: Oxford University Press, 1984); quotes at 94, 177.

85. *San Antonio Independent School Dist. v. Rodriguez*, 411 U.S. 1, 33 (1973).

86. Barnett, *supra* note 23, at 35 (footnote omitted).

87. *Id.* at 37.

88. Stephen Macedo, *The New Right v. The Constitution* 27 (Washington, D.C.: Cato Institute, rev. ed. 1987).

89. But cf. Henry Manne, *Insider Trading and the Stock Market* (New York: Free Press, 1966), in which the economic wisdom of a prohibition upon inside trading is questioned; Dennis W. Carlton and Daniel R. Fischel, "The Regulation of Insider Trading," 35 *Stan. L. Rev.* 857, 858, 866–68 (1983), in which they assert that capital markets might be more efficient in equating price with real value if inside trading were permitted. To do justice to Carlton and Fischel, I doubt that either of them would assert that inside trading, however beneficial economically, is a fundamental right.

90. Compare, e.g., *Miller v. Schoene*, 276 U.S. 272 (1928) with *Lucas v. South Carolina Coastal Council*, 112 S. Ct. 2886 (1992). See generally, Rubenfeld, *supra* note 70, "Usings," at 1077.

91. On the issue of privacy, see, for example, *Florida Star v. B.J.F.*, 109 S. Ct. 2603 (1989); on the issue of child pornography, see, for example, *New*

York v. Ferber, 458 U.S. 747 (1982); cf. *Osborne v. Ohio,* 110 S. Ct. 1691 (1990).

92. In recent years, a number of public and private institutions have begun to promulgate policies seeking to strike a constitutional balance between the rights of "hate speakers" under the First Amendment and the rights of vilified ethnic groups to pursue education free of such racial harassment. See, for example, Stanford University's policy on racist speech, which subjects such speech to disciplinary action whenever it "is intended to insult or stigmatize an individual or a small group of individuals . . . and . . . is addressed directly to the individual or individuals whom it insults or stigmatizes . . . and . . . makes use of insulting or 'fighting' words," defined as words "which are commonly understood to convey direct and visceral contempt for human beings." Stanford University Fundamental Standard Interpretation: Free Expression and Discriminatory Harassment, June 1990. The University of Michigan's policy was invalidated in *Doe v. University of Michigan,* 721 F. Supp. 852 (E.D. Mich. 1989), on grounds of overbreadth and vagueness. At least one chapter of the American Civil Liberties Union (Northern California) has adopted a similar statement of policy, which would permit racist speech on college campuses to be prohibited only when it "is specifically intended to and does harass an individual . . . and . . . is addressed directly to the individual or individuals to whom it harasses; and . . . creates a hostile and intimidating environment which the speaker reasonably knows or should know will seriously and directly impede the educational opportunities of the individual or individuals to whom it is directly addressed; . . . is enforced in a manner consistent with due process protections, . . . contains specific illustrations . . . which demonstrate when the policy does or does not apply, is proportionate to the gravity of the offense, and does not impose prior restraint upon expression." *ACLU News,* August–September 1990, at 2.

The academic literature on the subject is burgeoning. See citations collected in Calvin R. Massey, "Hate Speech, Cultural Diversity, and the Foundational Paradigms of Free Expression," 40 *UCLA L. Rev.* 103, 105n.3 (1992).

93. *Richmond v. J. A. Croson Co.,* 109 S. Ct. 706 (1989); *Metro Broadcasting v. Federal Communications Comm.,* 110 S. Ct. 2997 (1990).

94. Post, *supra* note 19, at 177.

95. See, e.g., U.S. Const. art I, sec. 8 (commerce clause) and art. IV, sec. 2 (privileges and immunities clause).

96. Cf. *City of Philadelphia v. New Jersey*, 437 U.S. 617 (1978).

97. Cf. *Southern Pacific Co. v. Arizona*, 325 U.S. 761 (1945).

98. See *Osborne v. Ohio*, 110 S.Ct. 1691 (1990).

99. For a discussion of some of the problems encountered when incorporating social science into legal adjudication, see David Faigman, "To Have and Have Not: Assessing the Value of Social Science to the Law as Science and Policy," 38 *Emory L. J.* 1005 (1989). For a discussion of these issues in the area of constitutional adjudication, see David Faigman, " 'Normative Constitutional Fact Finding': Exploring the Empirical Component of Constitutional Interpretation," 139 *U. Pa. L. Rev.* 541 (1991).

100. See, e.g., *CTS Corp. v. Dynamics Corp.*, 481 U.S. 69, 94 (1987) (Scalia, J., concurring). Justice Scalia criticizes the aspect of dormant commerce clause jurisprudence, which requires courts to assess "whether the burden on commerce imposed by a state statute 'is clearly excessive in relation to the putative local benefits.' " *Id.* He prefers the approach advocated by Professor Regan to the effect that the Supreme Court should invalidate, on dormant commerce clause grounds, only those state laws that "discriminate against out-of-state interests." *Id.* at 95. See Donald H. Regan, "The Supreme Court and State Protectionism: Making Sense of the Dormant Commerce Clause," 84 *Mich. L. Rev.* 1091 (1986).

Chapter Six: The Natural Law Component

1. John Hart Ely, *Democracy and Distrust: A Theory of Judicial Review* 50 (Cambridge, Mass.: Harvard University Press, 1980).

2. Benjamin Wright, *American Interpretations of Natural Law: A Study in the History of Political Thought* 339 (Cambridge, Mass.: Harvard University Press, 1931) ("[N]atural law has had as its content whatever the individual in question desired to advocate."). See also Clinton Rossiter, *Seedtime of the Republic: The Origin of the American Tradition of Political Liberty* 366, 375 (New York: Harcourt, Brace, 1953); Ely, *supra* note 1, at 51. Ely's example is the statement "no one should needlessly inflict suffering."

3. Among the academic contributions to this literature are Edward S. Corwin, "The 'Higher Law' Background of American Constitutional Law," 52 *Harv. L. Rev.* 149 (1928) (Part One); 52 *Harv. L. Rev.* 365 (1928) (Part Two); Suzanna Sherry, "The Founders' Unwritten Constitution," 54 *U. Chi. L. Rev.* 1127 (1987); Thomas Grey, "Origins of the Unwritten Constitution: Fundamental Law in American Revolutionary Thought," 30 *Stan. L. Rev.* 492 (1978); Thomas Grey, "Do We Have an Unwritten Constitution?" 27 *Stan. L. Rev.* 703 (1975). Notable examples of the Supreme Court's employment of natural law methodology within the rubric of constitutional adjudication include the opinion of Justice Chase in *Calder v. Bull,* 3 U.S. (3 Dall.) 386 (1798); *Fletcher v. Peck,* 10 U.S. (6 Cranch) 87, 139 (1810), which found the Georgia statute at issue a violation of "general principles which are common to our free institutions"; *Scott v. Sanford,* 60 U.S. (19 How.) 393, 407 (1857), which inferred from the framers' intent and structure of the original constitutional design the conclusion that African-Americans "had no rights which the white man is bound to respect"; Justice Miller's opinion in *Loan Ass'n v. Topeka,* 87 U.S. (20 Wall.) 655 (1874); *Griswold v. Connecticut,* 381 U.S. 479, 484 (1965), which located the right to privacy in "emanations from" the "penumbras" of certain of the enumerated rights in the Constitution; and *Shapiro v. Thompson,* 394 U.S. 618, 630 (1969), in which the Court refused "to ascribe the source of [the right to travel to any] . . . particular constitutional provision."

4. See Raoul Berger, "Natural Law and Judicial Review: Reflections of an Earthbound Lawyer," 61 *U. Cin. L. Rev.* 5 (1992); Helen K. Michael, "The Role of Natural Law in Early American Constitutionalism: Did the Founders Contemplate Judicial Enforcement of 'Unwritten' Individual Rights?" 69 *N. Car. L. Rev.* 421 (1991).

5. Philip A. Hamburger, "Natural Rights, Natural Law, and American Constitutions," 102 *Yale L. J.* 907, 908 (1993).

6. Use your own so as not to harm another's.

7. See Hamburger, *supra* note 5, at 909, 930–55; quote at 940. Hamburger states that "Americans . . . consider[ed] natural law a prudential or moral guide rather than a substitute for constitutional law."

8. *Id.* at 934n.77, quoting an Antifederalist who was plainly worried that

the claims of natural right would receive a deaf ear in the constitutional courts of the new federal government.

9. Lloyd Weinreb, *Natural Law and Justice* 1 (Cambridge, Mass.: Harvard University Press 1987) (emphasis in original).

10. *Id.* at 2.

11. H.L.A. Hart, *The Concept of Law* 181 (Oxford: Clarendon Press, 1961).

12. See Weinreb, *supra* note 9, at 97–126, discussing natural law theories of Lon Fuller, John Finnis, David Richards, and Ronald Dworkin.

13. See, e.g., John Barton, "Behind the Legal Explosion," 27 *Stan. L. Rev.* 567, 572–78 (1975).

14. Moreover, the trend toward positivism works to further erode the connection between law and cultural ethos. The cultural binding force of law is sapped because, in an increasingly positivistic world, "law is . . . *expected* to be artificial." Barton, *supra* note 13, at 574 (emphasis in original).

15. Grant Gilmore, *The Ages of American Law* 110–11 (New Haven: Yale University Press, 1977).

16. An example of this phenomenon might be a law banning married couples from using contraceptives. It is likely that there is overwhelming, but not universal, agreement that such a law is repugnant to our current cultural ethos. If so, it seems illogical to expect such a law to exist. But, of course, such a law did exist (albeit without much enforcement) in Connecticut until it was invalidated in *Griswold v. Connecticut*, 381 U.S. 479 (1965). The most likely explanation for the existence of laws contrary to the cultural ethos is that laws continue to exist long after the death of the cultural ethos which they manifested. A rule against perpetuities applicable to statutes might be a good idea. Cf. Guido Calabresi, *A Common Law for the Age of Statutes* (Cambridge, Mass.: Harvard University Press, 1982).

17. Grant Gilmore, *The Ages of American Law* 49 (New Haven: Yale University Press, 1977).

18. Oliver Wendell Holmes, Jr., *The Common Law* 41 (Boston, Little, Brown, 1881).

19. See generally, Kenneth Arrow, *Social Choice and Individual Values* (New York: Wiley, 1951).

20. Laurence Tribe, *American Constitutional Law* 12n.6 (Mineola, N.Y.: Foundation Press, 1988) (emphasis in original).

21. *Palko v. Connecticut*, 302 U.S. 319, 325 (1937).

22. Alexander Bickel, *The Least Dangerous Branch* 25, 26 (Indianapolis: Bobbs-Merrill, 1962).

23. *Brown v. Allen*, 344 U.S. 443, 540 (Jackson, J., concurring).

24. Canadian Charter of Rights and Freedoms, pt. 1 of the Constitution Act, 1982, Schedule B of the Canada Act 1982 (U.K.), ch. 11 [hereinafter Can. Charter], especially sec. 33. Either Parliament or a provincial legislature may declare that its legislation supersedes the fundamental rights guaranteed in the Charter. Such action is limited in effectiveness for five years, but a legislature may renew the declaration for an unlimited number of successive five-year terms. Thus, if a national or provincial legislative majority feel strong enough about a matter, guaranteed human liberties may be eliminated in perpetuity.

25. *Id.* sec. 1.

26. David L. Faigman, "Madisonian Balancing: A Theory of Constitutional Adjudication," 88 *Nw. U. L. Rev.* 641, 666 (1994).

27. 381 U.S. 479 (1965).

28. See Charles Black, *Structure and Relationship in Constitutional Law* (Baton Rouge: Louisiana State University Press, 1969).

29. Randy E. Barnett, "Unenumerated Constitutional Rights and the Rule of Law," 14 *Harv. J. L. & Public Policy* 615, 630 (1991); quotes at 630–31, 631n.52.

30. Bernard Siegan, *Economic Liberties and the Constitution* 324 (Chicago: University of Chicago Press, 1980).

31. Mary Ann Glendon, *Rights Talk* x, 171 (New York: Free Press, 1991).

32. Can. Charter.

33. *Regina v. Keegstra*, [1990] 3 S.C.R. 697, 735 (Dickson, C.J.) (emphasis added).

34. [1986] 1 S.C.R. 103.

35. *Id.* at 139.

36. Convention for the Protection of Human Rights and Fundamental Freedoms, 4 Nov. 1950, effective 1953, in Council of Europe, European

Convention on Human Rights: Collected Texts 4–5 (Strasbourg: Council of Europe, 1974).

37. 4 *European Human Rights Reports* 149, 164–65 (1981).

38. *Buck v. Bell,* 274 U.S. 200, 208 (1927).

39. *Michael H. v. Gerald D.,* 491 U.S. 110, 128 n.6 (1989).

40. *Poe v. Ullman,* 367 U.S. 497, 542 (1961) (Harlan, J., dissenting).

41. "No one acquires a vested or protected right in violation of the Constitution by long use, even when that span of time covers our entire national experience and indeed predates it." *Walz v. Tax Comm'n of New York City,* 397 U.S. 664, 678 (1970).

42. Laurence H. Tribe and Michael C. Dorf, *On Reading the Constitution* 100 (Cambridge, Mass.: Harvard University Press, 1991).

43. *Planned Parenthood of Southeastern Pennsylvania v. Casy,* 112 S. Ct. 2791, 2882 (1992) (Scalia, J., dissenting).

44. *Griswold v. Connecticut,* 381 U.S. 479 (1965).

45. *Roe v. Wade,* 410 U.S. 113 (1973).

46. *Planned Parenthood of Southeastern Pennsylvania v. Casy,* 112 S. Ct. 2791, 2881 (1992) (Scalia, J., dissenting); quote at 2881.

47. For some of the arguments germane to this point, see Calvin R. Massey, "The Locus of Sovereignty: Judicial Review, Legislative Supremacy, and Federalism in the Constitutional Traditions of Canada and the United States," 1990 *Duke L. J.* 1229, 1300–1307.

48. For discussion of additional examples, see *id.* at 1229, 1272–98.

49. 22 U.S. (9 Wheat.) 1 (1824).

50. *Id.* at 207–9. See also *Cooley v. Board of Wardens,* 53 U.S. (12 How.) 299 (1851).

51. *Payne v. Tennessee,* 111 Sup. Ct. 2597, 2609–10 (1991), quoting *Helvering v. Hallock,* 309 U.S. 106, 119 (1940).

52. *Id.* at 2610, quoting *Burnet v. Coronado Oil & Gas Co.,* 285 U.S. 393, 407 (1932) (Brandeis, J., dissenting).

53. *Smith v. Allwright,* 321 U.S. 649, 665–66 (1944).

54. *Payne v. Tennessee,* 111 Sup. Ct. 2597, 2609 (1991).

55. *Burnet v. Coronado Oil & Gas Co.,* 285 U.S. 393, 406 (1932) (Brandeis, J., dissenting).

56. Hamburger, *supra* note 5, at 930, 937, and 940.

Chapter Seven: Stewards of the Constitution

1. *United States v. O'Brien*, 391 U.S. 367 (1968).

2. See Randy Barnett, ed., *The Rights Retained By the People* 351 (Fairfax, Va.: George Mason University Press 1989).

3. Randy Barnett, "James Madison's Ninth Amendment," in *id.* at 7n.16.

4. Geoffrey Walker, *The Rule of Law: Foundation of Constitutional Democracy* 44 (Melbourne: Melbourne University Press, 1988). See also Laurence H. Tribe, "The Curvature of Constitutional Space: What Lawyers Can learn from Modern Physics," 103 *Harv. L. Rev.* 1 (1989); Calvin R. Massey, "Rule of Law and the Age of Aquarius" (Book Review), 41 *Hastings L. J.* 757 (1990).

5. Massey, Rule of Law and the Age of Aquarius, *supra* note 4, at 762.

6. *Id.* (emphasis in original).

7. Walker, *supra* note 4, at 47.

INDEX

Cooley, Thomas, 82–83
Corwin, Edward, 27, 29
Crosskey, William, 36, 38, 42, 231n. 53

Dartmouth College v. Woodward, 5–6
Dred Scott Case, 88
Douglas, William O., 3, 111, 193–94,
  224n. 17
Dudgeon v. United Kingdom, 197
Due process, 4–6, 15, 94, 99, 112, 131,
  147, 202, 210, 214
Du Ponceau, Peter, 83

Eighth Amendment, 119
Eleventh Amendment, 47–48; as ex-
  ample of constitutional cy pres, 100–
  102, 110, 245n. 12
Ellsworth, Oliver, 81, 131, 247n. 5
Equal protection, 99–100, 140–41,
  149–51, 210, 214; and affirmative
  action, 105; as example of constitu-
  tional cy pres, 102–4
Erie Railroad Co. v. Tompkins, 135–36,
  143, 145
European Convention on Human
  Rights, 197
European Court of Human Rights, 197

Faigman, David, 192, 197–98
Federal Farmer, Letters from the, 59–60
Federalist Papers, 63, 83, 237n. 5,
  241n. 52
Fifteenth Amendment, 104
Fifth Amendment, 4, 86, 119, 124
First Amendment, 90–91, 92, 119, 215,
  255n. 92
Fletcher v. Peck, 49
Fourteenth Amendment: and affirma-
  tive action, 105; and congressional

enforcement, 148–51, 252–53n. 64;
  and due process, 4, 92, 138, 147; and
  equal protection, 22, 102–4, 140–
  41; as example of constitutional cy
  pres, 102–4, 110; and incorporation
  doctrine, 99, 133–34, 138, 186; and
  privileges and immunities, 99, 243–
  44n. 1
Fourth Amendment, 119, 145–46
French-and-Indian War, 28, 116
Fugitive slave clause, 110–11

*Garcia v. San Antonio Metropolitan
  Transit Authority*, 144–45
Gerry, Elbridge, 56
Gibbons v. Ogden, 205
Gilmore, Grant, 181
Glendon, Mary Ann, 196
Goldberg, Arthur, 10, 91, 224n. 17
Gordon, Thomas, 32
Gorham, Nathaniel, 131
Griswold v. Connecticut, 11, 159, 185,
  190, 193, 224n. 17
Grotius, Hugo, 30–31
Guaranty clause, 111, 250n. 36

Haines, Charles, 46
Hamburger, Philip, 26, 175–76, 207–8
Hamilton, Alexander, 63–64, 83, 85
Ham v. M'Claws, 45
Hans v. Louisiana, 101
Harlan, John, 159–60
Harrison, Benjamin, 37
Hatch Act, 89
Hayburn's Case, 47
Henry, Patrick, 37, 58, 64
History, utility of, 21–23, 53–54, 199–
  201
Hobbes, Thomas, 127

Silent Rights